Allegories of America

CONTESTATIONS

CORNELL STUDIES IN POLITICAL THEORY

A series edited by
WILLIAM E. CONNOLLY

A complete list of titles in the series
appears at the end of the book.

Allegories of America

Narratives · Metaphysics · Politics

Frederick M. Dolan

Cornell University Press

Ithaca and London

First published 1994 by Cornell University Press.

Printed in the United States of America

Grateful acknowledgment is given for permission to quote from *The Changing Light at Sandover* by James Merrill, copyright © 1980, 1982 by James Merrill, reprinted by permission of Alfred A. Knopf, Inc.

⊗ The paper in this book meets the minimum requirements of the American National Standard for Information Sciences— Permanence of Paper for Printed Library Materials, ANSI Z39.48-1984.

Library of Congress Calaloging-in-Publication Data

Dolan, Frederick Michael.
    Allegories of America: narratives, metaphysics, politics / Frederick M. Dolan.
        p.   cm. — (Contestations)
    Includes bibliographical references and index.
    ISBN 0-8014-3006-2. — ISBN 0-8014-8200-3
        1. Political culture—United States.   2. Political science—United States—
History.   3. Fiction—Political aspects—United States.   4. Politics and
literature—United States.   5. Allegory.   I. Title.   II. Series.
E169.1.D65   1994
320.973—dc20   94-26097

*To my mother and to
the memory of my father*

Contents

Acknowledgments

An adequate acknowledgment of the individuals and institutions who have earned my gratitude for their support and encouragement would be embarrassingly long, and so I am more selective than my debts, in all strictness, allow. My colleagues in the Department of Rhetoric at the University of California, Berkeley, have created an electrifying environment for writing and teaching at the crossroads of the humanities and social sciences, and it is a pleasure to acknowledge their stimulus. Students from many disciplines, both undergraduate and graduate, prompted me to elaborate and revise some of the ideas and interpretations in play here when I tried them out in classes, seminars, and informal discussions. I am particularly grateful to David Dahl and Elizabeth Maddock Dillon, who served as my research assistants. William E. Connolly, Roger Haydon, and Janet S. Mais aided and abetted the transmutation of manuscript to book, and Stanley Aronowitz, Jane Bennett, Thomas L. Dumm, Philip Kuberski, Michael Shapiro, and Dana R. Villa provided incisive readings. I benefited greatly from a sabbatical leave supported by a Humanities Research Fellowship from the University of California at Berkeley and from a fellowship from the Doreen B. Townsend Center for the Humanities (also at Berkeley). Versions of parts of Chapters 3 and 4 appeared in the *Canadian Journal of Political and Social Theory* 12:8 (1988); *Diacritics* 20:2 (1990); *Contemporary Literature* 32:4 (1991), copyright 1991 by the regents of the University of Wisconsin and used by permission of the University of Wisconsin Press; the *Massachusetts Review* 32:1 (1991), and *Ideology and Power in the Age of Lenin in Ruins*, ed. Arthur and Marilouise Kroker (New York: St. Martin's Press, 1991), and I am happy to acknowledge these journals and publishers and their readers, whose responses were stimulating and helpful.

I am by no means certain that those who have put up with my preoccupations would care to be so identified. Nonetheless, for sharing with me their intelligence and wit, and for their constancy, I must thank, in some cases a second time: Marianne Constable, Maureen Dolan, Tom Dumm, Vicky Elliott, Phil Kuberski, Avital Ronell, and Dana Villa.

F.M.D.

Berkeley, California

Allegories of America

Allegories of America

In *Harlot's Ghost*, Norman Mailer's epic novel of postwar America, Harlot, an old hand at the Central Intelligence Agency answerable only to Allen Dulles, formulates a distinction between espionage and counterespionage. Espionage, he tells a group of CIA trainees, is "a middle-class activity." It "depends on stability, money, large doses of hypocrisy on both sides, insurance plans, grievances, underlying loyalty, constant inclinations toward treachery, and an immersion in white collar work" (p. 421). It is, in other words, thoroughly banal and straightforward, continuous with the routine duplicity of everyday professional life, utterly familiar and intelligible. But whereas espionage involves nothing more than a simple, self-aggrandizing violation of a trust, counterespionage is, in Harlot's estimation, "damnable." The world of counterespionage is "built on lies. Or, should we say, on inspirations?" and thrives on complexity, uncertainty, unintelligibility (p. 426).

Precisely because each of the great parties to the conflict between democracy and communism *expects* the other to lie, the game of counterespionage is played best by those whose loyalties are unknown, especially to themselves. Agent Hubbard, the narrator of *Harlot's Ghost*, spends the middle 1950s in Montevideo trying to corrupt a minor Uruguayan communist and finds that the more experience of the CIA he acquires, the less sure he is of its aims, the more uncertain he becomes of his own motives and those of his colleagues.

As the novel unfolds, the CIA becomes an utter mystery even to the most powerful within it; when disaster strikes, the first question is always whether the perpetrator was an enemy or one of their own. Because it *is* certain that at all times one is being lied to and manipulated, even the most unpredictable historical events are interpretable: the Sino-Soviet split, for example, is a "gargantuan production in disinformation" (p. 1203). These interpretations are inherently unverifiable, but that serves only as a goad to a virtually pathological "will to know": "The actors in this kind of venture tend to be adventurers, aristocrats, and psychopaths," Harlot acknowledges (p. 426). The arena of counterespionage—which, as Mailer's novel encourages us to believe, is paradigmatic for the texture of American life after World War II—is one of rumors, impressions, hypotheses, suppositions, opinions, appearances, of reflections whose aspects and attributes are continuously rearranged and reinterpreted to the point where lucidity and paranoia, freedom and totalitarianism, change places and merge.

Mailer's evocation of the character of postwar America brings together, in both content and form, some themes I explore in this book: the spaces opened up for power in an interpretively open world; the latent metaphysics of a politics entirely given over to phantasms and simulacra but whose actors are driven by the need to reduce the interpretive ambiguity of their world to the reassuring forms of a metaphysical allegory; the affirmation of America as a privileged locus of such experiences; and the indispensability of fiction for registering the complex ironies generated by this situation. In the chapters that follow, I survey strands of the American discourse on national identity, paying particular attention to this interpretative problematic. These readings rely on a persistent feature of claims Americans make about their national political life (a feature they no doubt share with other national communities), to the effect that the American political project secures a privileged spiritual or metaphysical value. At the same time, America's self-allegorization is also self-deconstructing, as reliant on tropes of self-creation and fictionalization as on that of the correct, mirrorlike representation of the real as a foundation for a national project. America's discourse of national identity incessantly negotiates the two poles of, on the one hand, solid foundations or grand narratives and, on the other, the ever-present threat of the collapse of absolutes.

My reason for carrying out these readings, however, is not solely a fascination with the twists and turns of American public discourses and their theorization. Holding these readings together is the conviction that such discourses allegorize the central problematic that post-Nietzschean and post-Heideggerian reflection offers to political theory: that of speaking, acting, and judging "without grounds," the withering away of transcendental normative principles invoked to anchor political actions, judgments, opinions.[1] In the historicodiscursive events we know as "America," the postmodern problematic assumes the form of a national myth; and American national ideology, from its canonical founding texts and speeches onward, can be shown to reflect and indeed perform the conundrums and complexities associated with the loss of grounds for action articulated first by Nietzsche and Heidegger and then by so many others. I attempt to illuminate that problematic by situating it in the context of discursive events organized by actual political conflicts, tasks, and judgments, as well as to illuminate America's political fantasies through the postmodern problematic, and so to explore and expose the limits of each. To this end, I exploit various interpretative or hermeneutic orientations and devices, from deconstruction to the analysis of ideology. Reading the discourse of American national identity, then, is motivated by a concern for this problematic, so although I have tried to learn from historians of American political thought, my approach has been driven by my fascination with the problems I seek to expose, not by a desire for historical comprehensiveness.

That problematic, to repeat, concerns the collapse of the very idea of a grounding theory of the political that might guide practice and judgment. Political philosophers have traditionally sought three advantages from a *theory* of politics. First, a theory provides an exhaustive, fully coherent account of some object of inquiry, placing its possessor in a position to make judgments about political life (and to assess the judgments of others) from the vantage of a synoptic knowledge. Second, a theory provides means for distinguishing the ideological discourse of quotidian political contestation from a political *truth* conceived as independent of continually shifting opinions and wills. Third, it clarifies political thought: by ordering and naming, by drawing boundaries and making distinctions, a theory separates the political from the nonpolitical, the public from the private, and so provides its possessor with a vocabulary of clear and distinct concepts with which to negotiate the confusion of public representations and discourses. These advantages enable the theorist to lay claim to a privileged, though no doubt frail and contested, authority in discussions of political life.

The founding gesture of political theory in this sense is Socrates' invocation, in Plato's *Republic*, of an invisible but theoretically intelligible realm of incorruptible forms, knowledge of which provides a foundation for political reflection that is inaccessible to the many and which serves to reduce the multiplicity of political opinions to a single, univocal metaphysical Good. As first Nietzsche, and later Heidegger, have taught us, "Platonism," in the extended sense of the will to search for and establish a disinterested, disembodied knowledge, has governed the West's most privileged inquiries and oriented them, since the birth of modernity, around the project of controlling the contingency of the world by recasting the latter as an ideal entity accurately represented before the subject's gaze. From Plato to John Rawls, thinkers have enlisted the powers of theory to render political life accessible as a whole, discussable in its clearly delineated parts, and subject to true judgments.

Many in the tradition of Western political thought have debated whether a theoretical account of politics was possible and what sort, but few questioned the enterprise of theoretical understanding as the master trope for the knowledge of politics as such. Then readers of Nietzsche and Heidegger began to do just that and therefore found themselves searching for modes of political reflection that neither reduce to the everyday, ideological discourses of politics as practiced nor appeal to timeless criteria of truth and certainty to judge such practice. *Allegories of America* aims to contribute to this discussion by assessing the successes and failures of some notable attempts to negotiate the dilemmas encountered in this search, but also, and more particularly, by exploring this problematic in specific discursive contexts of American political thought. Its method, admittedly, is one of studied indirection. My conceit, and the rationale for carry-

ing out a project such as this under the present title, is that narrating
the story of theory's self-deconstruction, and the attempt to fashion
strategies for facing the dilemmas attendant on that deconstruction,
can be seen as allegorical of broad features of American political
thought itself. If the task bequeathed us by such figures as Nietzsche
and Heidegger is, roughly speaking, the problem of finding a vocabulary for the identification and discussion of political matters in the
absence of assured foundations, methods, approaches, sources, and
procedures supplied by the canon of European metaphysics, then
one might approach their narratives (for they can no longer safely
be called *theories*) as allegorical of America's perennial anxiety over
its own identity and over what authorizes its actions, of America's
continually renewed attempt to found and refound a polity in the
absence of a legitimating or reliable foundational discourse.

I think of Nietzsche and Heidegger, and even more so their better
readers, as offering us *allegories* rather than *theories* in the etymological sense of the former term: these authors write narratives intended to contest dominant, public meanings attached to traditional
Western concepts and practices by discerning in the latter another,
larger significance. And just as they deconstruct the canon of Western metaphysics, I seek to put their allegories to work in American
political thought, culture, and ideology to effect, explore, and reflect
on parallel dislocations and disruptions of meaning. In America, to
put it bluntly, the postmodern or postmetaphysical problematic—
the problem of acting without grounds and in the absence of the
constraints of traditional absolutes—assumes the status of a national
mythology, so that Nietzsche's and Heidegger's narratives help reveal "another" layer of significance alongside the conventionally
established, public meanings of America. By the same token, putting
their postmetaphysical narratives to work in the context of American political thought helps to sharpen and focus the dilemmas these
narratives offer to political reflection in ways that a more straightforward theoretical argument might not capture. In sum, *Allegories of
America* explores the political stakes of the questionability of theory
by, in Slavoj Zizek's phrase, "looking awry"—thinking through concrete exemplars meant less to illustrate a theoretical thesis than to
provide perspective on it.[2]

Why question theory? The questionability of the theoretical enterprise, formulated most deeply by Nietzsche and Heidegger and
first brought to bear in a sustained manner on political thought by
Hannah Arendt, has since been forcefully restated by Jean-François
Lyotard, among others.[3] Nietzsche's "diagnosis" of theory as an expression of a dangerous Socratic will to "correct existence" lies behind what Lyotard presents as a conflict between the *pious* and the
pagan in the history of Western thought.[4] According to Xenophon,
Socrates' conversation concerned the need to distinguish "what is
pious, what is impious," and the foremost example of piety is Platonism, the essence of which lies in the assertion that justice or freedom
in their purity and perfection are *ideas*.[5] The corollary, says Lyotard,
is that they exist nowhere perfectly: for Platonism, justice "can be
accomplished only if it is first correctly thought out and described";
we require a *theory* of justice or freedom or equality to enable us to
establish these practices in actual political life. Lyotard emphasizes
that this theoretical (or philosophical) approach to politics, which
ties the evaluation of the political realm to the establishment of an
accurate theoretical description (of justice or freedom), makes essentially no reference to actual political contexts and indeed devalues
such contexts insofar as they fail to live up to the *truth* of the political,
as independently established with the help of reliable philosophical
procedures. Such procedures are *pious* because they inevitably imply
"the representation of . . . a lost origin, something that must be re-
stored to a society in which it is lacking."[6]

As Lyotard stresses, this "piety" goes far beyond Socrates and
Plato themselves and indeed determines virtually the entire history
of Western attempts to think the political:

> We are dealing with discursive orderings whose operations are dual,
> something that is characteristic of the West: on the one hand, a theo-
> retical operation that seeks to define scientifically, in the sense of the
> Platonic *epistēme*, or in the Marxist sense, or indeed in some other one,
> the object the society is lacking in order to be a good or a just society;
> on the other hand, plugged into this theoretical ordering, there are
> some implied discursive orderings that determine the measures to be
> taken in order to bring [society] into conformity with the representa-
> tion of justice that was worked out in theoretical discourse. (p. 21)

The essence of pietism, then, is the attempt to offer a complete, self-contained, context-independent, true description of some object that also serves as a standard by which to judge particular contexts and events. What makes this operation "pious" is just that the object of such theoretical discourse is by definition never fully actualized in any given state of affairs; it is always lost, absent, in need of recovery. But *that* fact, for Lyotard, is disastrous; for it opens the door to the nihilism preeminently explored by Nietzsche and regarded by him as constitutive of late, post-Enlightenment modernity. From the pious, theoretical, "philosophical" perspective, polities that are actually alive and kicking cannot but acquire a ghostly, "as-if" quality, as mere imperfect approximations of the true normative ideal. Though such a perspective is sustainable given a belief in a realm of truth that legitimates the actual as an imperfect approximation, the results are disastrous, as Nietzsche emphasizes, once the Platonic will to truth has devoured itself and its theoretical gaze has been exposed as only another mythology. In that event, given the absence of any perspective *other* than the pietistic, one is abandoned to a world of appearances that remain "mere" appearances, relatively valueless and without connection to a more substantial reality. Despite the best efforts of those who would "complete" the project of Enlightenment, the pietistic perspective is inseparable, in Nietzsche's view, from specifically modern logics of repression and nihilism because, for the pious, anything that departs from the principle of the ideal is by that very fact excluded, marginalized, or otherwise devalued.[7]

Lyotard's Nietzschean skepticism toward the very idea of a political theory suggests connections with some aspects of Heidegger's and Arendt's projects. For Nietzsche, theory is the symptom of a resentful desire to "correct existence," a desire that is limiting and repressive in its own right and issues eventually in what he calls "the devaluation of the highest values," the destruction of any and all unquestioned, authoritative principles of action and judgment.[8] Heidegger too, of course, is suspicious of the West's project of theoretical clarification, and indeed his diagnosis of the modern epoch of technology as the simultaneous realization and closure of Western metaphysics' project of accurately representing the world owes much to his encounter with Nietzsche's thought.[9] Arendt's skepticism toward a normative, "pietistic" theory of politics is rooted in her conception of free political action as initiatory, as that which brings into existence what could never even have been anticipated or imagined. For her, a norm could serve only to delimit the inherent open-endedness of action that she wishes to preserve.[10] Nietzsche, Heidegger, and Arendt all offer reasons to be suspicious of "theory" as the organizing trope of political thought and action and to attempt to articulate and explore the ideological effects of the search for grounds, principles, and transmundane sources to guide political action. The reference in Chapter 5 to "practicing political theory" does not so much call up the general problem of postmodern political theory as it does announce an attempt to *practice* it by putting the problematics of these authors to work in concrete texts, contexts, and discourses of American political thought, ideology, and culture: to read them "after" these theorists both in the sense of reading in their wake and in the sense of seeking to understand their ideas and formulations "otherwise," through alien contexts and concerns.

This book, then, works through the dilemmas presented by the questionability of the theoretical enterprise by exploring how theory is thrown into question in the context of American political thought, as a site in which the modern or postmodern problematic takes on the aspect of nationhood. Chapter 1, "The Fiction of America," highlights the theoretical significance of John Winthrop's attempt simultaneously to discover and to invent a metaphysical origin for the American nation in his sermon "A Modell of Christian Charity." Fixing the fabulous, fictionalizing dimensions of the Puritan project by drawing on the work of Jean-Luc Nancy and Philippe Lacoue-Labarthe on "the fiction of the political," this chapter articulates the "ontotheological" aspect of American national identity: Winthrop's sermon is shown to figure America as a peculiarly distilled, simplified, and even exaggerated political deployment of the fundamental tropes of European metaphysics as Nietzsche, Heidegger, and their late twentieth-century readers understand them. In Chapter 2, "America's Critique of Reason," I explore the contest between the purportedly Newtonian rationality of the Federalists and the "hermeneutics of suspicion" of the anti-Federalists in the public debate over the U.S. Constitution. That dispute is framed here in terms of the Habermasian ideal of a public sphere and its critics, emphasizing the limits of the "cynical" reason of unmasking and suspicion (with the help of Sloterdijk's and Zizek's philosophical and psychoanalytic understanding of modern cynicism). Anticipating some of the concerns of Chapters 4 and 5, "America's Critique of Reason" also demonstrates the unavoidability of fictions in opening up and preserving public spaces and exposes the dilemmas posed by the idea of a democratic public sphere.

"Cold War Metaphysics," the third chapter, shows how a variety of discourses claiming to represent the "real" America during the postwar period constitute an attempt (again reflecting the protocols of a foundationalist metaphysics dedicated to grounding action and judgment in correct representation) to reduce the complexity of the world to the measured forms of a grand allegory. Cold War discourse in America is metaphysical because it is organized around what Derrida calls "fear of writing," that is, the anxiety provoked by the effects of nonobligated or unmotivated linguistic signs. This chapter attempts to isolate "fear of writing" at a number of levels, from the intelligence estimates of the National Security Council and the scientistic ideology of postwar American political science to the political scandals and popular culture of the period. Framing the problem in terms of related but contradictory Hobbesian and Lockean strains in American political vocabularies, the chapter explores how the metaphysical dimensions of Cold War discourse push almost to the breaking point an American "identity crisis" organized around these two figures.

Chapter 4, "Fiction and the Dilemma of Postmodern Politics," exploits the fact that whereas our "official," "serious," "representational" discourses studiously avoid considering problems such as those articulated in earlier chapters, the fictional counterworlds of novelist William Burroughs and poet James Merrill make the loss of normative foundations, and the need to make strong political judgments, key themes of their major works. This chapter asks what it would mean to take their fictions seriously as thought and philosophy, its guiding question being Habermas's distinction between "serious" and "fictive" discourse. The reading of Merrill, especially, suggests that devices marginalized by Habermas as "fictive" harbor crucially important critical resources.

This last theme is taken up in the final chapter, "Practicing Political Theory Otherwise," which explores the appropriating of what the tradition marginalizes as "fictive" for the purposes of "serious" political discourse. The means for this exploration is a reading of Arendt's narrative practice of political theory as she applies it to the American founding in *On Revolution*. My aim is to articulate the significance of Arendt's highly idiosyncratic approach to the practice of political theory, one that takes the form of what she calls simply "storytelling." Through the figure of Arendt's reflections on the American Revolution, this chapter reflects on the inner and mutually illuminating relationships among and between the workings of foundationalist metaphysics, the practice of political theory, and the question of America.

To say that the approach I have adopted in this book puts me at odds with political theory as such is true only to the extent that one assumes traditional notions of theory—for example, that a clear line can be drawn between the fictive and the literal and that theoretical truths of the sort that yield insight into political life are invariably found with the latter, optional fancies with the former. Perhaps I can make this point more clearly by appealing to Michael Oakeshott's distinction between the "theorist" and the "theoretician" in order to suggest that my interpretations of ideology and metaphysics in American political discourse are an attempt to construct a kind of middle ground between the two. For Oakeshott, a theoretician is one who insists that acquiring a theoretical vocabulary about something can actually enhance one's ability to do the thing in question—as if a theory of morality would make one a better judge of moral conduct. That claim is what has given theory a bad name and theorists a dubious reputation; it is the reason, for example, that the cave dwellers of Plato's *Republic* wish to murder the returning theorist: instead of giving interesting reports about exotic travels which are valuable in themselves, the theoretician maintains he now knows more about their world than they do and that they therefore must adopt his vocabulary. The solution to this problem is to insist on the autonomy of theory, on its value as sheer storytelling and adventuring: if the returning theorist would limit his claim to being able to put what the stay-at-homes do in a different context, he could be accepted as a member of their community, though perhaps an eccentric one.

As appealing as calls for the autonomy of theory may be, and as necessary as they are in the context of an instrumentalizing society, in the end I find myself dissatisfied with an approach that, in Wittgenstein's famous phrase, "leaves everything as it is." Instead, I have chosen to explore the possibilities of the stance of the theoretician—one who wishes not just to return to the community and be accepted by it at the price of insisting that the journey need have no consequences for our self-descriptions but who cannot resist the temptation to redescribe the warp and woof of political discourse in light of these adventures. Such a stance entails all the risks Oakeshott describes, and my gamble is simply that it *can* be brought off, that there are ways in which the returning adventurer can tempt the stay-at-homes to hear him or her out and to feel the force of his or her redescriptions. This approach places me in the tradition of the theoretician rather than the theorist—"a deplorable character [who] has no respectable occupation." [11] From Oakeshott's point of view, I risk becoming a rank Platonist. The gamble is that the occupation of tempting readers to redescribe American political discourse in other terms can be a respectable one if it is done with the right touch, in the right manner. Does it all come down to manners? If so, I must try to mind mine. What can that mean, in this context, but exploring theses not to prove or disprove them but to discover the consequences of entertaining them?

CHAPTER ONE

The Fiction of America

In Hannah Arendt's reading of the founding of the American Republic, the Declaration of Independence is a model of how to resolve what she calls the "spiritual perplexities" that accompany the Enlightenment's sense of freedom from the authority of ancient traditions. According to her interpretation, the American revolutionaries faced, with inherited habits of thought, an entirely unprecedented concatenation of events beyond the capacity of that thought to address. The problem bequeathed by their sense of freedom from tradition was that such freedom brought with it the dissolution of the "absolutes" upon which political authority traditionally rested, thus raising the question of how to found a new republic in the absence of any divine or transcendental authority to justify and anchor the regime. The solution—highly unexpected, given the Enlightenment's antipathy to tradition—was to reinvent in modern terms the classical Roman idea that the act of foundation is itself authoritative.[1] According to Arendt, such a problem could not have arisen during the virtually unbroken "continuity of tradition" stretching from the first centuries of Christianity through the development of the European sovereign nation. In this tradition, the law, as command, needed "a divinity, not nature but nature's God, not reason but a divinely informed reason, . . . to bestow validity on it."[2]

The American escape from this tradition, in which the secular must be grounded in and ratified by the transmundane, occurred,

Arendt asserts, not owing to the development in America of a modern, posttraditional mode of thought but rather to the unexpected vagaries of political life in the New World as the early European settlers experienced it:

> From the weight and burden of this tradition the settlers of the New World had escaped, not when they crossed the Atlantic but when, under the pressure of circumstances—in fear of the new continent's uncharted wilderness and frightened by the chartless darkness of the human heart—they had constituted themselves into "civil bodies politic," mutually bound themselves into an enterprise for which no other bond existed, and thus made a new beginning in the very midst of the history of Western mankind. (P. 194)

In emphasizing the invention of America as the collision of European habits of thought and action with alien and inhospitable shores, Arendt repeats familiar tales of American "exceptionalism": bereft of traditional European institutions, the colonists could rely only on mutual promises as the basis of political stability, and hence they developed a political culture based more than any other on "promises, covenants, and mutual pledges" (pp. 181–82). European traditions came to grief faced with the sheer unprecedentedness of the demands of American experience.

In Arendt's account, this response to the New World led to a form of political authority in which the traditionally legitimating reference to absolute principles or transcendental imperatives was replaced by a practice of perpetual political transfiguration driven by the constant reinterpretation of the fundamental, founding, "constitutional" law. "The very authority of the American Constitution," Arendt writes, "resides in its inherent capacity to be amended and augmented" (p. 202). But delimiting the origins of the phenomenon of an almost infinitely plastic, augmentable, amendable interpretive authority to the experiences of the Europeans *after* crossing the Atlantic—as Arendt does when she insists on the trope of American exceptionalism, in which the raw experience of the New World shatters and relativizes European "absolutes" of long standing—needlessly brackets a whole field of prior American political discourse. The continuing presence of that discourse is, moreover, responsible for the persistent attachment of a sense of the sacred to an allegedly secular national project.[3] John Winthrop's sermon "A Modell of Christian Charity," delivered not *after* crossing the Atlantic but *during* the voyage of the members of the Massachussetts Bay Company, suggests that the problematics of an interpretive authority show up in many dimensions other than constitutional interpretation, which for Arendt becomes "the true seat of authority in the American Republic" (p. 200).

Winthrop's sermon, as it has come down to us, is paratextually marked as an *event:*

A MODELL OF CHRISTIAN CHARITY.
Written
On Boarde the Arrabella,
On the Attlantick Ocean.
By the Honorable John Winthrop Esquire.
In his passage, (with the great Company of Religious people, of which Christian Tribes he was the
Brave Leader and famous Governor;) from the Island of
Great Brittaine, to New-England in the North America.
Anno 1630

His discourse is dramatically *located* spatially, geographically, temporally, and authorially: the sermon is uttered by John Winthrop, governor of the Massachusetts Bay Colony, on board the flagship *Arbella*, in the Atlantic Ocean, during the voyage from England to America in 1630. To emphasize that the text *begins* by alerting us to these facts is, perhaps, to cheat a bit, as the manuscript on which it is based is not in Winthrop's hand. According to the editors of the *Winthrop Papers*, the original was probably copied and circulated for some years after the establishment of the community, by which time its founders were presumably being mythologized.[4] However that may be, it is possible to hear something other than mythologization in the simple emphasis on date, place, time, and occasion, because these are peculiarly *political* markers as well. Political discourses are preeminently concerned with particular times, dates, and places; with circumstances facing particular communities at particular moments. Dating and locating the speech would then not only signify an attempt to monumentalize the accomplishments of the founders of the community but also indicate the concretely *political* character of this speech. In singling out such facts as who they are, where they are going, and what they are doing, the subtitle of the sermon stands in a certain degree of contrast to the title in so far as it draws attention to the character of its audience as a body politic. As such, that audience is a community concerned less with timeless truths or metaphysical verities than with those truths embedded in histories, places, events; in intentions, actions, consequences.

The place named in the subtitle, however, is ambiguous: Winthrop's sermon is uttered "on the Attlantick Ocean," a geographic rather than a political space, and one situated, moreover, between two worlds: Great Britain and North America, Old England and "New-England." And this fact alone, I want to hazard, embodies and conveys something about the *kind* of political discourse Winthrop's speech is. Anachronistically relying on, and metaphorically extending to the political, Thomas Kuhn's distinction between "normal" and "revolutionary" science, we might distinguish normal and revolutionary political discourse.[5] As normal science involves approaching scientific inquiry guided by a paradigmatic exemplar and integrating puzzling and apparently idiosyncratic facts into the terms of a dominant, uncontroversial theory, so normal political discourse addresses political experiences and problems within the framework of settled practices, institutions, assumptions, concepts, and values. And as revolutionary science involves the invention of a new approach to scientific inquiry and a new theory that displaces the semantic horizon of its predecessor by way of accounting for anomalous facts, so revolutionary political discourse involves the reinvention of conventional terms of appeal, contestation, and adjudication. Normal political discourse relies on agreed-upon names, procedures, expectations; revolutionary political discourse aims to invent these. Of course there need be no simple relationship between revolutionary political discourse and revolutionary political action. Ancient discourses can obscure the birth of the new, and sometimes the old can be preserved only with the most radical transformation of its conceptual articulation. The relationship between political discourse and political action, as Marx shows brilliantly in *The Eighteenth Brumaire of Louis Bonaparte*, is always complexly ironic and overdetermined.

One form often taken by revolutionary political discourse, or by discourses that aspire to such an achievement, is the discourse of founding, and Winthrop's sermon conforms to that genre in not assuming the existence of a settled order but, rather, aiming to persuade others to accept the political terms it constructs and offers. The text of the *Modell* mentions its place of utterance, but that place possesses no traditionally sanctioned political significance. Speaking on the Arbella, in the Atlantic Ocean, to a literally unsettled group in the midst of a voyage away from one place of habitation and toward another, Winthrop speaks from a site designed for motion, not a fixed location but one whose meaning is wholly informed by its not being where it "should" be, by being on the way to somewhere else. Is it too much to find in the context of this event a dramatic sign of a departure from classical political assumptions?

Classically, political discourse is addressed to communities fixed in space and time; the fate of the polis as a whole is an overriding concern precisely because on it depend the lives of its associated members; it is impossible simply to fabricate a new polity as one makes a vase or a temple. Thus even where political action is thought to be in the service of or guided by the transmundane or transhistorical—bodies politic ideally serving the right growth of souls, as in Plato's or Aristotle's philosophical politics—the classical discourse of the political still remains tied to the concrete particulars and idiosyncratic histories of communities rooted in their own pasts. We see this, for example, in both Plato's and Aristotle's detailed examinations of their own societies and in Socrates' difficulties, in Book 5 of the *Republic*, in explaining how a good regime could be constructed out of the human material available from the less good regimes. Winthrop's gesture, in this context, is new, revolutionary, utopian; for his political discourse is situated in a place that is no *one* place, and it concerns not given, ineradicable features of a concrete society but motions, projects, possibilities, and voyages.

Above all, the forum of Winthrop's discourse signifies that the temporal rather than spatial dimension is central to Puritan understandings of what America and politics in America must mean. But while on the one hand Winthrop speaks from an indeterminate, unsettled place of "passage" (as the text puts it), on the other hand, he speaks with authority because he has already invested this passage with a highly specific and dramatically charged ideal meaning— so much so that he can as much as say what America is without the colony's having yet been truly founded. His subtitle defines "North America" as "New-England." North America, like everything else in the Puritan imagination, has a double meaning: an uncharted, uncivilized terrain in which new communities might be established without resistance;[6] also, the fulfillment of biblical prophecy, not only a new (and better) England but, more important, a New Jerusalem. Moreover, Winthrop's authority to define the mission of the Puritan colony as sweepingly as he does in the *Modell* is attributable to the vagaries of the company's charter, which, in neglecting to specify that its meetings take place in London so that policy would ultimately be governed by the Crown, made it possible for Winthrop to merge the roles of company head and colonial governor, company policy and state legislation.[7]

According to the charter, the owners of the Massachusetts Bay Company were empowered to

> make, ordeine, and establishe all manner of wholesome and reasonable orders, lawes, statutes, and ordinances, directions, and instructions, not contrarie to the lawes of this our realm of England, as well for settling of the forms and ceremonies of government and magistracy fitt and necessary for the said plantation, and the inhabitants there, and for nameing and stiling all sortes of officers, both superior and inferior, which they shall finde needful for that government and plantation, and the distinguishing and setting forth of the several duties, powers, and lymytts of every such office and place.[8]

It is difficult to imagine a more sweeping grant of authority than one that allows for the "settling of the *forms* . . . of government"; and the proviso that the colonists do nothing "contrarie to the lawes of . . . England" meant little, considering that the transfer of legislative authority to the colony itself left the colonists alone to determine what that might entail.[9] Because of these circumstances, it is not so much

Winthrop's discourse as his very persona that organizes the quite different (but, as we know, by no means incompatible or uncomplementary) institutional energies of trade, theology, and politics.

For all the powerful Crown and company backing of Winthrop's authority to found a community, however, that authority cannot be reduced to merely its official or statutorial aspects. Along with these we must register what might be called his *interpretative* authority, which consists in his ability to weave, from the elements of Puritan federal theology and the circumstances of the New World, a political discourse that is authoritative because it connects the intentions and prospects of the community's members to fundamental precepts of puritan federal theology. It is authoritative, that is, because Winthrop, as a master reader and interpreter of Scripture, grounds his claims about the nature of the political project upon which the group has embarked in God's Word itself.

The text of Winthrop's discourse begins by linking God's will with one of the politically most striking facts about the human condition, namely, inequality: "God Almightie in his most holy and wise providence hath soe disposed of the Condicion of mankinde, as in all times some must be rich some poore, some highe and eminent in power and dignitie; others mean and in subieccion" (p. 282). The series of stark contraries—rich/poor, mighty/lowly, power/powerlessness—is framed and softened, however, by the very grammar of the sentence in which they occur, which articulates them as the outcome of the singular event of God's holy will. The apparently basic fact of inequality, then, is really not so basic as it might appear, given that what is truly fundamental is that all humanity be as God ordains and that all are essentially one as expressions of God's plan. From this perspective, the differences in power and privilege which divide human communities are insignificant in comparison to everyone's shared identity as a child of God and participant in God's plan. Yet at the same time, the way in which such divisions are rendered insignificant also has the effect of establishing them as unalterable givens. No mere artifact of European society and history, inequality of wealth and condition enters into the way in which God has constituted humanity as social beings.

In singling out the problem of inequality by beginning with it,

Winthrop seems to make of inequality *the* political problem, at least from a secular point of view. Human beings differ from one another dramatically, so much so that their relationships with one another might appear to be essentially antagonistic; yet they must live together as God's people. Immediately upon outlining the permanence of inequality, Winthrop offers "THE REASON HEREOF," which is a rational demonstration of the truth of his claim that human inequality is an expression of God's will, and then supports it, soon enough, by paraphrases of specific biblical passages and accurate references to Scripture:

> I. Reas: *First*, to hold conformity with the rest of his workes, being delighted to shewe forthe the glory of his wisdome in the variety and differance of the Creatures and the glory of his power, in ordering all these differences for the preservacion and good of the whole, and the glory of his greatnes that as it is the glory of princes to haue many officers, soe this great King will haue many Stewards counting himselfe more honoured in dispenceing his guifts to man by man, than if hee did it by his owne immediate hand. (Pp. 282–83)

In the first place, then, mankind, as God's glorious creation, is more glorious to the extent that humanity manifests itself through a variety of human types and conditions than if all mankind were truly equal. Inequality of condition is simply an expression of the excessive plurality and variety that marks humanity in particular, and creation as a whole, as an artifact of God's pleasure. Winthrop goes on to offer two other ways in which inequality is consistent with God's will: the differences among men provide greater opportunities for God's grace and more varied opportunities for virtuous acts; and— what is politically most interesting—such differences constitute a mechanism whereby communities become more unified such that "every man might haue need of other" and "they might all be knitt more nearly together in the Bond of brotherly affeccion" (p. 283).

Winthrop's way of subordinating social differences to an end-governed whole manifests the familiar orientation of Puritan political theory toward the community (as the Church Visible, which in its turn points ideally toward the Church Invisible) as the ultimate referent of political thought, an orientation articulated by "federal" covenantal theology and its tenet according to which God enters into contracts with entire communities as such.[10] What I wish to underline here, however, is not Winthrop's substantive political theory so much as his method of deriving that theory and that method's links with persistent metaphysical motifs in Western political thought. In Winthrop's America, government is in large measure a hermeneutic problem, that of orienting oneself toward God's Word but also of bringing the Word to life in the practices and institutions of the community of those who believe the Word. The organization of both church and state, then, ought to be an attempt to mirror Christ's life as closely as possible in his absence, to make over the human world into a holy world as far as possible. The Christian community finds its essence by imitating the essence of Christ—that is, the *essential* meaning of Christ's appearance and life, not its external features.[11] The true meaning is recoverable and reproducible because it is, as Winthrop conventionally terms it, a "pattern" that recurs, a "type": the call of God; the period of doubt, temptation, and testing; the final breakthrough to faith pure and simple. The Christian state too, if it is to be intelligible *as* a Christian community, must vividly rely for its protection on faith in Christ alone.[12] The fundamental marker of fidelity to God's law is the theocratic structure of the community itself, where the final and ultimate authority is the church, in other words, God's laws, rather than the depraved human desires of our "bodye of Corruption."[13]

The Protestant project of recovery, as manifested in Winthrop's foundational discourse, thus obeys the mimetic logic that Philippe Lacoue-Labarthe has isolated as the persistent metaphorics of the Western tradition of political thought: the fundamental meaning hermeneutically recovered from the biblical text serves as the essential principle around which the Christian community is organized, formed, shaped, and brought to stand.[14] For Lacoue-Labarthe, Western metaphysics has been haunted by "a dream of the City as a work of art," a dream in which "the political (the City) belongs to a form of *plastic art*, formation and information, *fiction* in the strict sense" (p. 66), that is, in the sense of the forming or molding of available and malleable material; and it is in this sense that "an entire tradition . . . will have thought that the political is the sphere of the *fictioning* of beings and communities" (p. 82).[15] In the Western tradition, that is, the political is metaphysically delimited as the actualization or realization, in "this world," of values, norms, or commands possessing an absolute status as "otherworldly." It is a realization effected by means of politics conceived as rulership: the shaping of bodies politic in accordance with an ideal model, whether philosophically derived or religiously revealed. Thus Lacoue-Labarthe cautions against the inference that the "fictional" in this sense determines the political as sheer, unregulated invention: "The fact that the political is a form of plastic art in no way means that the *polis* is an artificial or conventional formation, but that the political belongs to the sphere of *techne* in the highest sense of the term, that is to say in the sense in which *techne* is conceived as the accomplishment and revelation of *physis* itself" (p. 66). The political as traditionally understood is the sphere of art, but in the sense of a making or fabrication controlled by a prefigured model with which subjects are enjoined to identify.[16] Winthrop's theocracy obeys this logic: members of the colony at Massachusetts Bay *become* a community by entering into a compact with God to ground the success of their endeavor in grace alone, but the community can only be brought into existence because, in some sense, it potentially already exists as a community (God's elect) as revealed through God's Word.[17]

In Winthrop's discourse, too, America is less a territory or place than a goal, a project, a making. The violence involved in such a conception of America—which dismisses as merely incidental or unessential the concrete histories of America and its inhabitants in order to reconfigure America as a *new*, that is, newly authenticated, England—is inescapable and by now, of course, widely acknowledged. As Congregationalists, Winthrop's Puritans cannot conceive of membership in the church apart from the *work* of faith and the publicly confessed self-scrutiny such work demands. The true church is not the church into which one is born but the one that is *made* when individuals who publicly confess their faith voluntarily join together to follow God's commands and enjoy his promises.[18] Winthrop's church is thus radically independent of the particular, local histories of nations, states, and traditions: "Since Christ's time," as he writes, "the church is to be considered as universal without distinction of countries." [19] No longer rooted to the soil, the theocracy is grounded in the terrain of human decisions, discourses, interpretations, and agreements—in art.

After appealing to an interpretation of Scripture to justify why God burdens man with the political problem (that of inequality and difference), Winthrop goes on to sketch the biblical doctrine on the "rules whereby we are to walk, one towards another" and the "law by which we are regulated in our conversation, one towards another." [20] Thus Winthrop proposes to derive from Scripture the rules regulating how we are to live together, to formulate a biblical political theory. The Bible narrates man's fall from grace and God's contrivances with the help of which man may be redeemed. Man, Winthrop points out, has known two "estates": that of "innocency," before the fall, and of "regeneracy," in which man is saved through God's grace by accepting Jesus Christ as savior. The law of the estate of nature is a conduct of life appropriate to paradise: as man was created in God's image, "all are to be considered as friends in the estate of innocency" (p. 283). The unity of the state is sundered with the fall and man's depravity. Because God's offer of redemption through the acceptance of Christ is not accepted by all, "the law of grace or the gospel . . . teacheth us to put a difference between Christians and others" (p. 284): the Christian community possesses a special privilege among human communities.

There are thus two laws of conduct: one deriving from nature or a state of innocence, another appropriate to man's current, divided estate, overshadowed by the distinction between the saved and the damned. That distinction means, among other things, that Christians are enjoined to make extraordinary sacrifices to ensure the success of *Christian* communities and their members; Christians can be expected to acknowledge that all of their personal gifts and possessions are rightly subjugated to the task of building and preserving the community of believers (pp. 284–89). Ideally, the work of the Christian community is to elide, as far as humanly possible, the terrible consequences of fallen man's deprivation of direct government by God by so arranging human artifices and agreements as to enforce God's law, not man's.

The true bond tying together the believers is not "force of Argument," but love, which is "the bond of perfection" that serves to knit the various parts of the body politic together (p. 288). "All true Christians are of one body in Christ," Winthrop writes, and "all the partes of this body being thus vnited are made soe contiguous in a speciall relacion as they must needes partake of each others strength and infirmity, ioy, and sorrowe, weale and woe." "This sensiblenes and Sympathy," he continues, "of each others Condicions will necessarily infuse into each parte a natiue desire and endeavour, to strengthen defend preserue and comfort the other" (p. 289). The history of the church, no less than the lives of Jesus and his apostles, exemplies this concern for others exercised "not for wages or by Constrainte but out of loue" (pp. 289–90). Christian love is pure and unconditional, then, but it is also *reciprocal* "in a most equal and sweete kinde of Commerce": "This loue is allwayes vnder reward it never giues, but it allwayes receiues with advantage" (p. 291).

Significantly, the mutuality of Christian love, the glue binding the ligaments of the Puritan body politic, is itself based on a law of identity: "The ground of loue is an apprehension of some resemblance in the things loued to that which affectes it, this is the cause why the Lord loues the Creature, soe farre as it hath any of his Image in it, he loues his elect because they are like himselfe, he beholds them them in his beloued sonne" (p. 290). Christian love, in Winthrop's understanding, is the expression or manifestation of God's will to absolute self-identity: God, we are to understand, would remain identical to himself, and love is the force of that will to identity, the desire to make oneself over in God's image and to merge one's identity with others so moved. "Of all the graces," then, "this makes vs nearer to resemble the virtues of our heavenly father." Winthrop goes on to observe that the peculiarity of the Massachusetts community will consist in the fact that there, the identification of every member of the community with God will be so complete as to overpower the forces that might drive the community apart or divert it from its true mission. The community is founded on its irresistible desire to model itself on "this louely body of the Lord Jesus," so that "by prayer meditacion continuall exercise at least of the speciall [power] of this grace till Christ be formed in them and they in him all in each other knitt together by this bond of loue" (p. 292): the Puritan community is a *work*, a community realizing its essence by modeling itself on an aesthetic image brought to stand as a transcendental absolute.[21]

The Puritan community, then, will imitate God's love by placing the concerns of a Christian community above all private considerations: "In such cases as this the care of the publique must oversway all private respects." But how can such an extraordinary display of God's power be achieved? Winthrop's answer to that question is bold: "That which the most in theire Churches maineteine as a truthe in profession onely, wee must bring into familiar and constant practise" (p. 293). Christian doctrine must be made real in the world; the saints must really act as God commands them; into Winthrop's mere "Conclusion," arising from "former Consideracions," that "loue among Christians is a reall thing not Imaginarie," life must be breathed (p. 292). Hypocrisy or backsliding is intolerable, however, not only because it is unchristian but because the reliance on God's love and the project of imitating Christ is the *essence* of this particular community, exhausting its very identity, thereby singling it out for God's special concern:

> When God giues a speciall Commission he lookes to haue it stricktly obserued in every Article. . . . Thus stands the cause betweene God and vs, wee are entered into Covenant with him for this worke, wee haue taken out a Commission, the Lord hath giuen vs leaue to drawe our owne Articles wee haue professed to enterprise these Accions vpon these and these ends, wee haue herevpon besought him of favour and blessing: Now if the Lord shall please to heare vs, and bring vs in peace to the place wee desire, then hath he ratified this Covenant and sealed our Commission, [and] will expect a strickt performance of the Articles contained in it, but if wee shall neglect the observacion of these Articles which are the ends we haue propounded, and dissembling with our God, shall fall to embrace this present world and prosecute our carnall intencions, seekeing great things for our selues and our posterity, the Lord will surely breake out in wrathe against vs be revenged of such a periured people and make vs knowe the price of the breache of such a Covenant. (P. 294)

The colony at Massachusetts Bay will not have been just any Christian community, then, but one that will have taken on itself the special task of manifesting, proving, and displaying to the world, as its explicit contract with God, that Christian love is "a reall thing not Imaginarie." A force to be admired and above all emulated by all the world, Christian love's very essence resides in its power, by sheer force of example rather than mere argument, to constitute a model for others to mime. It is for that reason that Winthrop calls on the members of the Massachusetts Bay Colony to make of their community a *model* of Christian charity: a "Citty vpon a Hill" scrutinized by all, it must make manifest that its members rely above all on fidelity to God's law, not man's, for ultimate protection. In complex mimetic logic, a circular chain is thus established in which Winthrop's community mimes God's law (as revealed in the Bible), and the world, through miming the Puritan community, is brought to God; an endless chain of similitude, resemblance, and identification governs the colony's theologicopolitical strategy.

America, then, insofar as it *is* still a "place" for Winthrop, is figured above all as the site of a demonstration, a *proof* that life can indeed be shaped in accordance with God's commandments as opposed to the corrupt ways of the European churches and states. But just to the extent that what is to be proved here is a *timeless* truth, registered *against* the temporalizing corruptions of tradition, history, and power, Winthrop's project will be intimately tied to such discourses; for it must then be unimaginable except as a hermeneutic project of wresting free the pure Word of God from the corrupt textual body of distorting commentaries, interpretations, and institutions built upon them—a project as endless as it is necessary. To see how this aspect of Winthrop's America is articulated, we must turn away from the substance of Puritan political theory as well as its metaphysical underpinnings in "the fiction of the political" and toward the problem of *how* Winthrop founds a community by *reading* the Bible.

Winthrop appeals to knowledge of God as revealed in the Bible, to the Word of God and to God's Scripture.[22] But although the biblical history of sacred events in holy time constitutes a grammar for the interpretation of mundane events in secular time (the time between Christ's departure and return), this script must be read and interpreted if its meaning is to be apparent. That one must *read* the Bible—that God's presence is not directly, immediately felt at each

moment—is itself the fall: if he would reestablish direct communication, man must decode the script of the Bible. But God's script is precisely a revelation that is intelligible to *fallen* man's understanding;
hence, recovering the authenticity of God's *word* demands a labor of
interpretation that isolates the spark of the divine in merely human
sentences. Given the idea of a federal covenant, then, there is the
most intimate connection between the interpretation of God's Word
as registered in the biblical text and the foundation, by the establishment of a specific contract between God and a people, of a political
community. And because God's *word* must be recovered by *human*
acts of interpretation which—just because they are human—are thus
eminently contestable, the "America" figured by Winthrop will of
necessity have been an interpretive polity that, despite all claims to
absolute authority, is always potentially unsettled and dynamic.

How is the meaning of the Word of God recovered from God's
script? Although God himself is irreducibly mysterious, he chooses
to make his intentions regarding man intelligible to him, and the
whole truth of those intentions is expressed in the biblical record of
divinely inspired revelations to human individuals. There is something of an ambiguity in the idea of *God's* word; for the words we
have are humanly constructed transcripts of the divine revelations
themselves, which thus call for interpretation to isolate the divine
Word in the flawed human script. As Martin Luther puts it, "The
Holy Scripture is the Word of God, written and (as I might say) let-
tered and formed in letters, just as Christ is the eternal Word of God
cloaked in human flesh. And just as Christ was embraced and handled
by the world, so is the written Word of God too."[23] This consideration determines the basic textual strategy of Protestant critique:
Luther and Calvin insist on returning to the original Word of God
in its purest and most singular meaning, freeing it from human additions and misinterpretations by means of commentary that itself is
always liable to error and contestation.[24]

Framed as a *return* to the essential meaning of God's Word, Protestant reformism presents itself not as the creation of new institutions but as a recovery of an earlier, older, more original state of
affairs forgotten, lost, or maliciously concealed and corrupted. Just
so, Winthrop's *Modell of Christian Charity* outlines a new commu-

nity, a New England located in the New World, which is presented as a recovery of the most ancient eternal truths: what God truly created, commanded, and promised. The political problem is thus, among other things, a problem of knowledge and interpretation— "Knowledge of God the Creator," as Calvin entitles the first part of his *Institutes of the Christian Religion* (1556–1559). If God is indeed the *author* of our experience, we must read with an eye to authorial intention, read in a way that allows us to grasp God's meaning rather than imposing our own and corrupting his text. Calvin's *Institutes* will thus recover the original authorial intention organizing the biblical script (and creation itself) so that we can know God by grasping how he commands us to live during the period between Christ's appearance on earth and the Last Judgment. The realization that the script of the Bible demands interpretation is somehow at odds with the presupposition that God's Word is complete and sufficient in itself, however, which accounts for a curious feature of Luther's and Calvin's texts, namely, the prefatory apologies for their having been written. Calvin, for example, asserts that "Holy Scripture contains a perfect doctrine, to which one can add nothing," and then goes on to produce fifteen hundred pages of commentary.

The Bible's "last word" is thus endlessly prolonged, but how is this project reconciled with the presupposition of the Bible's self-sufficiency? Again, by relying on the uneven distribution of natural talents, including that of reading the Bible correctly. As Calvin continues,

A person who has not much practice in it [reading the Bible] has good reason for some guidance and direction, to know what he ought to look for in it, in order not to wander hither and thither, but to hold to a sure path, that he may always be pressing toward the end to which the Holy Spirit calls him. Perhaps the duty of those who have received from God fuller light than others is to help those simple folk at this point, and as it were to lend them a hand, in order to guide them and help them to find the sum of what God meant to teach us in his Word. Now, that cannot be better done through the Scriptures than to treat the chief and weightiest matters comprised in Christian philosophy. For he who knows these things will be prepared to profit more in God's school in one day than another in three months—particularly as he knows fairly

well to what he must refer each sentence, and has this rule to embrace
all that is presented to him.[25]

Publicly offering his "additions" to the biblical text is consequently
enjoined on Calvin as his godly duty to those less practiced in "Christian philosophy." In any case, Calvin's abilities are due not to him but
to God, who will ultimately judge the worth of his work.

Calvin presents his commentary as explicitly "parasitic" and peda-
gogic; readers are to use it as an aid to their own readings of the
Bible, not as a substitute; in shedding light on the Bible by offering
its basic teaching whole, God is simply revealing himself once again
through Calvin. Indeed, if Calvin's commentary "supplements" the
Bible, the Bible itself is already supplementary to a message God
has installed in creation itself: if God is the *creator* or *author* of the
universe, the latter's immediate presence is by itself a sufficient revelation of God to man. Calvin's act of supplementation is thus done
imitatio Christi and indeed *imitatio Dei;* for in the wake of man's fall
from divine sponsorship, God has supplemented his original revelation with others (comprised in the Bible) to underscore his plans
for mankind. In a word, the persistence of sin requires some to help
others read the Bible right.

What form, exactly, will such assistance take? God's Word is a
totality not to be wholly identified with any *particular* sign, passage,
or event in the Bible. These latter, rather, are intelligible only in
terms of the complete message contained in the Bible as a whole,
which is why Calvin states that only one who knows "the chief and
weightiest matters comprised in Christian philosophy"—one, that
is, who possesses a unified understanding of the central teachings of
Christianity—will be able to *read* the Bible in the sense of understanding particular passages and the events they relate. Only a reader
who "has this rule to embrace all that is presented to him" will know
to "what he must refer each sentence" in the Bible: understanding the details presupposes a sense of the whole. That "sense of the
whole" is nothing less than Christian faith: a Christian initiates a
reading of the Bible by relying on faith in Christ. That faith supplies,
as it were, the terms of hermeneutic engagement: if Christ's appearance and his promise of redemption is the central event in history,

the Bible will then appear as an archive of figures, meanings, and events that recur endlessly because, in effect, they all say the same thing, either anticipating or remembering the moment and meaning of Christ's appearance. The role of the biblical reader is therefore to articulate the meaning of the whole to readers who might be unable to accomplish this for themselves, to enable them to begin the task of studying the Bible on their own.

Reform, then, is guided by the recovery of the original, pure, singular meaning of the Bible, a meaning generated by a process of interpretation which projects a total meaning from the apprehension of details and discovers in the detail a manifestation of the whole. We know the content of this recovery and reformation: the Protestants discover textual support in the Bible for clerical marriage, for a priesthood of all believers, and above all for the centrality of grace. The consequence, however, is that contestation and political innovation is virtually institutionalized, because of the inevitable contestability of any single formulation of the central teaching of the Bible and because any such hermeneutic formulation is stigmatized in advance as a merely human, partial, necessarily incomplete adumbration of God's Word, awaiting a more precise characterization or an alternative construction—as the dissents of Roger Williams and Anne Hutchinson emphatically show. As Luther writes, the Word of God comes to us having always already been "handled" by man; yet we cannot isolate the authentic Word of God except by "handling" it further. The fact that political authority is now oriented toward shaping the community in accordance with a true meaning that keeps changing with the vagaries of hermeneutic reappropriation installs in the concept of theocracy a perpetually renewed necessity to shape and *re*shape the body politic.[26]

At issue in the emergence of America in one of its earliest (European) incarnations—as a New England—is a peculiarly distilled, simplified, and exaggerated political deployment of fundamental tropes of European metaphysics. At bottom, this America is nothing but the practice of political *theory*, metaphysically understood: the hermeneutic isolation of a pure essence to be imitated, yielding a concrete effectuation that may serve as a model for others; an attempt to regulate practices by appealing to an aesthetically projected absolute that organizes a harmonious, self-identical, enduring unity. At same time, Winthrop's absolute is installed by a hermeneutic practice (the recovery of meaning from confused and humanly corrupted traditions) that contaminates its own purity, constantly deferring the moment at which unity will be achieved, always calling for a more authentic reading, always doubting its own insights. For example, crises the community faces lend themselves to interpretation as God's commentary on the always-ambiguous state of the covenant.[27] Already with Winthrop, America will have been figured as an interpretive polity, wresting true meaning from its corrupt human handling in a project that, of course, would prove ultimately to be of a virtually ungovernable intensity. Americans 150 years later would write a preamble to their Constitution that stands as a virtual refutation of the leader of the Puritan theocracy's warnings against "seeking great things for our selues and our posterity." But the break will not have been so absolute that Abraham Lincoln could not affirm, more than 200 years after Winthrop's discourse, that America is a nation dedicated to a timeless theoretical "proposition" and specially committed, moreover, to the project of breathing life into it, making it manifest, and demonstrating its truth. America will not only have "fictioned" the political but have taken up that fictioning as the very essence of its being as a community.

CHAPTER TWO

America's Critique of Reason

1

According to the first *Federalist* essay, the true significance of American civilization will have been its success at "establishing good government from reflection and choice": the rationalization of politics in the name of freedom. For Hamilton, Madison, and Jay, as for the eighteenth century generally, the desirability of a society governed according to the deliberations of reasonable individuals was obvious, though grave doubts were entertained about the extent to which such government was realizable. In the twentieth century, however, a growing awareness of reason's pathologies—the spread of forms of rule intimately linked to the accumulation of knowledge—has provoked many to question the very idea that reason and freedom are necessarily twinned and, hence, to contest the desirability of a rational society.[1] Habermas's interest in "rethinking the public sphere" is motivated in part by the resulting need to conceptualize other, nonfunctionalist modes of reason and deliberation. New forms must be appropriate to modern contexts of political, moral, and aesthetic practice in which authoritative, transcendent grounds situated outside the purely relative spheres of opinion and communication have been irretrievably lost. Nor can reformulations yield to the Nietzschean or Weberian temptation to erect sheer, arbitrary will as the fundamental ground of practical life.[2]

Shifting perspective from an isolated subject of objectifying reason to a picture of rationality modeled on dialogue, Habermas conceives of a *communicative* as opposed to purely *functionalist* reason. Deliberation among diverse equals is governed by normative ideals (of sincerity, mutual understanding and consensus, and rational defensibility) built into the formal structure of communication itself. He intends communicative reason to ground the concept of a democratic public sphere in which political decisions are shaped by the uncoerced deliberations of equal participants. Such a concept, Habermas believes, does justice to modernity's eschewal of otherworldly, transcendentally obligating imperatives for action while it preserves a place for the philosophical hope, traditionally mortgaged to the transcendental, that reason can guide human affairs to freedom.

Proponents of this normative, Habermasian concept of the democratic public sphere, according to which political legitimacy is measured by the ideal of decisions reached through reasoned debate among equal discursive partners in forums where what matters is the quality of the argument rather than the status or identity of the arguer, have recently had to defend themselves against self-styled "Nietzschean" critics dedicated to debunking them by "unmasking" the very idea of a universal, regulative norm *necessarily* aligned with pluralistic, democratic practices. Critics of the normative ideal of communicative reason, especially those influenced by Michel Foucault, worry that, under some circumstances, this criterion can entail the imposition of discursive practices that at once establish and conceal the domination of an embodied subject of reason. The criterion of uncoerced consensus, they argue, is not capable by itself of isolating each and every instance of domination, routinization, exclusion, or imposition likely to be destructive of the spontaneous, open, revisionary character we associate with a plural, democratic polity. In particular, it is blind to the necessary limitations entailed by any "regime of truth," no matter how free of coercion and manipulation its establishment may have been, and therefore it cannot serve as the fundamental analytic ground of an emancipatory political theory. Indeed, there can be no such fundamental ground; no assured theoretical perspective or analytic device to replace the irreducibly ad hoc, narrative practice of constructing, in Foucault's terms, the history of the present. The task of political theory, rather, is "to leave power no place to hide" (his phrase too), not even in the ideal of uncoerced consensus. Because truth is properly in the service of "life," as Nietzsche formulates it in the second of his *Untimely Meditations*, life must be allowed to break through even the norm of uncoerced consensus for the sake of previously unrecognized possibilities—if by "life" we are allowed to understand not only those needs or instincts whose repression Freud famously accounted a cost of civilization but, more broadly, the open contingency of spontaneous, value-positing interaction.[3]

But the question of whether the normative ideal of uncoerced consensus as the ground for a conception of the democratic public sphere can be defended against Nietzschean unmasking easily works to obscure an equally crucial matter. Let us assume that arguments appealing to the idea of an entirely noncoercive, objective practice of discourse can be debunked on the grounds that the Habermasian position relies on an absolute distinction between coercion and consensus, whereas Nietzsche (and Foucault) demonstrate how the autonomous subject of reason is *always* already subordinated to the very system of constraints that "produces" autonomy. The would-be debunker succeeds all too well owing to the *political* consequence of unmasking, which is what Peter Sloterdijk characterizes as the cynicism flowing from "enlightened false consciousness," the insinuation in our political culture of a tacit norm according to which the truth itself is cynically manipulated in public forums for private advantage. When unmasking the pretensions of objective truth or pure reason becomes an official ideology rather than a plebian mode of attack, the result is a political culture in which the claims and actions of public figures are automatically discredited while simultaneously clung to as necessary fictions. This amounts to an apt description of our reigning, fin de siècle, postmodern politics, where political appeals are incredible *just because* they rely on claims to universality, objectivity, or community that are no longer believable—even though they might not be recognizable as *political* appeals were they not to make such claims.[4]

If the ironic consequences of the attempt to expose the antipluralist effects of an ideology of reason seem familiar, it is because they amount to the political version of a dialectic initially identified by Nietzsche and extended by him to characterize European modernity as a whole: reason's commitment to objective truth leads it to undermine its own foundations by discovering the irreducible partiality of the *will* to truth.[5] The resulting nihilism stems from the fact that the debunker of reason stands, as in Nietzsche's figure from *Beyond Good and Evil*, in the shadow of the dead God: he or she no longer believes in the objectivity of reason but cannot shake off the conviction that objectivity is the only worthy standard of action and judgment. Nowhere is Nietzsche's ambiguous legacy to us *less* ambiguous than in our political culture's anxious conviction that beneath every proposal or idea claiming general application there is hidden a particular interest or a merely strategic necessity.

The situation described by Sloterdijk yields an apparent dilemma: preserve the normative concept of the democratic public sphere at the cost of betraying Foucault's injunction to leave power no place to hide, or unmask the philosophical ideologies and interests lurking beneath the reasoned search for consensus at the cost of undermining the conditions of democratic political life. To explore some of the contours of this dilemma, I turn to an exemplary historical deployment and unmasking of political reason: the defense of the U.S. Federal Constitution and the anti-Federalist critique of it. That conflict yields alternatives that closely approximate the opposition just isolated between reason and its unmasking. Following it, I hope, will allow us to reflect on the peculiar possibilities and limitations of American constitutional discourses for the project of a "postmetaphysical" understanding of politics.

2

American constitutional government as an emblem of the rationalization of politics? That interpretation sits uneasily with the standard account of the Federal Constitution, attributable to the *Federalist* itself, which views it as controlling the passions not by reason but other passions—"self-interest rightly understood," as Tocqueville formulates it, a principle that "uses, to direct the passions, the very same instrument that excites them."[6] But if the constitutional order itself relies on shrewdness rather than nobility, it would be difficult indeed to find a historical instance of political discourse more faithful to the normative ideal of the public sphere than the *defense* of the Constitution put forward in the *Federalist* essays, which carefully eschew appeals to status and identity in favor of rational argument alone.[7] In the opening essay of *The Federalist*, for example, Publius predicts that the "great national discussion" of the proposed Constitution will let loose a "torrent of angry and malignant passions." A correct view of the merits of the Constitution can be reached only if the participants in the debate rise above their passions and put aside, for the purposes of political deliberation, "any impressions other than those which may result from the evidence of truth" (p. 5). Publius's call for the application of enlightened reason to politics is, of course, much more than a response to the ills of American politics during 1787 and 1788; it also expresses an understanding of the modern political predicament. A dynamic society of conflicting interests and individuals supports little in the way of—indeed would seem to undermine—a moral community whose shared ends and commitments might constitute a relatively impersonal foundation for political legitimacy and coherency. Any such standards must, therefore, be discovered by reason guided by experience: in the place of a moral community, political science.

But is not the political reasoner himself afflicted with passions and interests? Publius addresses this worry by relying on a rhetoric of frankness: "I will not amuse you with an appearance of deliberation," he announces, "when I have decided. I frankly acknowledge . . . my convictions" (p. 6).[8] That Publius's prejudice in favor of the Constitution is named and acknowledged is meant to suggest that the reader need not inquire further into Publius's identity and can concentrate instead on his arguments. Throughout the *Federalist* essays, Publius returns to the theme that the people must put aside their passions and judge the Constitution according to the test of a disembodied reason, of logical coherence and strict deduction divorced from, as we might put it, the "constitution" (or position) of the *subject.*

Scholarly accounts of the public debate over the ratification of the Constitution stress the substantive political differences that divided the architects of the Constitution from those who opposed its ratification. Federalists feared the fragmentation and consequent domestic convulsions possible under the Articles of Confederation, while so-called anti-Federalists worried that their liberties would be swallowed up by a large national government.[9] Federalists argued that a weak central government and a system of fragmented state governments would leave America vulnerable to foreign political influence, while anti-Federalists were convinced that a strong national state would be tempted to support overseas adventures and require continuing military conscription to maintain, thus eroding democratic institutions. Federalists warned of the corrupt government that might result from popular demagoguery, while anti-Federalists countered with the tyranny of presidents appointed by "men of parts" in the "aristocratical" Senate. Most generally, while the anti-Federalists placed their faith in civic virtue; local traditions; and small-scale, representative governments whose electorate and political officials are bound together by the similarity of their interests and conditions, the Federalists imagined a rational administrative *system* that, they hoped, would operate relatively independently of the idiosyncrasies of particular publics, communities, and ideologies and might thus serve for some time to govern a complex, dynamic, rapidly changing, and expanding society.

The scholarly discussion assumes that, though there was disagreement over substantive issues, Federalists and anti-Federalists debated the issues on the basis of a common understanding of what counted as an acceptable political argument, claim, or interpretation.[10] But there is good reason to believe that the anti-Federalists rejected not only the proposed Constitution but Federalist political science as well. Whereas Publius insists on judging the merit of an assertion or argument according to canons of reason that reject ad hominem arguments, some anti-Federalists insisted that, in order to grasp the political meaning of an utterance, one has to take into account the *subject* of the enunciation as well as the enunciation itself. As "John DeWitt" puts it, "As a man is invariably known by his company, so is the tendency of principles known by their advocates—nay, it ought to lead you to inquire who are its advocates?"[11] For "DeWitt," it would appear, it is not sufficient to dissect the *arguments* of the Federalists, because such an approach relies on a separation of reason and passion which is fatal to genuine political understanding, where discourse, passion, and reason are intimately connected and cannot be separated, even analytically. Pure reason, applied to political speech, yields naïveté; political wisdom begins by placing political speech in the context of a passionate interpretative agon. This necessitates studying the motives of the speaker, which reveals, for "DeWitt," "ambitious men . . . who openly profess to be tired of republican governments" (3:25). With this in mind, "DeWitt" suggests reading the Constitution with the suspicion that it harbors "aristocratical tendencies," which he proceeds to locate in the way in which the House of Representatives alienates elected officials from the people and is subservient to the Senate and presidency.

We thus find two models of political reason, two hermeneutic approaches to the interpretation of political claims and proposals: one based on suspending local points of view and dedicated to attaining a perspective in which particular passions and interests are subordinated to the universal perspective of reason; another in which the political meaning of a discourse is accessible only through the tangled passions, motives, and interests of the speaker. The presence of these two models suggests that the dispute between Federalists and anti-Federalists ought not to be understood solely in terms of such controversies as the differences over the interpretation of Montesquieu, alternative conceptions of representation, or the question of republican virtue. Also to be considered is the "metatheoretical" problem of how political proposals are to be understood, analyzed, interpreted, and evaluated. Debating that problem gave expression to a "hermeneutics of suspicion" that not only rejected the possibility of a disengaged, theoretical understanding of politics but regarded the latter as, at best, a naive and untrustworthy guide for political deliberation and, at worst, a mask for baser, "human, all-too-human" motives and interests.[12]

Viewed in this light, the ratification debate takes on a distinctively contemporary significance, and the anti-Federalists can be made to enter contemporary debate, not only (as has been recognized) about the character of American democracy and the role of a powerful state but also about the nature of political reason and the scope and limits of unmasking critiques. Political theorists and historians of political thought have pointed to the perennial importance to American political thought of anti-Federalist reservations about distant central government and impersonal political machines.[13] But attention to the ways in which anti-Federalists scrutinized and assessed the claims and arguments surrounding the Constitution reveals a preoccupation with the implication of the subject in the utterance of political judgment. The anti-Federalists took issue not only with the national state designed by the Founders but with the latter's vision of a rational political science as well. They argued not only that the proposed national government was dangerously "aristocratical" but that the way in which it was presented and defended was unfaithful to the peculiar demands of *political* analysis and judgment. Or rather—as they rarely made such arguments explicitly—much of their analysis of the Constitution rests on such considerations. A reconstruction of anti-Federalist hermeneutics will serve to illuminate the meaning of claims about a "reasonable" state founded in something more durable, and allegedly more admirable, than the idiosyncrasies of embodied and contested identities.

For the Founders, establishing a *novus ordo seclorum* required a rigorous frankness, a new honesty about human motives, about the uncertainties of knowledge and the intractability of an irreducibly (though not entirely) self-interested human nature.[14] In return for honesty, however, a measure of order could be brought to the analysis of human affairs. As Morton White argues, Publius opposes the notion of apodictic certitudes or exact knowledge in the field of politics; such was the almost exclusive reserve of the natural sciences and mathematics alone.[15] But this does not mean that he eschewed the possibility of a more rational method for thinking about politics or that he felt the need to defer to traditional wisdom on such matters. In fact, Publius argued for a political science, and *The Federalist* follows such a logic.

Although it is a commonplace that the *Federalist*'s defense relied on "reason," the specific strategies have, however, been less carefully scrutinized.[16] Men and women of the previous century could refer to a deity personally engaged in the affairs of the world as the basis for their understanding of legitimate government, of course; but eighteenth-century Americans' thought tended to replace the Divine Contractor with an image of God as the Grand Architect— in Newton's terms, the uncaused first cause. "The business of natural philosophy," he proclaims in his *Opticks*, "is to argue from phenomena and deduce causes from effects 'till we come to the very first cause, which is *not* mechanical."[17] God is now a *Deus absconditus*, not only not immanent in the universe but no longer even within earshot of mortal man. Newton explains the operation of bodies as if the universe were a mechanism: rational understanding means picturing the universe as a machine whose parts function according to regular (hence predictable) routines. But although the mechanistic philosophy risks the celebrated and bemoaned disenchantment of the world, it also serves to bring one closer to God than ever was possible through the unreliable and degraded script of the Bible. Whereas the Bible offers God's revelations only through the finite and corruptible language of men, the motions of the heavenly bodies display God's revelation in utter purity. To the extent that natural philosophy could discover the nature of that original revelation, it could claim to be a more reliable guide to the deity than the Bible itself. Thus while Newtonians objectified the universe as a mechanism, they brought the knower closer to God. Moreover, enlightened political science also suggested a revision of the doctrine of *imitatio Christi*, the idea that the Christian should strive to live his or her life on the model of Christ's. Now the model deity was the Grand Architect, the builder of the perfectly balanced and regulated machine. Accordingly, the Founders would *design* a Constitution for the ages. As Woodrow Wilson puts it, "The makers of our Federal Constitution constructed a government . . . to display the laws of nature. Politics in their thought was a variety of mechanics. The Constitution was founded on the law of gravitation."[18]

In Newton's "method of analysis," one begins with a small number of simple, fundamental propositions that are then combined to form more complex hypotheses that can explain phenomena. The method of analysis is guided by experiment, that is, by observations made under precisely controlled conditions and referred to publicly accessible information and experience. If experiments yield data at variance with the hypotheses, the latter must be revised. Publius's rational demonstration of America's need for a stronger, more "energetic" national government follows the method of analysis closely. Thematically, the defense of the proposed constitution begins (significantly enough, from the perspective of the last half of the twentieth century) with an argument from national security: America must be united under a strong national government because only the unity of a powerful national state can preserve the security of the people in the face of two threats, foreign attack and civil war. America's celebrated commercial energy will threaten European nations, tempting them to exploit differences and divisions among the States in order to slow the American economic juggernaut, and rivalries and mutual suspicions on the part of the States themselves will result in civil war. The presentation and defense of this thesis follows the Newtonian approach of rational deduction and experimental verification. The necessity of a strong national government is first shown to follow from a generalization of observations of human affairs. The vision, in essence, is Hobbesian: individuals love power and will devour one another in its pursuit unless restrained by a strong authority, whether that of their own reason and will or of the state.[19] However strong may be current feelings of unity owing to the Revolutionary War, we can be certain that such sentiments will eventually give way to conflict between the States (*Fed.*, p. 28). Thus the prevention of civil war demands a strong central government.

Just as the states must be regulated by a strong national government in the interest of peace, so must the national government be powerful in relation to the rest of the world, in order to deter aggression (pp. 18–19). If it is human nature to act to obtain what one wants, nations, being made of individuals, act on the same basis; war is therefore an ever-present possibility. And as we have seen, war against America is likely to be especially attractive to foreign nations because it is inevitable that America will become a major economic competitor. The only way to deter foreign ambitions is through a strong military deterrent, which in turn requires an effective, independent national government for its coordination and deployment.

Publius, then, proceeds first by deducing conclusions from generalizations about observations: nations, like individuals, are by nature greedy, resentful, suspicious, and fearful, and resort to war to get what they want; protection from them requires a strong government. The deduction is then strengthened by introducing confirming observations from the historical record. In Federalist No. 4, the history of Greece provides evidence for the thesis that neighboring states without a central authority are likely to consume one another in conflict. And in Federalist No. 5, Great Britain is invoked: so long as she was divided, internal wars prevented her from achieving a position of world power. The resort to world history is analogous in political science to experiment and observation in natural philosophy. In *The Federalist*, political regimes and policies are a series of experiments that, by their success or failure, validate or disprove the principles they express. Precisely because reason and history coincide only rarely, historical evidence is an effective proof text for rational deliberation on the best polity: regimes that destroy themselves invalidate the principles on which they are established; those that flourish strengthen the principles on which they are based. The example of Britain serves both scientific purposes: so long as she remained divided, Britain lacked influence; after her unification, she was able to resist foreign domination and become a major world power.

Only when a combination of rational deliberation and scrutiny of the historical record supports a particular conclusion can one look for additional verification in popular opinion: "It has until lately been a received and uncontradicted opinion, that the prosperity of the people of America depended on their continuing firmly united, and the wishes, prayers and efforts of our best and wisest Citizens have been constantly directed to that object" (pp. 8–9). But lately, unscrupulous politicians have worked a change in public opinion; thus the necessity for rational deliberation and historical discrimination to determine who is correct. Upon deliberation, Publius concludes that the people, not the politicians, are right: "I am persuaded in my own mind, that the people have always thought right on this subject, and that their universal and uniform attachment to the cause of the Union, rests on great and weighty reasons" (p. 12). We thus have three terms: popular opinion, the results of rational inquiry, and views promulgated by unscrupulous politicians who seek to lead the people away from settled beliefs by appeals to vanity and fear.

Popular opinion and reason agree in this case, to the disadvantage of the politicians, who constitute the greatest danger to security when they appeal to the passions of the people. The right model of the relationship among the people, their leaders, and reason is shown in the people's reaction to the pronouncement of the Continental Congress in 1774. The people realized that the delegates were in a better position than they to judge and so deferred to their advice: "These and similar considerations then induced the people to rely greatly on the judgment and integrity of the Congress; and they took their advice, notwithstanding the various arts and endeavours used to deter and dissuade them from it" (p. 12).

The crucial point here is that in Publius's method of political science, popular opinion is never *decisive*. If it agrees with rational inquiry, such agreement may be taken as another indication of the likely truth of the latter: an opinion that is durable, long lasting, and in accord with reason is probably based on experience and judgment, not passion. The status of popular opinion in Publius's science of politics thus nicely allegorizes the constraints placed on the direct expression of the general will in the Federal Constitution.

Although scholars such as Morton White are surely correct to emphasize that Publius rejects the idea of a knowledge of politics as certain as that which science gives us of natural laws, then, Publius does nonetheless appeal to the *model* of scientific reason in the staging of his political reflections. Equally important, as Albert Furtwangler has shown, is that Publius solicits the attentions of a public inclined to be convinced by the sober reflection and cool logic he so masterfully deploys and thus offers a model for political debate for a public ready to be guided by "candor."[20] Accordingly, Publius urges his readers to control their appetites and subdue their passions in order rationally to decide the question of the new constitution. Federalist political science emphasizes cool logic, clear and unambiguous assertions, solid argumentation, and above all political claims that appeal to a disembodied reasoner striving to objectify his world rather than to immediate passions and affections, which are necessarily narrowing and parochial.[21] Disembodied reasoners are exactly what the anti-Federalists refuse to be; they also discover signs of passion in the body—that is, in the language and Constitution—of Federalist reason itself.

3

Suspicion is a virtue.

—Patrick Henry

When Publius employs mechanical metaphors or those drawn from mechanistic sciences, they are typically introduced self-consciously, flagged *as* metaphors whose fictional status is insisted upon. Publius takes care to maintain a finely articulated distance from any idea or proposition he entertains, and the effect conveyed is that of a subject of purely formal reason, committed dogmatically to no hypotheses in particular, accepting beliefs only after they have been carefully scrutinized and found worthy of acceptance. The discourse of the "disengaged subject of reason," as Charles Taylor has named that figure, enables Publius to speak as the citizen of a national state, concerned not with the parochial problems of a Maryland or Massachusetts but with the country as a whole, not only at the present moment but in the future; and with the human destiny as such, not with late eighteenth-century Americans alone.[22] Only rarely does Publius enter into the fray to deal with local or partisan issues, or even to rebut specific criticisms; rare exceptions almost always take the form of footnotes or asides.

In contrast to the cool, unruffled, earnest but distanced tone of the *Federalist* essays, the attacks of the anti-Federalists are often driven home with the aid of sarcasm, satire, irony, and hyperbole. It is true that, like Publius, anti-Federalists typically expressed a conventional distinction between excessive passion, which led men astray and prevented sound thinking, and reason, which must be sovereign. They did not wish their criticism to be taken as personal attacks against individuals and, like Publius, called for "candor" in the public debate over ratification. Rarely did anyone go as far as Rawlins Lowndes of South Carolina, who attacked "the depraved inconstancy of those who pant for change."[23] "A [Maryland] Farmer" goes some length to deny any such feelings: "The *Farmer* took the liberty to condemn and to expose the doctrines and errors of *Aristides* [pseudonym of Alexander Contee Hanson]; but with charity he imputed his opinions to defect of judgment, or want of information. . . . The *Farmer* could not possibly entertain any *personal* resentment against *Aristides*" (5:85).[24] Like Publius, many anti-Federalists expressed a sense of the historic nature of the decision over the Constitution, and they echoed his call for reason and deliberation. According to Samuel Chase, for example, "The question is the most important that ever came before an assembly for decision. It involves the happiness or misery of millions yet unborn. The decision requires all the consideration that the utmost exertion of the powers of the mind can bestow. The present and future generations will bless or execrate us. We [are] at a solemn crisis—and the magnitude of the subject requires that it should be deliberately considered and fully considered with temper and moderation."[25]

But despite his lack of personal resentment toward Aristides, the Farmer insists on referring to aspects of Aristides's temperament and personality to shed light on the political meaning of his arguments and claims, speculating that Aristides' "fancied superiority, and insolence of office" is at the bottom of Aristides' claim that the Farmer's opposition "proceeded from his desire *to pay* COURT to a gentleman who lately held the highest office in the State." The Farmer goes on to suggest that Aristides revealed his true identity to the public because "his vanity prompted him to believe, that his character would carry respect and authority" (5:87–88). Aristides' vanity and arrogance are not without substantive significance, however, because the burden of the Farmer's criticism is to refute Aristides' view that a bill of rights has the status of a grant of rights from a sovereign—an understanding that, the Farmer stresses, is shared by no one but "the prostituted, rotten Sir Robert Filmer" (5:5). By connecting vanity, arrogance, and love of power with claims that can appear consistent with a larger doctrine meant to justify the divine right of kings and a patriarchal state, the Farmer succeeds in bringing out latent shades of meaning, implication, and political significance in the fragmentary assertions of his interlocutor.

Anti-Federalists commonly noted that some of the greatest anxiety about popular rule, and the greatest enthusiasm for the way in which the Federal Constitution might impede direct popular participation in government, came from the most privileged individuals in the community. The Farmer again: "Is it not strange to hear the

Governor of Connecticut, gravely asserting in their convention, the novelty of government by representation, and pinning all his hopes of our future happiness, and exemption from evil on this new discovery! And yet the Governor of Connecticut is not only one of the worthiest of our citizens, but rather of uncommon information in a country, where very few are so independent in their fortunes as to afford much time to study" (5:22). More than sheer ressentiment was at issue, however; a variety of subjective characteristics of its defenders were claimed to reveal essential truths about the Constitution they defended. Refuting the objection "Merchants are for it," Samuel Chase noted, "Ans. consider them. Birds of passage." At issue here are instability and opportunism, not power, though Chase also answered the question "Why not *another convention?*" by asking, "Who is violent for it—Ans. Rich men and speculators and office hunters" (5:17).

One of the clearest expressions of unwillingness to forgo ad hominem arguments is found in the speeches of Patrick Henry. "Suspicion is a virtue," he argued, "as long as its object is the preservation of the public good. . . . Guard with jealous attention the public liberty. Suspect every one who approaches that jewel."[26] For Henry, reason can be a source of dangerous ambiguity in governments and constitutions; an overly "reasonable" government may be one in which a justification for tyrannical policies is always available. Before Charles I, the rights of Englishmen were ill defined, so that "power and privilege then depended on implication and logical discussion."[27] Clarity and simplicity are to be valued more highly, in politics, than reason; otherwise rulers will utilize the ambiguities in complex laws and traditions to usurp power. Another anti-Federalist, writing under the name of "Denatus," echoes that view: "The aristocrat, makes a parade of bombastical wisdom, says the land-mark was not evidently fixed upon the face of the ground, but only the ideal— The people seem satisfied—He studies their imbecility, and moveth the land-mark a little farther" (5:18).[28] And Melancton Smith finds that the proponents of the Constitution are themselves "suspicious" of the motives and intentions of their countrymen—and dedicated to spreading such suspicions: "Why . . . are we told of our weakness? Of the defenceless condition of the southern parts of our state? Or the exposed situation of our capital?" (p. 321). Scrutiny of motives and dispositions is all the more important because, even if one sincerely wishes to be frank and honest about one's prejudices, that is impossible. "Men are apt to be deceived," writes "Cato," "both with respect to their own dispositions and those of others. Though this truth is proved by almost every page of the history of nations, to wit, that power lodged in the hands of rulers to be used at discretion, is almost always exercised to the oppression of the people, and the aggrandizement of themselves; yet most men think if it was lodged in their hands they would not employ it in this manner," though they are frequently wrong (p. 331).

"John Dewitt" also insists, as we have seen, on the necessity of knowledge of the speaker for a true comprehension of the political meaning of his utterances. The representatives at the Constitutional Convention, he notes, "were delegated from different States, and nearly equally represented, though vastly disproportionate both in wealth and numbers. They had local prejudices to combat, and in many instances, totally opposite interests to consult. Their situations, their habits, their extent, and their particular interest, varied each from the other. The gentlemen themselves acknowledge that they have been less rigid on some points, in consequence of those difficulties than they otherwise should have been" (p. 193). "DeWitt"'s suspicions lead him to discover that the Constitution makes no genuine provision for popular representation—that "this blessed proposed Representation of the People, this apparent faithful Mirror, this striking Likeness, is to be still further refined, and more Aristocratical four times told." As for the security of the people, "They have none. Nor was it intended by the makers that the should have.... They do not design to beg a second time. Knowing the danger of frequent applications to the people, they ask for the whole at once" (p. 316). Candor, for many anti-Federalists, did not preclude suspicion; for Henry, as we have seen, it could be a virtue. Taken together, these fragmentary comments suggest both a picture of the Constitution very different from the one Publius presents and an approach to deliberation over political affairs strikingly at variance with Publius's. In that picture, Publius and his Constitution do not present the aspect of a pristine and balanced machine, amenable to rational explanation. Again and again, their suspicions lead anti-Federalists to discover in the Constitution and its defense particular interests, potentially tyrannical powers or tendencies, and local prejudices where only sheer law should be.

4

It is only the superficial qualities that last. Man's deeper nature is soon found out.

—Oscar Wilde

An essential strand of American political interpretation and judgment, then, relies on the strategy whose dialectic and dilemmas I isolated at the outset of this chapter: unmasking the particularity of desire beneath the professions of dispassionate reason. Viewed from that angle, the anti-Federalist suspicions indeed issue in an "unmasking" of the Law of the Constitution, namely, that Law which insists on appearing as pure, neutral, impersonal, and dispassionate. Publius's national government resembles nothing so much as the Freudian superego, that seemingly "other" voice of reason and duty: in Publius's optic the national government brings to bear order, dispassion, deliberation, and sobriety on the passionate, brittle, unpredictable state governments.[29] If Publius presents the Constitution (and his explanation of it) as an embodiment of a superegoic Law, however, it is not surprising that anti-Federalists could so easily identify moments at which the Law's universality is vitiated by the particular. There is an ineluctable aspect of the particular, and even more tellingly of desire, to the Law itself: the pleasure taken by the subject of the Law in arresting the desire of others.[30] Because the Law cannot be *pure*, disembodied duty, but invariably betrays a positive pleasure in doing or enforcing duty, there is found, in Slavoj Zizek's terms, a smear on the pure body of the Law which indicates the sadistic pleasure taken in limiting the actions of others. Indeed, it is precisely such marks of pleasure that must be concealed if the Law is to appear as universal and above the fray. Just such a work of concealment is what Federalist reason cannot acknowledge but what the anti-Federalist hermeneutics of suspicion strives to articulate.

It does so, as we have seen, by emphasizing the subject of the political utterance, insisting that the meaning of political speech requires attention to what the speaker is *doing* when he speaks. In Zizek's (Lacanian) terms, anti-Federalist hermeneutics thus attends to the "subject of the enunciation" as well as the "subject of the statement." Every utterance, according to Zizek (and Lacan), possesses a double register: it makes a claim about some state of affairs, and it issues a tacit communication to the other about how the speaker wishes to be recognized; it attempts, that is, to establish a certain *relationship* between subjects. As there is no guarantee that these two dimensions of the speech act will be in harmony, it is possible for the subject of the statement to come into conflict with the subject of the enunciation. In effect, Publius insists that, for the purposes of debating the merits of the Federal Constitution, he be treated as the subject of a statement only, and in this way he hopes to efface the "smear" of enjoyment on the pure body of the Law. The anti-Federalists insist on taking him also as the subject of an enunciation, that is, as one who, in insisting on these constraints, attempts to establish a relationship with the listener. In insisting that subjectivity be "bracketed," then, just what demand is being enunciated? Simply that he be taken as the bearer of pure, dispassionate, universal Law for another, as Publius represents himself to be. But that formulation already contradicts itself by betraying the *desire* to represent the Law to another, the pleasure taken in enforcing the terms of reason. Using Zizek's language again, anti-Federalist hermeneutics brings to light the *obscene* elements of American constitutional discourse. For suspicious anti-Federalists, Publius's rigid distinction between reason and passion is necessarily disingenuous to the extent that it conceals the national/ rational state's passion to control and administer the passions of others and, indeed, to reduce politics to control and administration.

Unmasking the duplicities of others, however, entails its own duplicities and self-delusions: the strenuous attempt not to be duped, to sharpen one's vision so as to penetrate all masks and disguises, does not succeed without its own epistemological costs. Punning on Jacques Lacan's *nom-du-père*, Zizek formulates these costs by explaining "How the Non-duped Err" in conferring upon publicly constructed identities the status of unreal fictions:

We effectively *become* something by pretending that we *already are* that. To grasp the dialectic of this movement, we have to take into account the crucial fact that this "outside" is never simply a "mask" we wear in public but is rather the symbolic order itself. By "pretending to be something," by "acting as if we were something," we assume a certain place in the intersubjective symbolic network, and it is this external place that defines our true position. If we remain convinced, deep within ourselves, that "we are not really that," if we preserve an intimate distance toward "the social role we play," we doubly deceive ourselves. (Pp. 73–74)

"The final deception," according to Lacanian theory, "is that social appearance is deceitful, for in the social-symbolic reality things ultimately *are* precisely what they *pretend* to be," Zizek concludes. The symbolic order in which one's public identity is constructed is *not* unreal; to assume that it is, or that there is a "real" identity hidden behind it, are equally pernicious errors.[31]

A related desire to affirm the distinctive reality of identities formed in public motivates Hannah Arendt's insistence on the distinction between wearing a mask that differs from your "self" and simple hypocrisy:

For Machiavelli, the one-who-is and the one-who-appears remain separated, albeit not in the Socratic sense of the two-in-one of conscience and consciousness, but in the sense that the one-who-is can appear in his true being only before God; if he tries to appear before men in the sphere of worldly appearances, he has already corrupted his being. If, on the scene which is the world, he appears in the disguise of virtue, he is no hypocrite and does not corrupt the world, because his integrity remains safe before the watchful eyes of an omnipresent God, while the virtues he displays have their meaningfulness not in hiding but only in being displayed in public. No matter how God might judge him, his virtues will have improved the world while his vices remained hidden, and he will have known how to hide them not because of any pretense to virtue but because he felt they were not fit to be seen.[32]

Wearing a mask that differs from your self is not hypocrisy because public identities have a life of their own; they do not merely "express," and are not reducible to, a private self or ego. If the anti-

Federalists accuse Publius of wearing the mask of reason, then, we might justifiably conclude of them that they err in the manner of the non-duped.[33] Publius is "pretending," but it is impossible, or at least risky, to pretend in public because one might always become what one appears to be. Indeed, Furtwangler speculates that precisely this was at work in the invention of Publius as an authoritative voice on the Constitution:

> In defending this new Constitution, Hamilton and Madison . . . began to explain it to themselves. Neither author was completely satisfied, or even tolerably hopeful, when he left the Convention. As a result, the act of writing a defense of the Constitution was an exercise in self-contradiction — or perhaps better said, self-persuasion. The task imposed on Publius required Hamilton and Madison to review the Constitution, to go over it once more in a spirit of candor, looking for strengths rather than defects.[34]

What emerged from that task was a public persona — "Publius" — quite different from any that Hamilton or Madison might ideally have imagined for themselves; but in this reading, Publius is a mask, an *acknowledged* fiction, not a disguise. Indeed Arendt emphasizes the American revolutionaries' "Roman" awareness not so much of privileged historicopolitical models they might emulate but of the dependence of revolutionary political activity in the modern period on modeling, emulating, and generally appearing on the stage of the political world in a character not necessarily identical to one's private, personal self.[35] From this perspective, Publius, the persona of the disembodied, dispassionate reasoner calmly surveying America's past, present, and future, cannot be unmasked — not because he wears no mask but because there is no question of his dissembling that he *is* masked.

Pace anti-Federalist suspicions, then, we ought perhaps to read Publius's frank avowal of prejudice as a declaration that he cannot *in fact* be the dispassionate, reasoned observer he nonetheless emulates; ought to read it, that is, as the Lacanian or Zizekian mark of the non-coincidence of the subject with itself. But let us here return to the dilemma with which this chapter began: choosing between unmasking the "stain" of desire beneath the veneer of dispassionate reason at the cost of degrading as "human, all-too-human" the practice of a nontranscendental politics based on discourse rather than on transcendental grounds, *or* taking the mask of reason at face value, as it were, at the cost of furnishing power a hiding place. Publius's *frank* role playing eludes both this dilemma's horns because the dilemma assumes a certain *intolerance* for fiction that Publius does not share.

Merely adopting an attitude that avows and tolerates the fictional quality of the roles and personae necessarily assumed by the political reasoner may not, however, be sufficient to hold at bay the corrosive dialectic of unmasking. Habermas, for example, acknowledges the artificial, fictional, counterfactual, "aesthetic" character of democratic political activity: such discourse proceeds under the sway of norms, rules, and constraints having a purely discursive, nonmetaphysical status. Habermas sees such artifices—in particular that of uncoerced consensus, or "rationally motivated agreement"—as "idealizing assumptions" essential to preserving the openness or contestability of the prescriptions governing practical life, prescriptions whose force lies solely in the extent to which their claim to validity can be rationally defended: "Communicative reason finds its criteria in the argumentative procedures for directly or indirectly redeeming validity claims to propositional truth, normative rightness, subjective truthfulness, and aesthetic harmony."[36] Such is the bedrock of our intuitions regarding the legitimacy of procedural or formal democracy as a political community characterized by its participants' commitment to the democratic way of life rather than to a single, substantive good or goal, no matter how universal or "true."

But for Habermas, such idealizing assumptions have the status of "presuppositions that the participants themselves have to make if communicative action is to be at all possible" (p. 197), even though these same participants know that "their discourse is never definitively 'purified' of the motives and compulsions that have been filtered out" (p. 323). Freedom, absence of coercion, and rational motivation, then, are all only "counterfactually" assumed by the participants; that is, the ideally constituted democratic political life remains, strictly speaking, *fictional*. In Habermas's theory, the stains of unreason, coercion, and inequality that inform actual discursive political practice will not wash; so long as his idealizing assumptions remain *ideals*, they render democratic political practice into a merely imaginary activity. As a result, they are powerless to immunize democratic politics against the nihilistic consequences of the true world becoming a fable, that is, the world as *mere* discourse, as it must appear to those who act in the shadow of the dead god of theoretical truths and critical ideas.

As noted, Habermas's conception has come under attack for the way in which it elides certain forms of distortion or unreason in its very commitment to the counterfactual bracketing of status and identity for the purposes of reasoned political argumentation. Nancy Fraser, for example, responding both to feminist and Foucaultian concerns, argues that such bracketing reflects a *masculinist* understanding of rationality, and she calls for a rethinking of the public sphere that makes room for the expression and celebration of diverse, embodied, classed and gendered discursive styles.[37] Jean-François Lyotard, for his part, proposes an ideal of multiplicity and difference (rather than traditional reason's identity and consistency) to guarantee and regulate the diverse and contending discursive arenas of postmodern society.[38]

Characteristic of such suggestions, however—including, suprisingly, Lyotard's—is that each takes the form of proposing a candidate for a critical idea to regulate a practice. In other words, all partake of the theoreticist grammar that Lyotard himself calls "pious": all formulate theoretical *ideas* that are then invoked to judge and shape actual political practice (see the Introduction). In this respect at least, and despite the fact that these proposals are typically formulated in response to the Foucaultian concern that the Habermasian position offers power a place to hide, Foucault's approach to thinking about political practice is very different; for he attempts to dispense with the question of an ideal situated outside and regulating practice *even* in its Habermasian version of formal conditions of communication. To be sure, Foucault at times does seem to endorse something like the Habermasian approach, as in his comment that consensus is "a critical idea to maintain at all times: to ask oneself what proportion of nonconsensuality is implied in . . . a power relation, and whether that degree of nonconsensuality is necessary or not, and then one may question every power relation to that extent."[39] More often, however, Foucault attempts to distance himself from an approach that would tie democratic political practices to the necessary assumption of a critical, regulatory ideal, as in this statement:

> In the serious play of questions and answers, in the work of reciprocal elucidation, the rights of each person are in some sense immanent in the discussion. They depend only on the dialogue situation. The person asking the questions is merely exercising the right that has been given to him: to remain unconvinced, to require more information, to emphasize different postulates, to point out faulty reasoning, etc. As for the person answering the questions, he too exercises a right that does not go beyond the discussion itself; by the logic of his own discourse he is tied to the questioning of the other. Questions and answers depend upon a game—a game that is at once pleasant and difficult—in which each of the two partners takes pains to use only those rights given him by the other and by the accepted form of the dialogue.[40]

Politics, for Foucault, is not an *idea* to be clarified and instantiated but a practice—better, a *complex* of practices—to be celebrated, feared, preserved, changed, contributed to, or resisted, as appropriate. If the piety of theory plays into modern cynicism and nihilism by constituting the public sphere, willy-nilly, as a site of illusion or deception or parody, Foucault seems to recommend that we not *judge* democratic politics by measuring it according to an ideal. Rather, he would have us *value* it by contributing to its preservation and vitality, and conceive democratic political deliberation not as a fictional approximation or pretense but as the actual realization of whatever capacity we have to speak and act.[41] To do otherwise, he fears, is to risk falling into the resentful Socratic project of "correcting existence," as Nietzsche characterizes it in *The Birth of Tragedy*.[42] If the political as participation, deliberation, display, or agonism is to persist, it will be because it is interesting enough, seductive enough, to win the loyalty of its participants. For Foucault, political life begins and ends as a "this-worldly" practice; its entire value lies in the fact that it is *practiced*, not in the extent to which it realizes an ideal.

In his insistence on treating politics as a practice rather than as an obligating idea, Foucault's attitude resembles Arendt's conviction that the value of political action is inherent in its performance. Employing Nietzsche's most characteristic trope, Arendt expresses this point by reversing the Platonic hierachy that, for Lyotard, constitutes piety: we uphold the ideal of equality, she asserts, not because its truth obligates us to do so but "because freedom is possible only among equals, and we believe that the joys and gratifications of free company are to be preferred to the doubtful pleasures of holding dominion."[43] Like Foucault, Arendt stresses the erotic appeal of political action, its seductiveness as a way of life. The "actual content of political life," she writes, is "the joy and gratification that arise out of being in company with our peers, out of acting together and appearing in public, out of inserting ourselves into the world by word and deed, thus acquiring and sustaining our personal identity and beginning something new" (p. 263). Finally, Arendt insists that politics—as freedom, that is, as democratic deliberation—is *nothing but* a practice or performance: "Men *are* free—as distinguished from their possessing the gift for freedom—as long as they act, neither before nor after; for to *be* free and to act are the same."[44] For that reason, "the phenomenon of freedom does not appear in the realm of thought at all" (p. 145). For both Arendt and Foucault, what the former calls the "element of coercion" that truth carries with it is dangerous, not so much for the forms of rulership or domination it elides, as for the nihilistic energies it organizes when the imperative to "correct existence" necessarily issues in the baleful conclusion that existence is always incorrect.[45]

5

Publius's role of disembodied reasoner, his references to a "new science of politics," and his reliance on metaphors drawn from the motions of planetary bodies are commonly adduced as evidence of the idea that the operation of American Constitutional government is grounded in nature's own laws of motion as discovered by Newton.[46] Paradoxically, this appeal to Newtonian *science* has the effect of offering *mythical* reassurance, because the citizen can feel that his political system is modeled on heaven itself.[47] What greater or more powerful obligating idea could there be, after all, than scientific truths expressive of the immutable, eternal cycles of nature?

The anti-Federalist hermeneutics of suspicion, however, urges us to examine the constitutional order as an earthly, passionate, this-worldly regime. Margaret C. Jacob has stressed the connection between paganism, pantheism, and radical republican thought in the seventeenth and eighteenth centuries, noting "the tendency on the part of republican thinkers to explain the ordered universe not by reference to an imposed, supernatural order, administered as it were by God's self-styled representatives, kings, oligarchs and the like, but by recourse to the notion that spirit lives in nature, in people as in all objects." Extending back to the Hermetic and Neoplatonic tradition, she writes, this pantheistic dimension, by the early eighteenth century, "had become central to the way thinkers operating in a republican tradition formulated their arguments for a secular order decreed by the interests and necessities of ordinary men in search of a balanced and representative system of government."[48] Jacob appeals to convictions held by those whom Lyotard refers to as the "lesser Greeks": that the world is a complex and ambiguous whole to be negotiated and balanced, not an ideal truth to be known and realized.[49] In Lyotard's "pagan" view, the world is characterized by a multiplicity of powers and vitalities, none of which has the final say and whose specific capacities, interests, and proper sphere of influence is always at least somewhat in doubt.

The pagan character of the Constitution is to be found in the doctrine of overlapping responsibilities, or "mixing powers," among the three branches of government as a way of securing independence without relying on mere "parchment barriers." As Jeffrey Tulis explains, although "powers were separated and structures of each branch differentiated in order to equip each branch to perform different tasks," so that "each branch would be superior . . . in its own sphere and in its own way," nevertheless, "the three objectives of government—popular will, popular rights, and self-preservation—are mixed twice in the Constitution: they are mixed among the branches and within each branch so that each objective is given priority in one branch."[50] Tulis rejects two influential interpretations of the separation of powers: one that regards the branches as strictly separated according to function and another, more plausible theory that the Constitution simply mandates a plurality of power centers to ensure that no one center dominates the regime. In fact, each branch is designed so as to be especially suited to a particular function or functions, but each is also concerned with the "specialties" of others (as in Congress and the presidency, both of which are concerned with national security). The result is a dynamic constitutional polity in which the borders separating one branch from another are continually made the subject of agonistic contestation: "The founders urged that 'line-drawing' among spheres of authority be the product of conflict among the branches, not the result of dispassionate legal analysis" (p. 43).

Line drawing, though regulated by the architecture of the Constitution, is passionate, open, and dynamic. There are no formulas for resolving disputes, only power and contestation, or, in Lyotard's (Wittgensteinian) terms, the invention of new moves in the constitutional language game. From this perspective, the "reasonable" constitutional order, smeared or not with obscene enjoyment, gives way to an order of multiple, warring gods negotiating and renegotiating their always already impure, always already violated spheres of influence. Lyotard defines this kind of paganism as a political regime in which "there is always some talking to be done" because there are no fixed criteria from which a conclusion can be reached, "no stable system to guide judgments." Although "a society that must decide what is obligatory" is the essence of postmodernity, such a condition was first articulated by the Greeks, whose mythology lets us see "a society of gods that is constantly forced to redraw its code."[51] In offering his definition of postmodernity, Lyotard only echoes Max Weber's evocation of an enigmatic, "disenchanted" paganism as characteristic of modernity:

> We live as the ancients did when their world was not yet disenchanted of its gods and demons, only we live in a different sense. As Hellenic man at times sacrificed to Aphrodite and at other times to Apollo, and, above all, as everybody sacrificed to the gods of his city, so do we still nowadays, only the bearing of man has been disenchanted and denuded of its mystical but inwardly genuine plasticity. Fate, and certainly not

"science," holds sway over these gods and their struggles. . . . Many old gods ascend from their graves; they are disenchanted and hence take the form of impersonal forces. They strive to gain power over our lives and again they resume their eternal struggle with one another.[52]

With the demise of the holistic world view established by Christianity and the separation of science, art, and morality into autonomous and incommensurable inquiries, we are placed once again in a "pagan" universe—one in which a *plurality* of forces struggle with one another, defining and redefining boundaries and experiences in a never-to-be-settled, open, and unpredictable encounter.

The Federal Constitution establishes a political arena for a "pagan" encounter of warring gods redefining their powers as they struggle. In this respect, the anti-Federalists are decidedly "modern" or "classical," whereas the Federal Constitution would already be postmodern, in Lyotard's terms. Following Montesquieu, anti-Federalists insisted that republican government flourishes only when based in a small community united by shared practices and understandings. As "Brutus" observes,

In a republic, the manners, sentiments, and interests of the people should be similar. If this be not the case, there will be a constant clashing of opinions; and the representatives of one part will be continually striving against those of the other. This will retard the operations of government, and prevent such conclusions as will promote the public good. If we apply this remark to the condition of the United States, we shall be convinced that it forbids that we should be one government. The United States includes a variety of climates. The productions of the different parts of the union are very variant, and their interests, of consequence, diverse. Their manners and habits differ as much as their climates and productions; and their sentiments are by no means coincident. The laws and customs of the several states are, in many respects, very diverse, and in some opposite; each would be in favor of its own interests and customs, and, of consequence, a legislature, formed of representatives from the respective parts, would not only be too numerous to act with any care or decision, but would be composed of such heterogenous and discordant principles, as would constantly be contending with each other.[53]

An independent and energetic government, for "Brutus," one capable of decisive action in the public interest, must be grounded in a set of shared practices, customs, and interests serving to unite a community. Sovereignty, for "Brutus" as for the tradition, implies indivisibility, unity, and above all univocity. For Publius, *that* kind of "organic" unity is precisely what is to be undone by the Federal Constitution, which substitutes for it warring powers establishing domains vis-à-vis one another in the absence of fixed criteria. Resorting once more to Lyotard, we might say that "Brutus" is a classicist who insists that a legitimate legislator must assume the position of "an author who can write while putting himself at the same time in the position of a reader, being able to substitute himself for his own reader, . . . whereas in what we call modernity"—what Lyotard will come to call *post*modernity—"he no longer knows for whom he writes. . . . When you cast bottles to the waves, you don't know to whom they are going." [54]

Are we to conclude, then, that American constitutional politics—politics as the continual renegotiation of "essentially contested" boundaries—is an adequate institutional expression of a purely performative, postmetaphysical politics? That would chime with Richard Rorty's attempts to imagine a postmetaphysical liberalism based on a pragmatic attachment to liberal democratic *practices* rather than on theoretically grounded principles of justice or morality:

> Democratic society can get along without the sort of reassurance provided by the thought that it has "adequate conceptual foundations" or that it is "grounded" in "human reason." On this [pragmatist] view, the most appropriate foundation for a liberal democracy is a conviction by its citizens that things will go better for everybody if every new metaphor is given a hearing, if no belief or desire is held so sacred that a metaphor which endangers it is automatically rejected. Such a conviction amounts to the rejection of the claim that we, the democratic societies of the West, know what we want in advance—that we have more than a tentative and revisable *Grundrisse* for our social projects. [55]

It would also chime with Foucault's and Arendt's attempt to value politics for its performative rather than its ideal character. [56] In the "pagan" view of the Constitution that I have adumbrated, the Constitution just is that "tentative and revisable *Grundrisse*" of which Rorty writes. The problem with that view, like the argument that the Constitution is "already" pagan, is that American politics has rarely, if ever, been able to do without metaphysical reassurance.[57] Consider, in this context, the following passage from *The Federalist:* "It has been frequently remarked, that it seems to have been reserved to the people of this country, by their conduct and example, to decide the important question, whether societies of men are really capable or not, of establishing good government from reflection and choice, or whether they are forever destined to depend, for their political constitutions, on accident and force."[58] In Publius's argument, the American nation is presented as the test of a thesis, a proof in a rational demonstration. If history, as Publius utilizes it, is a series of experiments putting various theories of government to the test, America must be the most far-reaching and profound *test* of the modern idea that governments can be designed by individuals not cobbled together by accident or force.

In this view, the Federal Constitution perpetuates the legacy of the the Puritan ecclesiastical polity: America is not only the story of Americans but an attempt to prove a thesis, to demonstrate something to the world public. Eighteenth-century America may no longer be a manifestation of God's grace, but it *is* the conclusion to a syllogism of sweeping applicability, a publicly visible proof of the viability of what Jacob Burckhardt, in another context, characterized as the emergence of "a new fact . . . in history—the State as the outcome of reflection and calculation, the State as a work of art."[59] Publius's figuration suggests a desire to see America as a *logic*, as the necessary, determined, predictable outcome of true premises about human interaction. It is, in other words, an *ideological* discourse in Arendt's sense, an expression of piety in Lyotard's: an attempt to align the meaning and worth of the human world with the coercive regulation inherent in the logical development of an idea or the sheer givenness of a fact. That is, it is a practice governed by a critical idea, one which, in this case, achieves an authentically national (indeed, given America's missionary self-understanding, veritably world-historical) dimension.[60]

CHAPTER THREE

Cold War Metaphysics

1

The United States, it has been argued, has known three revolutionary transformations in constitutional regime: the founding, the Reconstruction amendments, and the New Deal.[1] I would add a fourth: the post–World War II reorganization of government codified in the National Security Act of 1947, which coordinated military, intelligence, and economic planning in terms of the global struggle against communism. We are warranted in saying that this event marks a change in *constitutional* regime, first of all, because the act's implementation transformed the character of the executive branch by powerfully expanding the limited military authority granted the executive in the original Constitution. The president's status as commander of the armed forces is significantly altered when, as with the Cold War and its institutionalization through the National Security Act, the threats calling for military alertness and intervention tend to be continuous rather than episodic or extraordinary and when they predominantly involve subtle subversion rather than obviously demarcated lines of battle and engagement. More broadly, however, the Cold War was *constitutive* of American national identity. While it prevailed, its vocabulary shaped the nation's tasks, policies, and pursuits, forming a frame through which issues as different from one another as civil rights, dissent, culture, education, and the economy could be weighed together in terms of their significance for the nation's struggle with a worldwide communist movement.

If the Cold War was a fourth constitutional regime, however, it was certainly unlike the others in the extent to which, while it prevailed, policy, legislated or otherwise, was shaped by public fantasies and hysteria. To employ the title of one of Cold War novelist John Le Carré's novels, the Cold War was a "looking glass war" in which the enemy one fought was to an unusual degree an unverifiable creature of one's own imagination. The antagonists of the Cold War could never be certain that the enemy was not one of their own, reflected back to them in an uncanny register. Despite its limited focus on the world of spies and its British setting, *The Looking Glass War* provides, in fact, an excellent introduction to the fearful hermeneutics of ambiguity that structured the public discourse of the Cold War on both sides of the Atlantic. Fred Leiser, being prepared to enter communist East Germany by compatriots who heartlessly manipulate him, using him as a tool for purposes they themselves can hardly articulate, tells of the ambiguity of an earlier incident during World War II, as a morse code operator:

> "They were following the message, you see; they wanted to know where the safety signal came. It was the ninth letter; a back shift of one. They let me finish the message and then they were on me, one hitting me, men all over the house.
> "But *who*, Fred? Who's *they*?"
> "You can't talk about it like that: you never know. It's never that easy."
> "But for God's sake, whose fault was it? Who did it? Fred!"
> "Anyone. You can never tell. You'll learn that." (P. 191)

In the world of the Cold War, loci of agency can never be fixed; the answer to "Who's *they*?" is endlessly deferred. Living in such a world is largely a matter of reconciling oneself to the aleatory amorality that governs it. One's superiors might at any time deem it necessary, in the interests of security—or even of the current political administration, or perhaps nothing more than the continued dominance of one's own intelligence service over the others—that one be sacrificed, as indeed happens to Le Carré's protagonist.

Leiser's training, and eventual sacrifice, are organized entirely around the vaguest of nervous speculations. Rumors, accompanied by hazy and indistinct photographs, suggest—to an imagination in-flamed by the Cuban Missile Crisis, to members of a secret service that has been marginalized and is on the lookout for ways of enhancing their influence within the state bureaucracy—that the Soviet Union has moved nuclear missiles into East Germany. The evidence, however, is uncertain; its significance must be clarified. Indeed Leiser's masters emphasize that in sending him over the border, they are not attempting to accomplish a specific task but are merely seeking to fix the meaning of ambiguous information:

> Rumors, a guess, a hunch one follows up; it's easy to forget what intelligence consists of: luck, and speculation. Here and there a windfall, here and there a scoop. Sometimes you stumbled on a thing like this: it could be very big, it could be a shadow. It may have been from a peasant in Flensburg, or it may come from the Provost of King's, but you're left with a possibility you dare not discount. You get instructions: find a man, put him in. So we did. And many *didn't* come back. They were sent to resolve doubt, don't you see? We sent them because we didn't know. (P. 182)

Flushed with hopes for success, the spies who orchestrate Leiser's downfall dream of further operations: " 'I spoke to the Minister about it. A training center is what we need. He's keen on this kind of thing now, you know. They have a new phrase for it over there. They are speaking of ICOs—Immediate Clarification Operations.' " (P. 245)

The looking glass war, then, is driven by the need to resolve doubt, to sift through phantasms and shadows, to distinguish between the apparent and the real. The hermeneutics of espionage, as Le Carré presents it, is palpably humanistic: only by "putting a man in" can doubt be resolved. Le Carré's Cold Warriors are unmistakably Cartesian, tormented by fears of an evil demon capable of creating false images, but equally possessed of the conviction that doubt can be resolved, clarification achieved, immediacy regained. In fact, a double agent had faked photographs suggesting the delivery of Russian nuclear missiles to East Germany, knowing that the West would send a Leiser to investigate and hoping that he would be captured, to be put to domestic political use in a show trial. (This, at least, is the explanation that appears likely toward the end of the novel, though conclusive proof is never found.) The Western agents are aware of the likelihood that they are being duped but hope to use the opportunity to increase their influence with sister intelligence agencies by demonstrating their efficiency at "clarification." Leiser in fact travels to the scene, his efforts to resolve the doubt through direct observation leading only to more more rumors and further uncertainties, the operation as a whole plunging him and his superiors into just the immorality, ruthlessness, and cunning they condemn in their enemy.

If the Cold War, as Le Carré suggests, is a looking glass war—organized around the fear of phantasms and the need to clarify them, but always vitiated by a mingling of the antagonists' identities that insinuates itself into the very core of the conflict—there can be no better place to turn to for a theorization of this conundrum than "philosophy through the looking glass," as the thought of Gilles Deleuze has been characterized.[2] In *Logic of Sense* and *Différence et répétition*, Deleuze makes the concept of the simulacrum or phantasm the centerpiece of Postplatonic philosophy. According to Deleuze, the project of "reversing Platonism" is to be achieved through a renewed appreciation for the distinctive qualities of simulacra and phantasmas—the realm of ideas, categories, and attributes that are thoroughly relational and relative, which cannot be measured according to an independent or objective standard.[3] These are dangerous for Plato because they have no fixed identity or unchanging essence; or to put it differently, their identity can be expressed only in relative terms. The afternoon is warm compared with yesterday but cool compared with tomorrow; Alice is bigger than she was but smaller than she will be. Plato disparaged simulacra by claiming that good copies or icons bear an *inner* resemblance to the idea. They correspond not to outer appearances but to essential, unchanging, defining characteristics. A phantasm, in contrast, possesses a merely superficial resemblance. The real enemy for Plato, according to Deleuze, is the phantasm—for example, the Sophist, who superficially resembles a true lover of wisdom but, Plato insists, is not.

The task of modern philosophy, Deleuze argues, is to affirm what Plato demonizes: "to glorify the realm [*règne*] of simulacra and reflections."[4] This is done by affirming the unlimited, unfixable quality of that which is merely relative, whose identity is determined solely through comparison with other reflections with no appeal to absolute standards. In that world, paradoxes abound because it seems possible to attribute anything to everything and everything to anything: things are at once warm and cool, near and far, up and down, familiar and strange, good and bad, all depending on one's ever-changing terms of comparison. As Deleuze forcefully argues, celebrating the reign of simulacra must ultimately call identity itself into question; for insofar as it is constituted in the realm of simulacra and phantasm, who, what, and how one is shifts with the winds of opinion and reflection. The Platonic philosopher, in contrast, faced with the fluidity of identity thus opened up, responds first by appealing to a privileged realm of fixed essences and then by singling out some simulacra as legitimate because they somehow participate it that realm.

If "all of Platonism," as Deleuze writes, "is constructed according to this will to track down phantasms or simulcra" (p. 166), then Le Carré's spies are master dialecticians. And if the metaphysics of American espionage and intelligence differs from Le Carré's interpretation, it does so primarily with respect to the global character of the American sphere of activities. As Gen. Maxwell Taylor put it, the United States "must partake of the many-eyed vigilance of Argus—constantly watching in all directions in anticipation of the emergence of forces inimical to our national purposes."[5] Indeed, the metaphorics of General Taylor's injunction, which are typical, are revealingly Platonic. Given the unique threat posed by the Cold War, American government must survey the *whole* world: its gaze must be comprehensive, all embracing, synoptic, and range "in all directions." Moreover, its gaze must *penetrate:* it does not simply inspect superficial events but identifies constants beneath the variety of global events, deeper forces expressive of broad historical tendencies or sweeping political projects. Finally, the American gaze is tied to the specific *purposes* of the subject who employs it: it is deployed by an agency that orders and ranks events in terms of their utility for a shared *telos.*

The Platonic discourse of the Cold War works to intensify and accelerate the general tendency to speak of government as, quoting William E. Connolly, "the ultimate agency of self-conscious political action."[6] The state is figured as a *subject*, in particular, as an epistemological subject committed to guaranteeing the objectivity of the world. But this places us at once on the terrain of what Martin Heidegger characterizes as the ironic "end of philosophy": the bitter fruit of Plato's inauguration of the "humanization of truth"; the triumphant consolidation of the Cartesian subject, committed to "the unconditional rule of calculating reason" that is the will to power.[7] If the planetary technological regime, ordering the world by constituting it as an object scrutinized in its entirety by the subject's gaze, appears not to need philosophy, that is only because "philosophy is already its foundation": no longer merely dreaming of encountering the world as a stable object of representation and calculation, . modernity and its state, Heidegger observes, achieve this in actuality (p. 96).[8] But that would mean that the paradoxes involved in conceiving of the world as the object of representation, and the subject as the willful orderer and shaper of the objective world so represented, invade the allegedly nonmetaphysical, mundane, "realistic" spheres of foreign policy, national identity, and security. In what follows, I explore some of the implications of that conclusion.

2

A comfortable, smooth, reasonable, democratic unfreedom prevails in advanced industrial civilization.
—Herbert Marcuse

The integrity and vitality of our system is in greater jeopardy than ever before in our history.
—*National Security Council Memorandum No. 68*

The Demon is not the Other, the opposite pole of God . . . but rather something strange and unsettling that leaves one baffled and motionless: the Same, the perfect Likeness.
—Michel Foucault

Visitors at Alta Bates Hospital in the city of Berkeley are routinely handed a brochure, to be read during the elevator ride up to the patient's room, that instructs in comforting the sick. "Act naturally," it advises, and elaborates: "Touching with a hug or a handshake, and having eye contact with the patient[,] will show that you care." The intent may simply be to inform and heal, but the advice would not be out of place in a briefing book for invaders from Mars or foreign agents on how to pass as Earthling or American. A generation ago, someone who had to be coached in such fundamentals might have seemed freakish, a candidate for therapy, perhaps; but pathology has become the norm and has extended to the culture at large. That passing on the rudiments of an acceptable bedside manner is now felt to be a responsibility of "health care providers" hints, with elegant banality, at the essence of postmodern theories of simulation or hyperreality: social life is the reproduction of models, not the spontaneous origination or recovery of forms, and models must therefore be generously provided. We might nevertheless speculate on the patient's reaction, after having been soothed with appropriate touching by her or his loved ones, upon reading the instruction booklet. Would it not provoke some concern about the status of these signifiers of care and concern, and their bearers?

To what extent have such fears become generalized cultural topoi? According to an article that appeared on the front page of the the *New York Times*, single women have taken to employing private detective agencies to verify the claims, the representations, as it were, of potential partners.[9] They suspect that the men in their lives are misrepresenting themselves, to put it charitably, and, the agencies say, they are usually right. Regularly, men hungry for commitment, men with advanced degrees, temporarily benched but well-paid football players, heterosexual men, turn out to be womanizers, uneducated, ex-cons, gay. The emergence of a profitable service industry dedicated to the task of separating genuine from false representations suggests that the very notion of "representation" has become a pervasive source of popular anxiety and concern, though not one that is beyond the ability of information brokers to remedy. (According to one detective quoted in the article, all that is needed to ascertain the validity of most claims is the appropriate social security number, which can be used to "access" the requisite information from computer files around the world.) In a similar fashion, other information brokers—*Times* reporters, for example—make it their business to sift through the claims of contenders for political power, whose representations regularly turn out to be, not false, but insincere, designed to appeal to narrowly targeted, "uncommitted" sectors of the electorate. We might ask of the latter the question we put to the patient at Alta Bates: Shouldn't the news that politicians are being scripted by pollsters generate doubts as to their authenticity and the significance of their claims?

If contemporary experiences of healing, courtship, and politics generate such anxieties, it is because they occur under conditions that degrade what we might call the semiotics of morality: the imperative that outer, public appearances faithfully mime inner, private realities.[10] The most influential political formulation of this theme is surely Niccolò Machiavelli's description of the dissembling prince, the man of power who lives in a world of deceivers and so must master the arts of deception and the organization of appearances in order to survive. But anxiety over the breakdown of a reliable semiotics of morality receives its classic formulation in Jean-Jacques Rousseau's first *Discourse*, where he imagines an earthly paradise where men see into one another's hearts and no appearance intervenes between the self and the world, a vision that stands in stark contrast to the fallen world in which mediation, and hence dissembling, insinuates itself into human experience and makes a mockery of human pretensions to freedom and fidelity.[11]

Although Rousseau's vision of a purified social compact that allows for the transcendence of particularity (and hence plurality) and the expression of the "general will" has not become the political model of modern liberal societies, his articulation of the suspicion of a disjunction between the inner and outer is securely embedded in their moral cultures. From the perspective of this moral semiotics, it is a contradiction in terms to suggest that a trained handshake, for example, will "show" that one "cares," because, if people are to be *trained* in "natural" gestures, such actions will show only the training itself. The fear of simulation, then, is a concern that the outward appearances do not correspond to inner essences, and it generates strategies to distinguish the apparent from the genuine, simulations from representations. Taken to an extreme, it is a fear that no judgment, no distinction, is any longer possible; a fear, as Jean Baudrillard has expressed it, that there is no God:

> The transition from signs that dissimulate something to signs that dissimulate that there is nothing marks the decisive turn [toward a culture of pure simulation]. The first implies a theology of truth and secrecy (to which ideology still belongs). The second inaugurates an era of simulacra and simulation, where there is no longer any God to recognize His own, nor any Last Judgment to separate true from false, the real from its artificial resurrection, because everything is already dead and resuscitated in advance.[12]

Baudrillard is misleading, however, when he suggests that the "era of simulation" *comes after* and *supersedes* the "era of representation"; rather, representation and simulation would appear to enjoy a symbiotic relationship. As he goes on to argue, the technology of simulation has indeed largely been devoted to simulating the real and, in this way, obscures the epochal transition Baudrillard wishes to mark.

In Cold War America, ideologists of representation simultaneously stimulate the fear that representation is at risk from simulation and reassure us that the recovery of representation, the equation of sign and thing, of public and private, is still possible—just as the Manhattan detective agencies cited in the *Times* must maintain both that men are becoming better liars and that detectives possess the technology that will reveal the truth. Representation, in this sense, thrives on generally available experiences of unintelligibility and ambiguity, which ideologists can presume to resolve. It is in this broad cultural context that claims for the "subversive" character of contemporary strategies of reading and interpretation must be scrutinized. Paul de Man, for example, argues that "literariness" is subversive because it undermines the authority of texts and discourses, which rely upon the fiction of reference to an extralinguistic meaning or truth that is undone by the close reading of self-deconstructing texts.[13] It is by no means clear, however, that the gesture of undermining authority is in itself necessarily subversive. As one powerful critique of modernity argues, the destruction of believable sources of legitimate authority may well generate in the wildest, most uncontrolled manner the need for ideological fictions.[14]

In fact, the symbiosis of simulation and representation is central to postwar American political culture and, more specifically, to the Cold War—as distinguished from Soviet-American conflict, which it promises to outlive. The Cold War may have been declared at an end, but the culture it has yielded to the belligerents through forty terrifying and confusing years is not as easily dispatched by diplomatic communiqués. What is this culture? It is commonly characterized in terms of an anxiety, expressed in literature, cinema, journalism, and political discourse as a pervasive sense of impending catastrophe. Any survey of Cold War discourse yields ample evidence of what Freud, in 1917, described as the characteristics of a generalized neurotic anxiety: "a general apprehensiveness, a kind of freely floating anxiety which is ready to attach itself to any idea that is in any way suitable, which influences judgment, and lies in wait for any opportunity that will allow it to justify itself. People who are tormented by this kind of anxiety always foresee the most frightful of all possibilities, interpret every chance event as a premonition of evil and exploit every uncertainty in a bad sense." [15]

So much for the experience; what is the object of this fear? Freud's answer is not readily paraphrased, but in the simplest terms, he claims that the neurotic is afraid of oneself, of one's own desires. Initially, Freud saw anxiety as the ego's attempt to defend itself against an impulse that has earlier been repressed but now threatens to come to the fore. In this sense, anxiety alerted the ego to the need for redoubled efforts at repression. Later, reversing himself, Freud came to see repression as the effect, rather than the cause, of anxiety. Fear of castration during the oedipal phase, he speculated, represented fear of the consequences of oedipal desire, which was resolved by the repression of this desire. Whatever the causal direction, however, anxiety is symptomatic of a repressed wish, an index of something the subject wishes but cannot acknowledge as its own desire. In the most general terms, then, one might say that neurotic anxiety is a fear of oneself, of one's integrity or identity (or the integrity *of* one's identity). That fear is experienced as a fear of some external threat to that identity—as in projection, for example, where the unacknowledged desire is attributed to an alien Other who must be suppressed.

In this last sense, the Cold War may be said to satisfy Freud's definition of a neurotic symptom: fears of the communist threat mask a deeper anxiety over the development of American political life. Critics of Cold War cinema, for example, have frequently interpreted the repugnance for impersonal communist collectivization as the projection of concerns about the power of an increasingly statist, bureaucratic, and conformist postwar America. Such diagnoses, however, often eschew political theory for the eroticized formulations of psychoanalysis, miming the very displacement of politics that they expose. Is it possible to read the anxiety of Cold War culture in a more concretely political manner?

We can begin to do so, I think, by distinguishing between two typical narratives in Cold War cinema, both relying on the theme of invasion. In such early Cold War films as *Them! The Day the Earth Stood Still, The Blob, The Thing, Godzilla,* and *The Attack of the Fifty Foot Woman,* a community—usually, if not invariably, small-town America and its values of family life, privacy, and self-reliance—faces a threat to its integrity. Sometimes the threat is of extraterrestrial origin, sometimes the result of science gone awry; but it is always a localized, definite, and in some sense, intelligible hazard. Typically, the central issue is to discover how to kill the alien. Often, as in *Them! Godzilla,* and *The Day the Earth Stood Still,* this demands the coordination of scientific knowledge and military muscle, and the plot frequently turns on whether scientists and warriors can overcome their mutual suspicion and work together. Such films allegorize one of the central achievements of Cold War culture: a union of the scientific and military establishments under the rubric of "national security."

In a second class of film, also revolving around invasion, the invader is difficult to locate or identify because it operates through a strategy of simulation or replication. In one classic example, *The Invasion of the Body Snatchers* (1956), pods from space duplicate the bodies of small-town Americans, replacing the originals with externally identical but deindividuated replicants. Similarly, in "The Hundred Days of the Dragon" (an *Outer Limits* television episode broadcast in 1963), Chinese secret agents plot to replace powerful leaders of American politics, journalism, and business with externally perfect "substitutes." And in *Invaders from Mars* (1953), to take yet another example, extraterrestrials surgically alter the brains of parents, teachers, and children, destroying their individuality and transforming them into impersonal agents of planetary conquest. In each instance, the duplicates are accurate enough to convince all but close family members, and even they are unable to articulate precisely what is "wrong" with their loved ones. Rather, the problem is thematized as an inexplicable lack of feeling, of inner conviction, which the alienated relatives mark in terms of *their* inability to feel love for the duplicate.

The question raised by this kind of film is not How do we kill the monster? but How do we know who is real and who a mere simulation? Real Americans are independent and self-reliant, but the victims in these films have been subordinated to higher powers and are individuals in appearance only. This fear of simulation—the fear of not being able to tell the difference between independent individuals and agents of larger powers—is also detectable in the logic that governs the most important legal instrument of the Cold War, the National Security Act of 1947. In setting up new institutions deemed necessary for countering postwar communism—a threat not anticipated by the authors of the Federal Constitution—the act supplements the powers available to the president by putting under his control an elaborate apparatus for the coordination and projection of military, political, and economic power, all largely removed from congressional and public control.

Behind the act lies the assumption that U.S. security was threatened by Soviet attempts at *subversion*, not by military attack. (The idea that conflict between modern states relies on subversion as much as on direct military engagement was an important issue in official U.S. discussions of Nazi Germany, which prepared for its military attacks against Austria, Czechoslovakia, and Poland by sending secret agents to infiltrate, disrupt, and demoralize. This was a staple of wartime propaganda, as in Frank Capra's contributions to the World War II documentary series *Why We Fight*, for example; after the German defeat, the Soviets assumed the role played by the Nazis.) According to George F. Kennan, whose "Long Telegram" from Moscow in 1946 established the terms in which subsequent U.S. strategy would be discussed, the Soviets were too weak militarily and economically to engage the West directly and could therefore be expected to resort to indirect means. Because the communist "system can handle only individuals who have been brought into complete dependence on higher power," Kennan telegraphed, "in foreign countries Communists will, as a rule, work toward destruction of all forms of personal independence, economic, political or moral."[16] The "underground operating directorate of world communism," according to Kennan, will achieve this by infiltrating and bending to its purposes legitimate groups and organizations, such as "labor unions, youth leagues, women's organizations, racial societies, religious societies, social organizations, cultural groups, liberal magazines, [and] publishing houses" (p. 58). It is important to understand what Kennan is asserting here *politically*. The "groups," "clubs," and "organizations" to which he refers amount to nothing less than the manifold voluntary associations that constitute a liberal democratic society, whose spontaneous activity a liberal democratic constitution is designed to protect from interference by the state. The political significance of these groups is rendered fatally ambiguous in Kennan's Cold War discourse, because it is no longer certain that their activities *are* spontaneous and independent. A liberal magazine, a social organization, a women's club, a publishing house—do they embody the latitude given to individual action and association in American democracy, or are they fronts—substitutes, replicants, pods—dedicated to reducing Americans to dependence on higher powers by undermining their confidence in their society? Within the terms of Kennan's discourse, there is no way to know. We cannot even tell by evaluating the sincerity of the members of these organizations, who, Kennan stresses, will be "genuinely innocent of conspiratorial connection with foreign states" (p. 58).

The Cold War casts a terrible ambiguity on the institutions American government is established to preserve: Are they vital emblems of freedom, or illusions concealing a deeper work of corruption? When we look at our labor unions, our free press, our political and civic clubs, do we see spontaneous associational life, or a deadly replication of such spontaneity, something that appears alive but really is not? That the difference between the American and the un-American is encoded as the difference between life and death, vitality and morbidity, is a reflection of deep-seated assumptions of liberal political thought, which relies on the idea of a "natural" individual whose powers and capacities preexist the derivative constructs of society and polity. Put most starkly, the liberty protected by the liberal state is the capacity to act at will; essentially, *to live*. Liberty, as Locke expresses it, "is the . . . power in any agent to do or forbear any particular action, according to the determination or thought of the mind." [17] To be sure, liberty is a dangerous power: liberty of thought can lead to incorrect and improper ideas and inferences and, by extension, to a rejection of God's law and to eternal damnation (secs. 56, 70 passim). But this does not vitiate the metaphysical equation of liberty with life. For Hobbes too, despite his radically different view of the scope and character of the state, political power is dedicated to ensuring a vitality associated with life: the sovereign is to maintain "felicity," that is, "continuall prospering" or "Motion," which is equivalent to "Life it selfe." [18] If liberal government is designed to minimize state restrictions and controls, this is legitimated not simply by a particular community with a concrete history but by life *as* life, in its growth, continuity, and spontaneity. And in America, therefore, as the best-realized liberal polity, human activity is least obstructed and individuals are most alive. Accordingly, threats to America are not so much threats to a "way of life" as to life itself, in its purest and least mediated or corrupted form.

The ambiguity of the Cold War polity is further complicated by the fact that, in order to respond to Soviet subversion, the United States itself must be transformed: *democracy* emerges as one of the many impediments to a full-scale mobilization against Soviet subversion. As Paul Nitze put it in National Security Council Memorandum No. 68 (NSC 68, the blueprint for global planning during the 1950s), "dissent among us" is a major threat to the containment of Soviet subversion, since the latter requires the full mobilization of the population, which "will be asked to give up some of the benefits which they have come to associate with their freedoms." [19] Accomplishing this task, Nitze emphasizes, will require that agencies of the executive branch engage in propaganda campaigns to persuade the public to make the necessary sacrifices: "Information," he writes, must be "made publicly available so that an intelligent popular opinion may be formed"; and "the initiative in this process lies with the Government" (p. 403). Kennan had argued along the same lines: "We must see that our public is educated. . . . Press cannot do this alone. It must be done mainly by Government" (p. 62). Again, it is important to stress the *political* meaning of these recommendations: the government, and, in particular, the executive branch, is to shape public opinion directly so as to recruit the electorate for "containment."

Nothing could be farther from the idea of a liberal democracy, where the state is viewed as an instrument of public will, rather than as its manager. It is not simply that citizens have no way of knowing whether they are looking at the exuberance of American freedom or a communist plot. Given the requirement that the state intervene in the formation of public opinion, it is always possible that such "freedom" may reflect the protocols of the CIA, NSA, or FBI as much as of the KGB. Films such as *Invasion of the Body Snatchers* and *Invaders from Mars*, then, evoke a very specific political anxiety, namely, the fear that we are no longer in a position to know whether American life is American or un-American. They articulate the problem of identifying "real Americans" who have independent existence and vitality and distinguishing them from nefarious imitations under the control of alien powers.

The argument of these films hearkens back to Puritan anxieties over the relationship between the visible and invisible churches; indeed, under Cold War political theory, America appears to have much more in common with the Puritan ecclesiastical polity than a constitutionally limited representative democracy. The "visible church," built by men on earth, was never identical, the Puritans feared, to the true spiritual church, which embraced those singled out by God for eternal life. Only God could infallibly sort out the apparently regenerate from the truly damned, though the elders did their best to exclude the unregenerate from the church, if not from its authority. This led to the institutionalization of elaborate practices of public avowals, confessions, and tests of sincerity by which members proved faith to the congregation. Max Weber has stressed the importance of Protestant uncertainty to the strong sense of private, individual fatality necessary to the emergence of a capitalist culture, but a consequence of even greater importance for us works in the opposite direction, making of the self something representable, arguable; a kind of rhetorical self.[20] In just this manner, postwar culture has relied on public tests for signs of the authentic American: naming names, and the loyalty oaths of the 1950s; and today, drug testing (reported to be favored by a majority), the loyalty oath of the 1990s. More generally, these films could be said to represent a secular version of the Puritan anxiety over the meaning of prosperity in the New World. Just as the Puritans could never be certain whether material success was a gift of the covenant or the consequence of forsaking the covenant for the pursuit of worldly goods, so postwar citizens can never know whether dissent, contestation, and difference are signs of vitality or of the beginning of the end.

From the early 1950s, increasingly efficient mass media delivered seductive and alluring images of American life—representations of increasingly doubtful authenticity, whose unverifiability led inexorably to greater and greater hysteria over the question of how to differentiate between the real and the simulated. Miles Orvell has tracked the emergence of this sense of urgency about losing or maintaining contact with "reality" and "authenticity," as opposed to derivative imitations, in American culture before World War II; the need for an original *American* culture that did not rely on European precedents was, of course, a central Transcendentalist theme.[21] The Cold War preoccupation with whether American life is real or artificial, however, is powerful enough to cut across, or absorb, ideological differences. The right-wing articulation of simulation as fear of communism, and the left-wing articulation of simulation as fear of consumer capitalism, are equally workable (or unworkable) attempts to think, judge, and protest the transition to a society of sheer artifice, where the model, as in Baudrillard's influential formulation, not the original, is the only source of authority.

Herbert Marcuse's *One-Dimensional Man*, published in 1964, articulates precisely the fear of simulation we find in Nitze, Kennan, and other Cold Warriors. According to Marcuse, what appears to be a society with minimal state coercion is in fact a closed world of programmed needs, of elections that do not need to be rigged; but, as he emphasizes, what is *truly* terrifying about advanced industrial society is that even the critical theorist cannot say with conviction that it is either free or unfree. It is both "unfree" *and* "reasonable": unfree because its members are subject to higher powers (for Marcuse, the media and the corporations); reasonable because this dependency provides for their needs as they experience and articulate them. Although this appears as a *choice* and is therefore legitimate—an instance, however corrupted, of freedom, a "token of . . . progress," as Marcuse puts it—the substance of this choice calls into question the validity, the reality, of the freedom it allegedly expresses, calling forth explanations in terms of the shadowy, impersonal manipulations of "the establishment" and its ability to offer *substitute* freedoms in the form of "institutionalized" or "controlled" desublimation:

> Technical progress and more comfortable living permit the systematic inclusion of libidinal components into the realm of commodity production and exchange. But no matter how controlled the mobilization of instinctual energy may be (it sometimes amounts to a scientific management of libido), no matter how much it may serve as a prop for the status quo—it is also gratifying to the managed individuals, just as racing the outboard motor, pushing the power lawn mower, and speeding the automobile are fun.[22]

Marcuse's vision of a consumer capitalism that renders revolution irrational because opposition to the regime is no longer based in concrete, widely experienced needs is ably realized in John Carpenter's film *They Live* (1988), whose fidelity to the narrative structures of 1950s cinema demonstrates how few thematic adjustments are necessary to effect the change from right to left criticism of simulation. The protagonist, rendered jobless by plant closings in Colorado, migrates to Los Angeles to find work as a day laborer on a construction site. He obtains, from some ill-fated scientists who have stumbled onto an alien plot to take over the world, specially treated sunglasses that enable him to see that what appear as the exuberant signifiers of Reaganite prosperity are in fact instruments of control and domination. Advertisements for Caribbean vacations and computers, he finds, are really urging the reader to "Marry and Reproduce" and "Obey," and books and magazines convey messages to "Consume," "Watch TV," and above all, "Stay Asleep." Eventually penetrating

the nerve center of the alien enterprise, which is located, appropriately, in the bowels of a television studio, the protagonist learns that
the aliens are here because "they're free enterprisers . . . the earth
is just another developing planet, their Third World." Like American imperialists, the aliens achieve their goals by placing in power a
comprador class, easily recruited from among the swollen oligarchy
of the Reagan years. "Our projections," an alien tells an assembly of
collaborators, "show that by the year 2025, not only America, but the
entire planet, will be under the protection and the dominion of this
power alliance. The gains have been substantial, both for ourselves,
and for you—the human power elite."

The sunglasses of *They Live* enable their wearers to distinguish
the aliens among the apparently real humans; those who appear to
be privileged, model citizens leading the good life seem corpselike,
machinelike—dead. Marcuse, too, fears that the dazzling consum-
erism of Cold War culture masks a deeper attraction to death and
destruction:

> Assuming that the Destruction Instinct (in the last analysis: the Death
> Instinct) is a large component of the energy which feeds the technical
> conquest of man and nature, it seems that society's growing capacity
> to manipulate technical progress also increases its *capacity to manipulate
> this instinct*, i.e. to satisfy it "productively." Then social cohesion would
> be strengthened at its deepest instinctual roots. The supreme risk, and
> even the fact of war would meet, not only with helpless acceptance,
> but also with instinctual approval on the part of the victims. (P. 79)

Thanatos, as Freud teaches, is essentially a drive for stasis, for rest
and stillness, for the nonorganic. Stanley Kubrick, in *2001: A Space
Odyssey* (1968), depicts this face of postwar anxiety. In the film, the
astronauts embody the human consequences of the development of
technological society. The latter is shown to have required extraterrestrial inspiration, as a result of which prehuman ape-men learned
to use bones as weapons to survive. After successfully killing his
enemy, the most cunning ape-man hurls his weapon into the air,
where it dissolves into a spacecraft high above the Earth. The dissolve
implies that there is nothing to say about the intervening history:
humanity was simply working out the consequences of technologi-

cal mastery, which enabled it to survive—but nothing more. This apparently Nietzschean theme (underscored in the film by Strauss's *Also Sprach Zarathustra*) is finally ironic, however, considering that taking the step beyond survival requires further alien intervention. What appears as a spontaneous quest for knowledge and mastery (the exploration of space) turns out to be a desperate struggle to regain proximity to—dependence upon—higher powers.

It is in the interior Jupiter mission scenes of *2001*, however, that the postwar death instinct is most relentlessly portrayed. Astronauts Bowman and Poole occupy an environment constructed entirely out of security concerns, exhaustively designed to enhance survivability in hostile Outer Space, and exquisitely responsive to its inhabitants' needs and requests. The astronauts do almost nothing except stare silently at the blinking lights of the control panels and video display terminals, on which we occasionally catch reflections more vibrant and alive than the men themselves. (In contrast with their monotonous and functional conversation, the ship's computer, HAL, is animated and sincere, interesting, and even believable, despite its somewhat breathless enthusiasm. When Bowman and Poole are roused to act, it is in response to HAL's initiatives.) In this sense, *2001* continues the Gothic tradition exemplified by E. T. A. Hoffmann's *The Sandman*, in which Nathaniel (owing to confusions engendered by his possession of a telescope that—unlike the sunglasses of *They Live*—reverses the truth) mistakes Olympia, an automaton, for a real woman. Caught in illusion, immobilized by the contemplation of her apparent beauty and vitality, Nathaniel becomes still and infirm himself. Hoffmann's story supplies the essential trope of Cold War political culture from Nitze to Marcuse to Kubrick: that gazing at the mere *image* of democracy is turning postwar citizens into deadened observers rather than vital participants.

The emergence of postmodern ideologies can be seen, in this context, as an attempt to execute an end run around the fear of simulation by claiming that the anxiety is futile because the distinction between the real and the artificial is itself an artifact of a necessarily *constructed* experience, that the real was an illusion all along. Indeed, the success of postmodern ideologies suggests that the fear of simulation has become routinized, ritualized, and trivialized through repetition over the period from the mid-1940s through the 1970s, which may help to explain why the United States and the Soviet Union announced, at the close of the decade of the 1970s, the end of the Cold War. Soviet leaders, recognizing, presumably, that oppressing Eastern Europe with tanks, nuclear weapons, and secret police did little to advance research into the particle beams, information technologies, and general digitization of reality that now drive the global economy, declared that political regime obsolete. The United States, for its part, bankrupted by the costs of maintaining the global military occupation called for in NSC 68, also stood to gain from a formal declaration that the Cold War was over.

But the maneuver was probably a feint; the end of the Cold War need not mean the end of Cold War metaphysics. The carefully nurtured ambiguity characteristic of postwar culture does not simply disappear; it is articulated in new ways. Thus, shortly after the official end of the Cold War, Arizona's Republican senator John McCain thematized the post–Cold War world as one in which the United States faces a swarm of small but irritating pests. According to McCain, "We need to recognize that our future military priorities lie . . . in projecting power to deal with a constant series of small crises in the developing world."[23] The appropriate military technology for the new world order, according to McCain, is the aircraft carrier, which "has proved to be the ideal political instrument in a world where fixed bases present steadily greater political uncertainties, in contingencies where we need to work in partnership with friendly states but when the deployment of combat units on their territory presents political problems, and in those cases where we need to establish a convincing military presence without taking sides" (p. 47). Using the very liminality of the seas to guarantee an American "presence," the aircraft carrier is the appropriate postmodern politicomilitary weapon because it can operate freely in a world bereft of clear and distinct borders, territories, and legitimacy; it is, indeed, the twentieth-century successor to the *Arbella*. Summing up such considerations, William H. Webster, onetime director of Central Intelligence, notes, "As the hard edges of the world recede, the threats we face have become more numerous, more diffuse, and more difficult to define. Intelligence is critical as policy makers determine what course to follow in a world which may well become more dangerous because less predictable."[24] In grasping that U.S. security is driven by the postmodern political world's *refusal* to yield a clearly defined and marked threat, Webster reveals a shrewd practical understanding of postwar culture and its capacity for ideological invention. That culture depends, not on a *Soviet* threat, but, in Oliver North's pithy phrase, on a "dangerous world" whose institutions and public modes of representation resist any reliable interpretation or assigned meaning.

Cold War metaphysics appropriates "literariness," in de Man's sense, for wholly unexpected ends, foregrounding the semantic productivity of representational language to exploit the instability of the world as an object represented by the subject. Securing a reliable, objective world yields to the anxiety that the world's objectivity reflects nothing more than the subject's will to order, uniformity, and routine, and thence to the conclusion that objectivity itself is altogether unfounded and contingent, a simulation dependent upon highly variable and unreliable capacities of artifice and fabrication. If we ask who is the political theorist par excellence of the world brought into being and maintained by the artificial polity, the theorist who most resolutely and with the greatest drama articulates the political implications of the *fragility* of such artificial and fabricated bodies politic, the answer is surely Thomas Hobbes. At the very birth of modernity, he imagined with unequaled vivacity the political costs attendant upon telling the truth, once the truth was defined as uniformity and consistency in the use of words. Hobbes, however, is arguably an odd figure with which to conjure in exploring the sources of an American political metaphysic, inasmuch as, in America's own mythical self-understanding, the theory of legitimacy authorizing American government is the *refutation* of Hobbes found, we are assured, in John Locke's political philosophy. Nevertheless, as we shall see, Cold War discourses in America are more fully illuminated by Hobbes than by Locke.

3

Thus Satan, talking to his nearest mate,
With head uplift above the wave and eyes
That sparkling blazed; his other parts besides
Prone on the flood, extended long and large,
Lay floating many a rood, in bulk as huge
As whom the fables name of monstrous size,
Titanian or Earth-born, that warred on Jove,
Briareos or Typhon, whom the den
By ancient Tarsus held, or that sea-beast
Leviathan, which God of all his works
Created hugest that swim the ocean-stream.
Him, haply slumbering on the Norway foam,
The pilot of some small night-foundered skiff
Deeming some island, oft, as seamen tell,
With fixéd anchor in his scaly rind,
Moors by his side under the lee, while night
Invests the sea, and wishéd morn delays.

—Milton, *Paradise Lost* 1

Paradise Lost, completed little more than a decade after the publication of Thomas Hobbes's *Leviathan* (1651), reasserts the sea-beast's sinful deceptiveness. For Hobbes, the dissolution of the metaphysical underpinnings of rule by divine right occasioned the construction of an "artificiall man . . . of greater stature and strength than the original" (p. 81). Although the breakup of the ancien régime appeared to cast man out of his religiously guaranteed order and into a world bereft of sure moorings, "man" might build a landing of his own were he to rid himself of the scholastic fantasies that kept him ignorant of his powers as a God-like artificer. *Leviathan* performs this task in part by ironically inverting the story of Genesis: far from Edenic, humanity's original abode, in Hobbes's origins story, is the harsh and unruly state of nature, from which to be cast out is a blessing; and "that sea-beast / Leviathan," classic symbol of Satan, becomes man's true and only savior. In Milton's epic, the shifting, unreliable leviathan is mistaken for an "island" to which a sailor adrift might anchor himself, escaping the turbulent winds and the dangers of the night. Man's attempt to anchor himself in the ground—that is, in matter rather than spirit—binds him intimately, Milton suggests, to Satan's revolt against God and so, in effect, to a perpetual de-anchoring or falling, a permanent confusion of the profane with the sacred. Hobbes aims, however, to show that the Satanic revolt was well considered; for what man left behind when dismissed from paradise was none other than God's "natural" world, nature being, for Hobbes, "the Art whereby God hath made and governes the world" (p. 81). In nature, however, as Hobbes teaches us, man's life was in fact solitary, poor, nasty, brutish, and short. The state—man's artificially created ground—is the truly limitless power, greater, potentially, than God's Nature.

The leviathan-state cannot simply *replace* the anchor of God, however, because Hobbes's attempt to *invent* a new anchor and a new ground relies on the privileging of capacities that are adrift owing to qualities inherent in the ground-creating, world-interpreting being, Hobbes's "natural" individual. With the same gesture that liberates this individual's creativity, Hobbes constrains it by insisting on total obedience to his self-created state, reinvesting in the notion of sin and the baleful consequences of revolt—not against God, now, but against the state. Despite their chronological order, *Leviathan* might profitably be read as an inversion of *Paradise Lost* (it does, in fact, invert the biblical mythology Milton was reinventing), a kind of black mass in which the punishment for disobedience is being cast out of the paradise of the well-ordered society and into God's stateless, indeed hellish, Nature. With the grounding of the only possible paradise in the deceptive sea-beast of human art, the ground is permanently unsettled. Like Milton's Satan, man with his artificial leviathan has been driven into the deep, into the "darkly chopping sea" of Dionysian uncertainty:[25] the covenants out of which human societies are made will respond to the constant seductions of man's own nature, or what Hobbes calls his "passions." Because the artificer that makes the leviathan can always undo it, obedience to state authority emerges as both absolutely necessary and absolutely impossible to guarantee. Hobbes's solution to this politicometaphysical problem is an elaborate and delicately balanced network of disciplines, constraints, and controls as the paradoxical condition of man's "freedom" and "power."

This Hobbesian conundrum is clearly at work in the final and most bizarre episode of the Cold War: the Iran-Contra affair, in which the executive branch used funds from nominally private arms sales to Iran to support efforts to overthrow the Sandinista government in Nicaragua. In their attempts to explain and justify their actions, President Ronald Reagan, Lt. Col. Oliver L. North and his cabal, and anonymous Pentagon strategists succeeded in building a discursive bridge leading back behind Locke to Hobbes. They did not, however, fix the groundless ground that haunts Hobbes's project. Instead, they pushed to the limit the American anxiety over our schizophrenic coupling of radical freedom with subjection to Nature. For the most striking aspect of the congressional debates surrounding the Iran-Contra affair was their enigmatic incoherency. Faced with Congress's passionate defense of the public's right to scrutinize the government's actions, coupled with scrupulous avoidance of any leads suggesting improper actions by the Central Intelligence Agency, it is difficult not to conclude that most members of the investigating committees sensed that their world no longer reflected the theory of constitutionally limited representative democracy they all-too-hesitantly invoked. It was as if the vocabulary of democracy itself had been placed under erasure: the committee members could not *not* speak of democracy, but neither could they fully convince themselves of the contemporary relevance of democratic principles. The Iran-Contra affair staged a revealing political identity crisis: Is America a Lockean or an Hobbesian society?

Hobbes's approach to the problem of politics is well known: willfull, self-regarding, and mutually suspicious individuals are to be regulated by the absolute law of a sovereign power constructed, in the absence of a transcendental authority, by themselves alone. The difficulty with Hobbes's "solution" is that though it is introduced to forestall an anarchic war of each against all, the system of concepts organized by the sovereign's laws is itself a source of chaos. Hobbes's sovereign performs its duties by the "making, and executing of good Lawes," but laws, of course, may be misunderstood. The need to interpret the sovereign power's commands is another source of inconstancy, threatening the commonwealth. Neither brevity nor verbosity are of any use; for "the written Lawes, if they be short, are easily mis-interpreted, from the divers significations of a word, or two: if long, they may be more obscure by the divers significations of many words" (p. 322). By multiplying the senses of a text, interpretation creates more problems than it resolves: "For Commentaries are commonly more subject to cavill, than the Text; and therefore need other Commentaries; and so there will be no end of such Interpretation" (p. 326).

Misunderstanding the sovereign's commands can be mitigated, for Hobbes, only by insisting on the "literal" sense of the law: "That, which the Legislator intended, should by the letter of the Law be signified." Disputes over the scope and meaning of the law are to be settled by the sovereign power alone. More than brute force, however, lies behind the sovereign's authority over the meaning of its words. It is not simply the sheer power of sovereign intention that adjudicates disputes over interpretation but the "perfect understanding of the finall causes, for which the Law was made" (p. 322). The sovereign's intentions, obscured by the "divers significations" of his words, can be saved, once more, only by a knowledge of politics that is "purged from ambiguity" and embodies a "perfect understanding." The problem of interpreting the commomwealth's laws, then, is referred to sovereign intention as the content of the law, while the problem of interpreting sovereign intention is referred to the "laws" of a new political science. The mainspring of civil order remains as fragile as the ever-threatened line between passion and delirium—no more, finally, than a "*Fiat*," as Hobbes puts it in the Introduction to *Leviathan*.

Leviathan attempts to establish an unambiguous political vocabulary on the basis of figures whose multiple meanings necessarily thwart any such project. At each stage, the hoped-for "constancy"—whether political, psychological, or metaphysical—appears compromised by the resources of the figures in which Hobbes chooses to state it and thus must be guaranteed by supplementary measures. Political action is concentrated as much as possible into the sovereign's law-making duties; law making, to circumnavigate the passions, must attain the status of a science; and finally, the imperative of guaranteeing a "felitious" sphere of individual action necessitates a comprehensive education for obedience. This route, however, merely returns us to the passions and to Hobbes's recognition that the artificiality of the covenants that make up political order among natural individuals demands that these be enforced by the sword, by a power able to "keep them in awe."

That the indispensable unity of the sovereign rests on a delicate weave, easily unraveled, helps to explain Hobbes's hostile reaction to the suggestion that the sovereign be subject to law. This idea is "repugnant," he writes, because it would lead to an infinite chain of equivocation, "continually without end, to the Confusion, and Dissolution of the Commonwealth" (p. 367). Yet this Hobbesian repugnance toward subjecting executive power to the law was, during the Cold War, voiced with extreme shrillness in what at the same time commonly supposed itself to be the most authentically Lockean political culture, the United States. The conundrums following upon Hobbes's demand that individuals make an almost *unconditional* grant of authority to the state appear less problematic for a political theorist such as Locke, for whom political authorities hold the people's power conditionally, on trust. Hobbes's unholy coupling of human powers with the despotic state, as the discourse of liberal authority would have it, is nothing more than an expression of bourgeois pessimism which more reasonable thinkers, on whom we rely to articulate our political identity, saw through. But Lockean liberalism, as we have seen, encounters its own specifically political forms of undecidability. At the center of both Hobbesian and Lockean accounts is the contract, the promise—the individual's promise not to use his unlimited natural right to invade others so long as all other individuals make the same promise. Accordingly, the great fear of contractarian experience is that one or more of the parties to the contract will make a *lying promise*, a circumstance that pushes hermeneutics close to the center of political judgment: now, political life demands ways of discerning sincerity, and liberalism demands a political semiotic that can tabulate the reliable signs of the sincere promise.

Precisely this riddle of promising and keeping promises is stressed as central to the definition of semiotics as a discipline by Umberto Eco, who defines the field as "a theory of the lie."[26] Semiotics, which treats "sign-functions" abstracted away from their referential dimension, is the study of whatever can be used to *depart* from the real. Eco's paradoxical definition of a discipline devoted to telling the truth about lying captures the character of modern political theory as Hobbes sees it. For Hobbes, sheer human artifice could fashion a simulacrum of the "natural" order, but the cooperation on which this art depended relied in turn on promises that were likely to be overwhelmed by the passions. As promises are, ontologically speaking, so thin, the necessary partner of consent is state coercion, which at its roots is that which moors us to the deceptive sea-beast, leviathan, the only ground for which we may hope.

This dialectic of consent and coercion was analyzed by Nietzsche in "On Truth and Lies in a Nonmoral Sense," where he emphasizes the will to conformity implied by the notion of a social contract. Individuals "by themselves," Nietzsche writes, will in the ordinary course of events rely on subterfuge, camouflage, and the lie for survival. Through "boredom and necessity," however, they might contract to live according to certain rules, that is, promises. The essence of the social contract is to tell the truth—with truth defined as conformity to the conventions of the group—to "lie according to fixed conventions."[27] Later, in *On the Genealogy of Morals*, Nietzsche detailed the forms of discipline required to produce a creature—the modern, guilt-ridden, self-scrutinizing individual—with a memory capable of keeping promises. Like Hobbes, Nietzsche emphasizes the paradox of the promiser: the language of commitment, stability, and trust lends itself most easily to deception and ruses. Contractarian societies, therefore, encourage ambivalence toward the promise, alternately grounding it in a dangerously unmanageable human will and in a Nature that can overcome the hazards of the former. The founding document of the American polity, the Declaration of Independence, conforms to this pattern: it celebrates the capacity of individuals acting with others to alter, invent, and establish new forms of political association; but, consistent with a theory of the individual's right to go against and control nature, it is careful to ground these capacities in "the Laws of Nature" and "Nature's God."

The discourse of Ronald Reagan is perhaps the most vivid expression of liberal anxiety over the promise. Indeed, for Reagan, the enemies of the United States are precisely those who cannot keep promises. Referring to the leaders of the Soviet Union, Reagan claims that "they reserved these rights to break a promise, to change their ways, to be dishonest, and so forth if it furthered the cause of socialism. . . . Promises are like pie crusts, made to be broken."[28] Accordingly, Reagan's objections to the Sandinista government in Nicaragua centered not on that government's human rights violations but on the charge that the Sandinistas *broke a promise:* they, Reagan alleges, "literally made a contract" with the Organization of American States for support in return for "true democracy."[29] In such statements, the stress is less on the absence of true democracy in Nicaragua, which is accorded the status of a mere symptom, than on the alleged fact that the Sandinistas broke a promise—that is, they violated a principle central to legitimate government as the discourse of liberal authority understands it.

But at the same time, the state over which this Lockean liberal presided for eight years relied overwhelmingly on what one of Reagan's operatives called "great deceit": "I think it is very important for the American people to understand that this is a dangerous world; that we live at risk and that this nation is at risk in a dangerous world. And that they ought not to be led to believe . . . that this nation cannot or should not conduct covert operations. By their very nature covert operations or special operations are a lie. There is great deceit, great deception practiced in the conduct of covert operations. They are at essence a lie."[30] For Oliver North, it is imperative that Americans "believe" that their government can and should engage in "great deceit," even though such a practice violates the ideas of legitimate government embodied in the U.S. Constitution. The "dangerous world" in which we live demands resort to "covert actions" or "special operations" that "are at essence a lie." The covert action, however, possesses the epistemological and moral status of a *noble* lie, forced upon the liberal democracies by the difficult choice between "lives and lies" and by the fact that those, such as North, who possess an esoteric knowledge of the nature of the threat to American freedom are hampered by an unwieldy bureaucracy, a misinformed Congress, and an apathetic public.[31]

Still, taken by itself, North's testimony leaves unclear the basis on which the citizen of a polity dedicated to open contracts and sincere promises may instead devote himself to "great deceit." Would not a more consistent strategy have simply alerted the public and its elected representatives to the danger? One of those hundreds of ignored government strategy documents, "Prospects for Containment of Nicaragua's Communist Government," dated May 1986 and issued by the U.S. Department of Defense, if read not as a prosaic planning study but as political allegory, suggests *why* the character of our "dangerous world" is such that liberal principles of legitimacy no longer apply. It provides the theory that North did not explicitly pronounce but upon which he acted.

Containment, as we have seen, referred broadly to the postwar commitment of the United States to prevent the spread of communism. In the debate over how to accomplish this goal, two camps quickly emerged. The document's title obliquely refers to the debate between proponents of "rollback" and a less extreme variant that became known simply as "containment." In this sense, containment envisaged a political deal in which the Soviet Union and the United States enjoyed tacitly recognized spheres of influence, and it necessarily assumed that both parties were capable of honoring treaties, that is, of making contracts and keeping promises. Proponents of rollback understood the Soviet Union as incapable of such fidelity; in Reagan's terms, that nation reserves the right to lie, cheat, and steal in the pursuit of communist expansion. In addition, rollback, by its nature, involves military conflict because an adversary that does not recognize the sanctity of contracts cannot be a party to a political solution. In arguing that the prospects for merely *containing* Nicaragua's communist government are bleak, the study is an implicit call for a military solution: rollback.

The document begins by noting differences of opinion in Congress over U.S. policy toward the Sandinista regime, differences that came to the fore in the wake of Reagan's lurid speech in March 1986 accusing Nicaragua of providing a "safe haven" for terrorists from around the world: "The President's request to Congress on aid to the Nicaraguan Democratic Resistance has led to an extensive debate in Congress. There is a difference in views as to how effective an agreement would be in providing the needed security for Central America."[32] The document first stresses the liberal, democratic context of U.S. policymaking: there is a "difference in views." But it goes on to insist that despite differences over policy, all parties to the debate agree that the Sandinista government is a threat to be combated and that though some in Congress "maintain that a greater effort should be made to secure a political agreement which would serve to contain Communism in Nicaragua," "many . . . recall the failure of previous treaties and agreements with the Communists." "Prospects for Containment," then, will jog the necessarily short political memories of liberal subjects.

This task is accomplished in a section misleadingly entitled "Historical Perspective." The title is misleading not because the accounts it presents are historically inaccurate (they are, in fact, grotesquely oversimplified) but because the study purports to deal with U.S. policy toward Nicaragua although not a word is devoted to relations between these two countries. Rather, "historical perspective" means reviewing situations in which the United States entered into political agreements with "the Communists," who, in the vernacular of the document, constitute a kind of Jungian archetype that everywhere and always remains the same. As "the Communists" are always the same, the behavior of any one communist entity is entirely predictable. If the further assumption that the Sandinistas are communists is also accepted, no further inquiry is necessary into the historical peculiarities of U.S.-Nicaragua relations; for Sandinista policy is therefore determined by their being part of "the Communists," not by their being Nicaraguans.

The discussion then turns to violations of treaties the United States has entered into with communists, which amount, of course, to communists' having broken their promises, just as, according to Reagan, they affirm their right to do. In the case of Vietnam, for example, North Vietnam "began illegal subversive operations in South Vietnam immediately after signing the 1954 Geneva Accords," although "Communist military violations of the Geneva Agreement began to escalate sharply only in the late 1950's, when Hanoi started to infiltrate armed cadres and supplies into Vietnam." The same is true, according to "Prospects for Containment," of "Communist belligerents" in Korea, other Indochinese countries, and Cuba. True to form, the Nicaraguan communists violated their agreement with the Organization of American States after assuming power in 1979. The communists, then, are *hoi barbaroi*, a group that cannot keep promises and hence is not fit to enter into the contractual arrangements familiar to Lockean liberals.

Not only do the communists fail to keep promises; they actively utilize the *rhetoric* of promising—likely to be seductive to members of liberal polities—to pursue the expansion of communist power. As Reagan has it, for communists, promises are made *in order to be broken*. Equally repugnant to liberal sensibilities is the fact that the communists *plan* to break their promises: the Nicaraguans "never intended to honor the[ir] pledge" to the Organization of American States, and the Vietnamese and Korean communists "were planning the infringements even as they were negotiating." The mere fact that the communists do *plan* is a telling mark of their difference from us. Strictly speaking, a liberal polity cannot plan; it only establishes a framework of order which leaves individuals free to plan their own lives as they see fit. The communists, with their Five Year Plans and historical inevitabilities, even plan to break promises.

The communists, then, plan with no regard for past promises and use promises only as a rhetorical device with which to manipulate liberal polities. The Sandinistas, therefore, can be expected to violate any Central American peace treaty they enter into. The questions then become What would a Central American treaty call for? and What Sandinista violations are likely to occur? The key element of any such treaty, the Pentagon emphasizes, is the stipulation that the governments of the region refuse to allow foreign troops or military advisors on their soil and refrain from supporting insurgencies in neighboring countries. Under the circumstances, this would have entailed that Soviet and Cuban troops leave Nicaragua and that the United States discontinue its support for El Salvador, Guatamala, and Honduras. On the theory that the communists plan to break promises, there can be only one reason for the Sandinistas to agree to such an arrangement: to induce the United States to withdraw from the region while they secretly pursue a military buildup that would enable them to become masters of the region. As the Pentagon imagines it, "The Nicaraguan government would sign a Contadora agreement. . . . The Nicaraguans would circumvent and violate the agreement in order to maintain or increase their military strength and to . . . support . . . Communist insurgencies throughout Central America. Nicaragua would seek to conceal its violations as long as possible. The U.S. and other Central American nations would fully abide by the agreement."

Constrained by contractarian principles, the United States would abide by its promises while the Nicaraguans secretly break theirs, resulting ultimately in the communist conquest of Central America. What, under the circumstances, are the liberal authorities to do? The United States could not simply announce its refusal to abide by a treaty supported by the governments of the region. Yet to observe the agreement while the communists secretly subvert it is to accept communist rule of Central America, in the long run. Although the Pentagon stops short of drawing this consequence explicitly, the document encourages the conclusion that the United States must, like the communists, secretly violate the agreement by supporting what it calls the "Democratic Resistance Forces" (the Contras) covertly with the methods developed by North. Faced with an entity incapable of participating in contractarian life, the United States has no choice but to resort to "great deceit."

The strategy North adopted in his testimony to the congressional committees investigating the Iran-Contra affair was to present the great deceit as natural, realistic, and self-evidently justified. Although the U.S. Constitution grants the executive branch limited powers in foreign affairs, North speaks as if it were self-evident that the president is "in charge" of foreign policy. Congress need not be informed of government action in that area, according to North, because the president is accountable directly to "the people." North makes it clear that the great deceit is not limited to the communist enemy but includes all elements of the liberal polity (e.g., the press and Congress) that threaten the implementation of the covert policy: the deception was staged in part, he says, "to limit the political embarrassment."[33] All of this is, by definition, legal, because it is done at the behest of the "commander in chief," who, once again, acts in the interest of the nation as a whole and not the parochial interests represented in Congress.

The logic of containment, as expressed in North's testimony

and in "Prospects for Containment," specifies the conditions under which the United States moves from Lockean commitments of limited, open government to a Hobbesian state of near-total authority and detailed administration of citizenship: for what were North's public lectures and slide shows—and indeed, his testimony—if not an exercise in "nurturing the habits of compliance"? Yet a nagging politicoepistemological question remains: If state policy must be secret, how can it be ratified by the people? Senator George Mitchell raised this issue in the course of his questioning of North: "If, by definition, covert action is secret and [the president] doesn't tell them about it, there's no way the American people can know about it to be able to vote him out of office" (p. 674). Covert action emerges as a vulgar Platonism in which a system of hierarchical, Hobbesian state authority is masked for the multitude by a display of images staged for the purpose of confirming the people's sense of living in a Lockean society of maximum individual freedom and government on trust. Thus the inescapable duplicity of North's presentations, emphasizing Soviet designs on Central America while at the same time implying that the United States was doing no more for the "Niacaraguan Democratic Resistance" than allowing them to die for their country. In public, North spoke as the citizen of a liberal polity, making arguments in favor a particular policy, while privately he was orchestrating a war his "intelligence" told him was necessary but toward which the public remained unsupportive.

Containment depicts a "dangerous world" in which liberal principles are put "at risk" to the precise extent that liberal polities adhere to them. Containment—in both its moderate and extreme versions—sees the postmodern political condition as demanding private, Hobbesian action coupled with public Lockean rhetoric. At the limit, containment even threatens to dissolve the distinction between public and private upon which liberal authority thrives. Many of North's associates, such as Richard V. Secord and Albert Hakim, were private individuals implementing state policy, while the state resorted to private funding and operatives because what it wanted to do was illegal. The implosion of the private into the public enabled all to deny responsibility: government officials could truthfully say that no appropriated funds were going to support the Contras, even though the policy of support was worked out in the White House; citizens, violating the law at the behest of the executive branch, could plausibly say they were doing so as patriots coming to the aid of their president. Perhaps North, Secord, Hakim, and even Reagan are neither private nor public figures but an undecidable, postmodern amalgamation of these terms, figures capable of simulating the public and private according to necessity. In a complementary way, containment gives us a new American state that is neither Lockean nor Hobbesian but both in the sense that it is committed to staging itself in either mode according to the demands of state power. In the last analysis, the Iran-Contra affair is but a symptom of an American identity crisis, a crisis, precisely, *of* identity: the repressed Hobbesian identity of freedom and control, or again, of the uncertainty and unreliability of a world "governed," rigorously, by a subject's shifting passion for objectivity, order, and security.

4

No prophecy is necessary to recognize that the sciences now establishing themselves will soon be determined and guided by the new fundamental science which is called cybernetics.

—Martin Heidegger

The essential connection between control and communication—epitomized in the feedback process, and highlighted in Norbert Weiner's term "cybernetics" for the study of the processes of steering and communication—has been . . . widely recognized among political scientists.

—Karl W. Deutsch

The dominant and most fertile intellectual innovation of our own age has been that of information feedback.

—David Easton

In "The Age of the World Picture," Martin Heidegger questions a question dear to students of politics in mid-twentieth-century America: What is science? The "essence" of modern science, Heidegger says, is "research." In scientific research, "knowing [*das Er-*

kennen] establishes itself as a procedure" (p. 118). Yet research for Heidegger is not, as this statement seems to imply, limited to following a method or rule. Rather, the fundamental accomplishment of science (an accomplishment that, despite the latter's ideological understanding of itself, links science to the completion of Western metaphysics) is the invention of a world to which methods and rules may appropriately be developed and applied. This world, once established, appears as "fixed," "sketche[d] out in advance." This does not mean that much about it is *known* in advance but that the basic character of the world is predefined so as to make the scientific procedure used to approach it seem rigorously appropriate: there is a "binding adherence" [*Bindung*] between the object of inquiry and the practices of the inquiring subject (p. 119). These two moments of scientific procedure—the projection of a world that is available to be researched, and the measurement and calculation of that world—are inevitably collapsed. By "forgetting" the constitution of the "ground plan" upon which science rests, by ignoring the historicity of his or her discipline, the scientist can imagine charting a world that is somehow obligated to submit to scientific representation. In Heidegger's words,

> Knowing, as research, calls whatever is to account with regard to the way in which and the extent to which it lets itself be put at the disposal of representation. Research has disposal over anything that is when . . . [n]ature and history become the objects of a representation that explains. Such representing counts on nature and takes account of history. Only that which becomes object in this way *is*—is considered to be in being. We first arrive at science as research when the Being of whatever is, is sought in such objectiveness. (P. 127)

Scientific discourse, then, must first constitute a world approachable by procedures of representation. How is this accomplished? By thinking of the world, Heidegger says, as a collection of objects on display; as a picture, or better, as something naturally complicit in the work of representation. Thus, "world picture," for Heidegger, "when understood essentially, does not mean a picture of the world but the world conceived and grasped as picture. What is, in its entirety, is now taken in such a way that it first is in being and only is in being to the extent that it is set up by man, who represents and sets forth" (pp. 129–30). This task, according to Heidegger, is dedicated to getting a grip on the world by simplifying it, in the form of a clear and distinct representation that can be composed and handled according to codifiable and transmissible rules. Such a world, in other words, is under the sway of a *subject:* "That the world becomes picture is one and the same event with the event of man's becoming *subiectum* in the midst of that which is" (p. 132). By organizing for the subject a picture-world in terms that have been made familiar and which may therefore be manipulated with confidence, scientific discourse incites irresistible fantasies of power and control.

Heidegger's assessment of the age of the world picture, however, implies more than this: that the world is *valued* as something that allows itself to be pictured by and for a subject; that the world is cultivated and preserved as an object gratifying the subject's will to power. Science wants a disposable world: one disposed to be represented, and disposable *as* representation, granted existence only to the extent it meets the knower's need to order and explain and discarded when it ceases to do so. But despite the generally acknowledged status of the United States as the most advanced modern scientific civilization — to say nothing of its notoriety as *the* "disposable" society of waste and consumption—Heidegger insists that the study of "Americanism" can shed no light on the meaning of the gigantic—or perhaps, more plausibly, that the naïve criticism of gigantism as originating in an uninhibited and corrupting American commercial empire impedes our ability adequately to conceive of this phenomenon. Thus Heidegger stresses that " 'Americanism' is something European" (p. 153). The essence of the desire to dispose of the world by putting it at the disposal of representation is deeper, Heidegger is certain, than anything suggested by the idle talk of American vulgarity. By now, however, I hope that the reader suspects that the topoi of "Americanism" which Heidegger wishes to exclude from the task of thinking might serve as exceptionally vivid symptoms of the history of metaphysics. In this section, I interrogate the significance, from the perspective of Heidegger's problematic, of the efforts of American political scien-

tists and journalists after World War II to recover, for the uses of
the subject, an objective picture of the political real.

Textbook histories of American "empirically oriented" political
science typically plot the emergence of a "behavioralist" approach
to the study of political life, whose hegemony is later challenged by
a generation of "postbehavioralists," both impatient with what they
regard as its empty formalism and anxious to confront more directly
the social and political conflicts of the 1960s. The lure of a *science* of
politics derived, of course, from complex historical, social, and dis-
ciplinary energies, and the postwar attraction of such procedures as
systems analysis, game and decision-making theory, and cybernetics
was overwhelming not only for students of politics but for anthro-
pologists, sociologists, economists, and above all, national security
think tanks at the RAND Corporation and the Pentagon, as well.
David M. Ricci suggests that such "scientific" approaches seemed
momentarily to accord with an optimism prevalent in American culture at large about the reasonableness or rationality of American
democracy itself: "The mid-century liberal matrix . . . suggested
that true understanding of democracy must rest upon an analogy
between science and society, that is, between a scientific method for
seeking the truth and a political method for making decisions, between a scientific community of scholars checking each other's work
and a political community of citizens assessing each other's interests."[34] "Assuming that the starting conception of science was correct," he goes on, "occasional references to this analogy reinforced
a conviction that political systems functioning along similar lines
must be desirable," an optimism that became less tenable as American society grew less governable over the course of the 1960s and
as the scientific study of politics itself uncovered phenomena (unin-
formed and apathetic voters, for example) that seemed to undermine
what democratic theory called for.

Readings such as these, while essential, rely on a figure commonly
encountered in narratives of postwar America: a catastrophic interruption of routine; the crisis of an unanticipated encounter with
a reality that shatters ideological complacency.[35] Critical intentions
aside, the trope is, in a sense, kind to behavioralism, as it allows

for the re-interpretation of positivist vices as virtues: the political scientists' inability to predict the conflicts of those years secretly confirms their celebrated scientificity and the cool rationality demonstrated in their refusal to turn prematurely from the *Fundamentalontologie* of theory building to the *Gerede* of political contestation and debate. But this refusal, as we shall see, was ironic. Struggling, during the Cold War of the 1950s, to free themselves from a tradition of political thought they experienced as arrogantly divorced from the real world, behavioralists agreed that political life could be understood more authentically if they constructed a neutral conceptual framework for the disinterested accumulation of reliable political knowledge. They succeeded, however, both in inventing a discourse of political surveillance more than adequate to the Cold War and in refurbishing such ideologemes as expertise, masculine toughmindedness, and truth-as-representation. This result can be seen, I suggest, not only by studying how the optimism about science and society broke down but through the meaning of "the starting conception of science" itself, the need to dispose of the world by seeing it as disposed to be represented.

Behavioralism is in the Emersonian tradition of breaking with tradition, which is viewed as empty convention and dull habit. For Emerson, the "rotten diction" of middle-class society, with its stale routines of work, church, and family, obscured the more fundamental truth of the unity of nature disclosed through nature's *original* language. For the behavioralists, likewise, the persistence of a too respectable, academically enfranchised tradition of political thought implied that the student of politics was abandoned to ambiguous signs with deceptive and uncontrollable effects, necessitating the *recovery* of the authentic and original language of political life, the discovery of a "motivated" political sign through which reliable representation and politics would be linked. In his *The Political System: An Inquiry into the State of Political Science* (1953), David Easton called on political scientists to turn away from textual prattle and scrutinize directly the laws of the real political "system." But like earlier (and later) epistemological escape projects, Easton's encounters an obstacle: the disclosure of political reality must take the form of an *interpretation* of the real. The burden of Easton's behavioralism, then, will be the quest for a "conceptual framework" that can regulate the play of overdetermined political signs and ensure the steady convergence of knowledge upon its extratextual referent. Instead, in the name of "reliable knowledge," Easton elaborates a *text*, in the de Manian sense: a *combinatoire* of tropes continually oscillating between literal and figurative senses, always just shy of the hoped-for univocal meaning.

The behavioralist moment in political science is long past, of course, and few would now defend the behavioralists' ambitions and claims as they were originally formulated. But if behavioralism is now regarded as naïve political science, it remains a sign of sophistication in the mass media. Its *jargon*—a rhetoric in which particular political associations are treated as "systems" with varying degrees of "stability"—has become firmly entrenched in the metaphysical language of journalists and their counterparts in the national security bureaucracy, a reliable sign of the "objectiveness" of international affairs themselves. This is the language we heard during the 1960s in discussions of the "pacification" of Indochina, where "human factors" such as the "flow of refugees" were to be "systematize[d]" and the "will of the regime" was considered as a "target system," and that is heard no less in the post–Cold War world of nameless and numberless threats to our "purposes," as when Defense Department officials speak impersonally of "projecting power" into or "signalling" Iraq.[36] Although representative of the behavioralist movement in postwar political science, however, Easton cannot be considered typical. As Ricci shows, the behavioralists, despite their attraction to the science-society analogy, never achieved a consensus about what "science" was.[37] Nevertheless, the construction of a behavioralist vocabulary is staged most vividly in Easton's work of the 1950s and early 1960s, and a re-examination of his behavioralism, therefore, offers a point of departure for a genealogy of an ideological language of international affairs which is shared by journalists and national security officials. The study of Easton's rhetoric of rationality discloses a set of problems through which relationships among and between social theory, metaphysics, ideology, and international affairs become accessible.

Easton's *The Political System* was one of many expressions of dissatisfaction by political scientists after World War II with unreliable theories orchestrated by a "voluminous and genteel tradition" that confronted the would-be student of politics with an unmanageable variety of vague concepts, ambiguous ideas, conflicting approaches and methods, and uncertain results. For Easton, "reliable knowledge"—the goal of political science—derives from systematic, empirically grounded theories that describe and explain the universal regularities of their objects. The possibility of such knowledge has lately come under suspicion, Easton acknowledges, but the reasons are spurious. What is needed is a "conceptual framework" to guide empirical investigation, one that would replace the battle of interpretation with a settled procedure for discovering the truth about politics. Equally necessary is a clearly defined *object* of empirical investigation. Coherently integrated, a generally accepted conceptual framework and a clear and distinct object of political analysis would enable the discipline to avoid the twin evils of fragmented fact collection, on the one hand, and utopian speculation on the other. A search through past theory yields the discovery that the distinctive and invariant subject matter of political science, and therefore the proper object of scientific investigation, is "the authoritative allocation of values in a society." The conceptual framework is what Easton later called "the most fertile intellectual innovation of our own age": cybernetics.[38]

Such an investigation is concerned with what *is*, not with what *ought* to be. The scientist's "values," however, which derive from emotional reactions to factual states, may, unidentified, interfere with the search for the universal regularities of the political system. So the values must be "clarified" by the construction of an imaginary ideal polity, bringing barely perceptible subjective preferences to light and enabling the correction for bias necessary to the successful prosecution of the research program. This task was once the raison d'être of political theory, which has since declined into the transmission of *past* political theories (historicism, as represented, for Easton, with intentional irony, by the work of Leo Strauss). Recast in terms of the enlightened search for political knowledge and established on a sound empirical and theoretical footing, political science will rejuvenate political theory in the traditional sense, by enabling the latter's clarification of subjective preferences to correct for bias in empirical theory, as its ever-increasing stock of reliable knowledge gives substance to the perennial political debate over means and ends.

There is a lapsus in Easton's apparently seamless narrative: the discovery of empirical regularities is deferred in favor of, once again, a forced march through past theory. Because of the interpretative "overload" caused by the "fragmentary" and "heterogeneous" character of the discipline's disorderly language, the prevailing attitude in political science is not the measured application of scientific method but, rather, "emotion or faith and . . . tradition."[39] *The Political System*, then, will illuminate the path out of emotion, faith, and tradition toward the measured gaze of pure science. But how is the need for such a turn demonstrated? In arguing against the traditionalists for a scientific subject whose gaze is not obsessively turned toward beguiling linguistic entities, Easton, apparently unconcerned with his inconsistency, asserts in effect that scientific method possesses the warrant of *tradition:* "From the seventeenth to nearly the end of the nineteenth century, the western world became increasingly imbued with a faith in . . . scientific method to solve social problems, empirical and moral" (p. 7). He admits that *faith* in science is no guarantee of scientific results. By his reading, the "western world," having escaped tradition and convinced itself of the necessity of a scientific approach to politics, fell victim to another form of blindness: mistaking the rhetoric of scientific speech for the substance of scientific method. Because scientists presented their results as deductive systems, political theorists concluded that all that was necessary was to cast their imaginings about political order in suitably deductive form, as Hobbes did in *Leviathan*. A good part of Easton's analysis in *The Political System* is devoted to separating true science from its impostor. Although true science must be "theory-driven," however, its metaphysical center remains "original research spurred by the quest for experiential knowledge," with "the use of controlled, first-hand observation as the basis for understanding" (p. 10). The quest for direct knowledge reached its peak, by Easton's account, in the nineteenth century: Comte, Marx, and Spencer constitute a "torrent of rationality" along with which—just as with custom, tradition, or faith—converts are swept (p. 11).

The more Easton characterizes science as based on direct experience, the more he relies on the language of faith, emotion, and imagination to describe the enterprise. Rather than making an inductive argument for a science of politics, he presents science as a tradition, one of attention to the senses, of "special, painstaking application to the facts of experience—the positive data of experience as opposed to the negative or airy data of pure imagination" (p. 11). Behind the apparently univocal name "science," then, lies an unacknowledged double usage. When it is a question of the hazards of tradition, "science" names the act of turning away from the habits of tradition toward direct, unmediated experience. But when it is time to describe the particulars of this turn, we are presented with accounts of conventions considered essential to inquiry: the principle of utility, the assumption of a rationally intelligible world, and techniques of controlled observation. Each, as Easton describes in detail, has a history and tradition of its own and is related to a larger framework of beliefs and practices characteristic of the "western world."

Unable to control this ambiguity—science as a pure, desocialized gaze and science as a practice rooted in traditions and institutions—Easton resorts to terms and phrases that appear to bridge the gap. "Controlled observation" is one such phrase, suggesting a blend of mutual vigilance over the distorting prism of subjective preferences, and the uncoerced, observing individual. "Reliable knowledge" is another, which etymologically betrays the element of faith in Easton's knowledge: to rely on something is precisely *not* to question but rather to trust. "Rely" once meant "to bind together" and was used to refer to the assembling or *rallying* of soldiers or followers. This sense is still active in Easton—and the behavioralist movement as a whole—whose program for a science of politics is imagined as a collective project involving many organized and coordinated researchers, as opposed to the idiosyncratic productions of "the single scholar in the library," as Robert A. Dahl characterized the old-fashioned political theorist.[40] "Reliable knowledge," the phrase Easton repeatedly uses to refer to the goal of political science, is, etymologically, knowledge produced by a *team*, under the direction, say, of a leading method. By comparison, the volumes of traditional political theory are too varied and inconsistent to be "rallied" to a single project. The image of organization as the most productive mode of theoretical life is a persistent one in the behavioralist literature, and one of the most problematic aspects of traditional political theory for behavioralism was, perhaps, the resistance to organization posed by its texts and their traditions of interpretation.

Easton's most important hinge between unfettered observation and the canons of inquiry is "theory" itself, whose acquisition is an interpretative act—the result, as we shall see, of sensitively *reading* the history of political theory. Managed correctly, this reading justifies the reader in quitting reading to discover the empirical regularities of the real political world.

The essential condition of reasoned discourse, Easton (echoing Hobbes) emphasizes, is semantic stability. Concepts that organize a political theory, such as "dictatorship, class, [and] sovereignty," become problematic when "students . . . use them apparently with reference to the same social phenomena but in fact with reference to considerably different things." When this occurs, the concepts become "ambiguous" and "imprecise," with the consequence that "definitive confirmation or invalidation for any given time is impossible." This leads to a horrifying undecidability in political science: "One set of political scientists can argue that planning and dictatorship are unalterably associated; another can demonstrate the contrary. One can maintain that the separation of powers acts as a restraint on political power; another can prove that it really makes possible the capricious and irresponsible exercise of power. . . . For each principle supported by considerable evidence there is a contradictory one supported by evidence of equal weight."[41]

Nor has the attempt to discover a definite object of political analysis prevented the excess of signified over signifier that so appalls Easton: the definition of the field as "the science of the state," for example, "only succeeds in substituting one unknown for another"; there are, Easton reports, "over 145 separate definitions" (p. 107). The impedimenta to reliable knowledge, then, were the undisciplined signs of a discourse that had severed its ties with political reality. But recovering the real demanded first of all another act of interpretation; one more extended read. The object of political analysis, for Easton, could be located by surveying the history of political thought and locating some stable, underlying property shared by attempts to define the political.

Easton's candidate, as I have noted, is "the authoritative allocation of values," but of more interest than the fruitfulness of this category are the problems it raises for Easton's strategy. Easton himself supplies us with the means to identify such difficulties. In his critique of nonstandardized discussion, he warns of the possibility that names can take on a variety of meanings (they can be used to "demonstrate the contrary"), so that on Easton's own assumptions, whether or not political theories coincide with the world they ostensibly refer to will be a matter of sheer chance. Yet he proposes to extract his concept of the political from the very literature he castigates as unreliable.

Easton gestures toward grounding this return to the text in observable fact. Social science was born, he tells us, when "investigators" began to "look at certain constellations or clusters of elements in the concrete world" and discovered "a special coherence or system" "In the concrete world of reality," he continues, some things are "more prominently associated" with politics than others. These things (Easton lists "government organizations," "pressure groups," "voting," "parties," "classes," and "regional groups") "show" a "marked political relevance" (pp. 97–98). Easton's resort here to a rhetoric of the senses—of political things that *show* themselves and that are *marked* with inscriptions we know how to decode—is odd, however, in that, as before, he elsewhere provides us with arguments against such evidence. We have no way of knowing, he later insists, from the "apperceptive mass of behavior" alone, what is and is not politically relevant.[42] If this is so, Easton seems to rely for identification of the political upon the traditional bequest he elsewhere depicts as unreliable. Thus he concludes in spite of himself that the discovery of a common property shared by all the studies proffered by the tradition yields not only information about the adventures of a frequently duplicitous discourse but insight into the *nature* of politics "in the concrete world of reality."

This Janus-faced conception of the behavioralist enterprise—science as the elaboration of a conceptual framework derived from the logic of past political inquiry, and science as the reflection of an innocently observed "coherence" that is legible in the real world of politics itself—leads Easton to waver between literal and figurative uses of the terms he chooses to describe political life. Despite his acute awareness of the dangers of ambiguity, he slips repeatedly from the stance of the reader to that of observer. "We are trying to find a convenient way of describing very roughly the limits of political research," he writes of his reading of the literature of political science, but he continues, adopting the position of an observer of the "behaving system": "trying to identify the major properties of the political aspects of social life."[43] Similarly, Easton the reader concludes that "neither the concept of the state nor that of power in general offers a useful gross description of the central theme of political research," while the observer immediately adds that we must therefore explore "suitable concepts for identifying in broad outline the major political variables" (p. 124).

Easton's divided intentions are no less evident in one of his more emphatically theoretical works, briefly mentioned above, *A Framework for Political Analysis*. On the one hand, a "system" is a theoretical construct, "the most recent development in a long line of changing approaches to the understanding of society" (p. 22). On the other hand, the construct is especially applicable to politics because the latter somehow already *is* a system, albeit a peculiar one, necessitating that "we distinguish those interactions in society that we shall characterize as the components of a political system" (p. 48). On the one hand, a system is the merest metaphor: "It is always possible to borrow the conceptual apparatus of other disciplines and apply them analogically to the data of a different field" (p. 2). On the other hand, the political system is an actually existing thing, an "adaptive, self-regulating, and self-transforming system of behavior" (p. 26). Easton distinguishes between "empirical behavior we observe and characterize as political life" and the "set of symbols through which we hope to . . . explain the behavior," insisting that "it is of the utmost importance to keep these two kinds of systems distinct" (p. 26). Yet this differentiation cannot succeed. By Easton's own analysis, the "empirical political system" is *already* symbolic, composed of actions we have "*learned to call* political" (p. 68, emphasis added). Although a theoretical apparatus is so frail and arbitrary a construct that "we may arbitrarily decide to consider a duckbilled platypus and the ace of spades as our political system," we are blocked in this mad project by what the *tradition* establishes about the limits of the political system (p. 32).

Easton's decision to regard *some* conventional ideas about politics as wisdom and insight rather than error or omission relies on an implicit theory of naming that departs strongly from his official suspicion of names as shifting, peripatetic, and unreliable. In this second, tacit theory, names are straightforward and honest, only picking out features of objects that are really there. As Easton puts it, there are "numerous organizations and institutions in which the quantity and saliency of political activities are so great that these structures are recognized as primarily political in nature. The fact that they are given political names identifies them as structures heavily freighted with political consequences for the society" (p. 42). In favoring, for some purposes, a realist theory of the political sign as the faithful representative of the referent it stands for, Easton neglects an alternative linguistic analogy. Consider, for example, Jacques Lacan's theory of the sign, in which the signifier "stands" for the repression or absence of its signified content. What if the self-professed political *names* in which Easton places his trust conceal an *absence* of the political, as in the corporate usurpation of the "political parties, legislatures, and various kinds of interest groups" that Easton elsewhere takes to be obviously legible political "units"? Easton's occasional indulgence in realism neglects the possibility that, in the technologically advanced countries of the late twentieth century, the political sign possesses a predominantly *ironic* or *parodic* quality.

Easton's "framework for political analysis" is drawn from cybernetics: politics is a "self-regulating system" (more specifically, a "conversion process") that maintains its "stability" by changing form to cope with "demands" ("inputs") that it converts into "authoritative decisions" ("outputs").[44] According to Georges Canguilhem, "cybernetics" as a term for the science of politics was first coined by André-Marie Ampère, who derived it from the Greek *kubernan* (to steer, guide, or govern). Ampère's justification for introducing the term is that in the Greek language the word had already passed from strictly nautical or navigational usage to the political, as we know from Plato. In his *Essai sur la philosophie des sciences* (1834–

1843), Ampère distinguishes cybernetics and the "theory of power" as the two parts of "politics properly so called" (p. 139).[45] Whereas the theory of power deals with the causes of the various possible forms of political regime, cybernetics deals with "the *art of governing in general*" (p. 141). In Ampère's usage, the art of government is devoted to the stability, safety, and security of the society as a whole. When Easton (along with other behavioralists) embraces cybernetics as the "latest conceptualization" in systems thinking, then, it is not without a certain irony, as the term had been attractive to positivist systematizers of knowledge one hundred years earlier.

The effect of the cybernetic vocabulary in political science is to recode as "natural" what modern political theory since Hobbes had insisted was artificial, namely, the intentional invention, through compacts, of society and government seen as systems of rules and laws. That is, no doubt, the real accomplishment of the picture-world of cybernetic politics: it gives back to politics what the latter's secularization had taken from it, lending to political activity a natural shape assumed before any particular empirical discoveries that might be made about it. In other words, it accomplishes what Heidegger asserts is the essential moment of science as research for a social science modeling itself on the "natural" sciences. Hannah Arendt comments that the discourse of cybernetics allows for "materialist" control fantasies as easily as idealism allowed for control fantasies: "Materialists play the game of speculation with the help of computers, cybernetics, and automation; their extrapolations produce, not ghosts like the game of the Idealists, but materializations like those of spiritualist séances. What is so very striking in these materialist games is that their results resemble the concepts of the Idealists. . . . Such notions are neither science nor philosophy, but science fiction."[46]

Accordingly, behavioralist political narrative replaces terms firmly rooted in the history of political discourse and expressive of its historical variability ("statesman," "tyrant," "sovereign," "citizen") with putative invariants that can be kept constant through narrative shifts of time and place ("demands," "authorities," "allocations"). The behavioralist political scientist is the author of a story whose subject is all possible polities. But the difficulties of naming the invariant elements of political life—difficulties recognized by Easton himself—

forces the scientist continually to remind himself that, although on the road to reliable knowledge, he has not yet arrived. All of Easton's assertions about the political system are provisional, and "further research" is inevitably called for in a fastidious discourse of qualification. In this respect, the attitude of the empirical political scientist resembles Hegel's Unhappy Consciousness. Convinced of the abstract possibility of attaining knowledge of the Unchangeable, but despairing of ever actually doing so, the Unhappy Consciousness (like the empirical political scientist) views any knowledge attained as partial, flawed, and transitional. In relation to the scientific ideal, work actually accomplished is of vanishing significance, so that "consciousness of . . . existence and activity . . . is only an agonizing over this existence and activity, for therein it is conscious . . . only of its own nothingness."[47]

Taken together, these readings suggest that Easton's drive to escape the distortions of traditional texts and compose political life as a picture-world that satisfies the needs of the scientist-spectator is only superficially comprehensible as a demand for clarity and rationality in political discourse. The possession of an empirical theory empowers political scientist by enabling him to speak sensibly about politics; its perennial absence is a constant source of shame and powerlessness. If we reformulate Freud's question and ask "What do political scientists want?" the answer, of course, is an empirical theory. The question then becomes What *is* an empirical theory, such that it generates intensely ambivalent reactions of attraction and repulsion? Freud suggests an answer: an empirical theory is a fetish. Although the fetish, as Freud analyzes it in his 1927 essay "Fetishism," compensates for the fear of castration by denying the fact of sexual difference, it is also a constant unconscious reminder of the apparent reality of the threat of castration. The unacknowledged awareness of the artificiality of the fetish, Freud suggests, accounts for the ambivalent attitude of worship and hatred that the fetishist harbors for his fetish.[48]

If the search for the highly prized object of an empirical theory lends itself to psychoanalytical explanation, the frequently expressed concern over the absence of a specialized, authoritative, expert political knowledge might serve as a clinical symptom. Easton's objections to traditional political theory stem from a fear that ambiguous concepts, poorly integrated research programs, and contradictory but equally authoritative political judgments render political science impotent, incapable of the reliable achievement of knowledge. As any fetish must, behavioralist empirical theory both denies and asseverates this "castration": on the one hand, it provides the only route out of the pseudoknowledge of tradition and toward reliable scientific knowledge; on the other hand, measured against his ideal of reliable knowledge, Easton's scientist must continually stop himself from speaking on the grounds that no real science of politics has yet been achieved. The pursuit of a theory, then, endows the behavioralist with a reassuring identity as an expert authority on political affairs, but the fetish of theory constantly calls his identity into question.

How, under the circumstances, can the political scientist's identity as an expert authority be upheld? By undercutting the claims to truth of *non*empirical theory, so that the trope of authority becomes the scientist's strategic *withdrawal* from discourse—as in the expert's refusal to gratify his constituency's desire for definitive assertions on the grounds, say, of inadequate data. The *refusal* to offer deep political knowledge becomes a sign that the expert operates on the terrain of the real, as opposed to that of desire and imagination in which anything and everything may be said. Examples of this perverse trope of authority can be found throughout Easton's writings; for example, in the unhappy discourse of qualification just discussed. But it is most accessible, perhaps, in Easton's style, which occasionally reaches for an excessively chopped, blunt, brittle mode of address, one drained of metaphor which, at times, is uncannily reminiscent of Alain Robbe-Grillet's *chosisme* in its attempt to expunge all emotional connotation.

We should note, finally, that in Freud's account, the drama of the fetish is eminently iconographic. Its establishment turns upon unexpected sightings, feverish scrutiny, single-minded curiosity, suspicion about hidden truths, and a determination to bring out into the light of day the visible, observable object. Thus the stress as Easton relates his project on an observed and *seen* political system—one that has been caught in the act, as it were, and is no longer veiled by tradition. Once again, theory is caught in a double role: symbolic of the transparent rendering of the behaving political system; symptomatic of an insatiable curiosity about a political truth that is always suspected of having been withheld.

The interpretation of theory as fetish in Easton's behavioralism allows us to identify the gender of the political scientist. A fetishist can only be a *man*, whose insecurity about the foundation of his own identity in the possession of a theory-fetish requires the ritual disparagement of the soft, easy, yielding folds of traditional political theory, in which anybody can say whatever he or she likes, in contrast to the manly mastery of rigorous methods that obey the strictures of the natural sciences. But the use of psychoanalytic concepts should not be taken to mean that behavioralism was a private affair; rather, viewing behavioralist theory as a fetish allows us to connect its discourse to the public language of the postwar national security state.

Easton castigates old-fashioned political science, which concentrated on particular institutions such as courts, legislatures, and pressure groups of particular countries, as local, parochial, and "culture-bound," calling instead for a science of the political system "in general." Old-fashioned political science is the natural accompaniment of a self-absorbed society caught up in a domestic economic crisis and undertaking sweeping reform, as was the United States before it entered World War II; Its discourse takes for granted the finality and closure of a nationalist narrative as "the most inclusive unit," in Easton's terms, for the interpretation of political action. The natural corollary for a science of politics "in general," on the other hand, is an outward-looking polity, caught up in the burgeoning affairs of an emerging international society. More specifically, I suggest, the ideological context of the demand for a vocabulary of the political system in general is the postwar international crisis, the Cold War. Such doctrines such as "rollback," "containment," and "counterinsurgency" might be read as sketches for a metaphysics of contemporary world history as a permanent crisis requiring constant supervision and, if necessary, intervention.[49]

Easton registers this change in perspective as one demanded by good scientific practice. Prewar political science was "biased" in favor of particular institutions because it assumed a stable political environment without showing how this was possible. Such an approach is useless "where the system itself is threatened with destruction, as in highly unstable systems."[50] Whereas the parochial approaches of "decision-making, coalition strategies, game theory, power, and group analysis" are "partial theories of allocation," the systems approach throws into relief "allocation . . . in general" by *assuming the system to be in crisis* (pp. 474–76), thus building into the very center of political science the new discursive conditions of postwar international life. In a political rehearsal of Cartesian method, Easton resorts to hyperbolic doubt about the survivability of any system of authority.

Whatever else it may have been, the Cold War was an interpretative grille through which the U.S. leadership projected itself into history by defining the world as the scene of a network of emerging nations, politically unwieldy, and threatened with destructive internal conflict bound to be taken advantage of by a potential enemy. In this context, Louis Althusser's influential theory of ideology, as the construction of a preordained harmony between qualities naturally possessed by a subject and the role established for it by the larger narratives through which relationships to others are disclosed, may be seen as an extension of Heidegger's concept of *Bindung*, or binding adherence, between subject and world. The Cold War provided for just such a complicity between the nature of the agent and its tasks: unparalleled among the industrial powers in military and economic might, only the United States possessed the requisite treasure and political will to assume the role of manager of stability on a global scale. As then assistant secretary of state Dean Acheson, arguing in 1947 for U.S. assistance to the government of Greece, characterized the United States vis-à-vis its allies with respect to the task of countering Soviet power, "*We and we alone* were in a position to do so."[51]

Once the U.S. government had assumed the role of "stabilizer" of an international "system" of order, all unanticipated change carried the charge of an implicit challenge or threat (Easton's "stress" or "demand"); the role therefore required an effective discourse of surveillance and supervision, one that could take as its object the entire comity of nations ("allocation in general"). To repeat Maxwell Taylor's phrase, U.S. leaders' "attention must partake of the many-eyed vigilance of Argus—constantly watching in all directions in anticipation of the emergence of forces inimical to our national purposes."[52]

It is necessary, furthermore, to acquire some conceptual purchase on the field of nationalities, ideologies, and histories that U.S. leaders felt called to manage. As an abstract vocabulary that provides a set of terms through which political change under densely individuated circumstances may be coordinated, Easton's behavioralism provides a discourse in which one can seem to survey the totality of a world system. Setting as its goal "a unified theory of politics that embraces national, comparative, and international approaches," political science teaches that postwar history can be handled in economical and dispassionate terms: the international system is, after all, "just another type of system . . . comparable in all respects to any other."[53]

The systems vocabulary posits a reassuring manageability to a world in permanent crisis, and the masculine resolve to face danger coolly comports well with the alienated masculine identity we discovered in behavioralism's fetish of empirical theory. Easton's political scientist fits well the peculiar character of the male "crisis manager" spawned by the national security state. As one witness describes the type, "Toughness is the most highly prized virtue, . . . and it is cultivated in hundreds of little ways. There is the style of talking[:] . . . fact-loaded, quantitative, gutsy[, with a] . . . machine-gun delivery. The man who could talk fast and loud often proved he was 'on top of the job.' Speed reading too became a kind of badge of prowess."[54] The male crisis manager's badge of toughness is his mastery of reified language, like the *chosisme* of Easton's behavioralism in which political action becomes "input" and "output." The crisis manager is not so much a man as an adolescent boy, whose tough talk is a fetish that screens him from fears of inadequacy to "project power."

The description just given refers to the "Kennedy operators," but their jargon of inauthenticity is shared by most operators of the national security state and their congressional and media interlocutors. In testifying before the congressional committees investigating the Iran-Contra affair, for example, arms broker Richard Secord characterized the interpretation of international affairs as "HUMINT" (for "human intelligence"), intelligence itself as a "product," and the supply of terrorist armies as an "enterprise." The state system must be protected, according to Secord, from congressional investigations that rob the president of his "covert tool," which must be veiled from scrutiny to protect him from "embarrassing" consequences. The Iran-Contra revelations, Secord lamented, by publicly exposing the inadequacies of the president's "tool," have ensured that "the whole world is laughing at us." [55]

Despite its role in revealing (but simultaneously, of course, *reveiling*) the presidential tool, the journalistic language of international affairs mimes that of the boyish crisis manager and the behavioralist political scientist. A *Newsweek* cover story of late 1985, for example, reports that the Philippines under Ferdinand Marcos has become the most "*destabilizing* problem . . . on the Pacific rim." [56] The cover describes the Philippines as "Another Iran"; the text itself predicts it will turn into "another Saigon" (p. 31). In news-speak, differences between three countries are immaterial; what matters is their common property as systems: the degree of stability. Like Secord's story of his meeting with CIA director William Casey, in which one discussed Nicaragua and the other Iran, and each believed the other to be referring to the same country, Eastonian behavioralist discourse allows for the elision of differences to make way for a world of fictional manageability.

According to Heidegger, "the American interpretation of Americanism by means of pragmatism still remains outside the metaphysical realm." [57] Yet the story of Easton's behavioralism suggests the essence of metaphysics: *Verfallenheit*, or fallenness, whereby Dasein becomes completely identified with the simultaneously frozen and malleable discourses that structure its existence. In *Being and Time*, the immediate expression of *Verfallenheit* is the anonymous but "tranquilizing" language of *das Man*, which presupposes the prevailing universe of discourse and its horizon of interpretation. The discourse of *das Man* tranquilizes because it covers over the radical contingency of Dasein's finitude with "idle talk, curiosity, and ambiguity" that represent Dasein's world as secured once and for all. It enables Dasein to indulge in curiosity about the world and to accept with equanimity the ambiguity of its knowledge, on the basis of a more fundamental acquiescence to the prevailing projection: in the Easton case, an ideological projection of a historical crisis secured in advance (though never fully) by masculine expertise. For Easton himself, Heidegger's "gigantism," or the technological sublime, becomes virtually self-sufficient, utterly devoid of the need for the stoicism that Weber recommended as the only responsible attitude toward the modern will-to-truth's self-destruction of its own intellectual accomplishments. The political scientist celebrates his own self-destructive inability to calculate what the progress of calculation might yield, the inevitable disposal of his picture-world of politics at the hands of younger scientists with faster computers:

> What we have now is a mere infant's step, a crude beginning in the way of mechanized facilities. New generations of successively more complex computers of almost unimaginable capabilities are already on the horizon. Their invention and perfection will take place at the hands of a new generation of young scholars who will be the first to talk machine language from their earliest exposure to arithmetic and mathematics in grade and secondary schools. Unlike their predecessors, it is they who will feel entirely at ease with and confident about their relationships to and mastery of the computer. The growth in the introduction and use of such machines for storing and processing information must indeed assume the shape of a steep exponential curve.[58]

The chief irony here, of course, is the zeal with which those most aggressively putting themselves forward as concerned about "the concrete world of reality"—the claim common to national security operatives, journalists, and political scientists—should be so drawn to discourses devoted to transfiguring that world into a disposable picture for the pleasures of the subject. In its search for a language that might replace the battle of interpretation with the security of a foundation, Easton's behavioralism, and the broader Cold War discourse of which it is a part, ask to be read as an episode in the completion of metaphysics.

CHAPTER FOUR

Fiction and the Dilemma
of Postmodern Politics

1

A prime source of the political anxiety inspired by the rejection of theoretical piety is the fear that, Being having been revealed as a text, the special authority enjoyed by agreements reached through discourse governed by universal rational procedures is lost. Those who in the name of reason would instrumentalize and objectify have lost their moorings; but so too have those for whom reason signifies openness, contestability, and continuous revision and who therefore insist that the call for the democratization of society can be uttered in the name of reason. In *The Philosophical Discourse of Modernity*, Jürgen Habermas argues that underlying these two senses of reason is a distinction between two aspects of language: the serious and the fictive (pp. 185–210, 294–326). In serious discourse, what is said is uttered in the understanding that the speaker may be called upon at any time to defend his or her views or proposals with rational arguments; in Habermas's terms, a statement's "validity claims" may be "redeemed." In fictive discourse, these expectations are "bracketed," so that the aesthetic, self-referential, playful aspects of signification may predominate. Against deconstruction, which questions the coherence of the opposition between the serious and the fictive (or between what he also terms the "action-coordinating" and "world-disclosive" aspects of discourse), Habermas argues that this distinction is no arbitrary theoretical construct nor a habitual, traditional linguistic practice (pp. 198–204).[1] Rather, it isolates attitudes and idealizations participants in communicative action necessarily hold when they enter into relations with one another (p. 198).

Governed by the expectation of rational defensibility and the ideal of universal argumentative norms, serious, action-coordinating discourse makes of communication a problem-solving instrumentality capable of coordinating action because of the "binding illocutionary force" with which it connects participants to one another. Seriousness, for Habermas, is the norm; the expectation of redeemability structures and informs everyday, ordinary communication. Fiction, then, must be thought of not simply as a deviation from the ordinary, an extraordinary and specially demarcated lifting of the constraints and expectations governing normal communication, but as a deviation that is "parasitic" upon those very constraints because they are necessary for the establishment of the realities that fictional citations only mime.[2] The poets and novelists whose fictions tempt us to redescribe familiar experience in new terms and who, at the limit, are said to invent entirely new perspectives from which to judge and value our experience, are far from being Shelleyan "unacknowledged legislators" of the sort monumentalized in Nietzsche's "metaphysics for artists." In fact, they must ultimately prove their worth in terms of the continuous "learning processes" and "ongoing test[s]" of ordinary *serious* language; for its perspective, just because it is not merely local but appeals to norms that transcend any particular context, remains decisive (pp. 195–210).

Against this Habermasian argument, deconstructionists point to the way in which the allegedly serious, literal discourses of everyday life are in fact permeated with symbolic, fictional constructs and conventional, ritualized meanings. If the communication of a meaning demands linguistic convention, then *all* communication is play-acting, all meaning fictional, all reason "mere" convention.[3] Reversing the traditional (indeed, Platonic) hierarchy that Habermas defends, in the Derridean optic, the serious turns out to be a special case of the fictive, an especially well-accepted, believable, satisfying fiction: "illusions," in Nietzsche's words, "which we have forgotten are illusions."[4] Here, the extraordinary fiction is not the result of bracketing the expectation that validity claims can be redeemed; rather, it is the shock of the new, that which not only departs from everyday *consensual* reality but also compels solely in virtue of the depth and originality of its vision.

The problem Habermas finds in this view strikes at the prime source of political anxiety surrounding the claims of deconstruction, namely, that such a "leveling" of the distinction between serious and fictive discourse assimilates political and moral judgment to aesthetics, "to 'the Yes and No of the palate', as the organ of a knowledge beyond true and false, beyond good and evil" (p. 96). If discourse is fictive, it cannot be serious; if it is not serious, it cannot be political. Therefore, if the postphilosophical abandonment of rational foundations carries the day, genuinely political discourse is ruled out because in place of the seriousness of binding illocutionary force we have only the light, irresponsible play of "illusion, deception, optics, the necessity of the perspectival and of error" (p. 95). We are faced, then, with an opposition in which superficiality, irresponsibility, and playfulness are ranged against the serious business of constructing binding agreements (binding *because* they are true) that are taken seriously inasmuch as they are at all times open to criticism and revision on the basis of further reflection and experience. Worlds can be poetically disclosed only at the cost of restraining oneself from entering into serious political enterprises; political action occurs only under the sway of the ordinary, the literal, the everyday.

Habermas inveighs against Derrida's blurring of this distinction in large measure because, were the poetic, world-disclosive aspect of language to become dominant, then rational, deliberative politics would be superseded by "the transsubjective will to power . . . manifested in the ebb and flow of an anonymous process of subjugation" (p. 95). That is, the *critical* dimension of reason—its insistence on openness, that everything be subject to universal argumentative norms—would be lost to the project of democratization. In this opposition between action-coordinating and world-disclosing discourse, the place and function of *theoretical* judgment is clear to Habermas: On the side of action-coordination, it mediates between the various specialized, expert serious discourses. It translates among them, and in virtue of its single-minded concern with consistency and argumentative force, it insists on the testing and demonstration of the worth of various competing claims to attention. It ensures that the competing claims of diverse communicative practices be ultimately answerable to the paradoxically noncoercive force of argumentation rather than to the "qualities of texts in general" (p. 190).[5]

The question, then, becomes How might one think of the contestability of political claims, visions, proposals, or agreements without relying on the foundation of a *critical idea* (that everything be subject to revision based on rational argumentation) as its essential possibility condition? In this chapter, I read postwar American literature to explore the possibility that the qualities of openness, revision, contestability, and questionableness cut across Habermas's distinction between the serious and the fictive. Such qualities can also characterize fiction, which, in the hands of such writers as William S. Burroughs and James Merrill, fails to respect the bracketing of validity claims that Habermas insists it must *nor* to rely on a "pious" appeal to a theoretical or critical foundation or framework for evaluation and adjudication. Nor is this a matter of asserting that the fictive, the nonserious, is really dominant in all discourse.[6] It is to say, rather, that for these writers, distinguishing between the serious and the nonserious, the real and the fictive, the authoritative and the nonsensical, is problematic and uncertain. It is facing up to that uncertainty that leads them to articulate strategies of interpretation and modes of judgment adequate to the demands imposed by such indeterminacy. Burroughs and Merrill, I suggest, invent ways of offering and contesting strong political judgments which operate entirely outside the framework of the Habermasian distinction between the serious and the fictive and his image of the theorist as a stand-in or interpreter mediating various specialized discourses and subjecting all to the demands of logical consistency.

2

It is difficult to imagine two writers more unlike one another: Merrill the aesthete, struggling always to distance himself, through sheer stylistic mastery, from a linguistic adventure that becomes ever more disturbingly "real," and Burroughs the avowed antiaesthete who would philosophize, if he must, not with Nietzsche's hammer but a Ruger .357 magnum. There is a remarkable thematic resemblance, however, in their work of the late 1970s and 1980s. Both create audacious, sweeping, visionary texts that formulate provocative diagnoses of a global political crisis seen from a distinctively American point of view. The late twentieth century, for Burroughs and Merrill alike, can be understood as the general corruption of the human species, to be remedied by means of a severe biologic purge. Both writers, the aesthetic commitments dividing them notwithstanding, strive to enact a dramatic departure from the ideologies of literary modernism and its cultivation of a private symbolic order to supplement the insufficiencies of a publicly unintelligible world. And the visions of Burroughs and Merrill both are as disturbing as they are aggressively nonsensical, challenging Enlightened, reasonable, scientific civilization in ways that seem alternately ridiculous (asking us to entertain the possibility of ghosts, flying saucers, and time travel) and obnoxious (attacking democracy and lamenting the worthlessness of the masses).

More important than any thematic similarities, however, is the way in which Burroughs, the public "literary outlaw," and Merrill, the master of the strictures of poetic grammar, have foregrounded the resources of fiction—in particular, narrative devices—for the purpose of articulating a vision of cosmic order and social decline in which distinctions between the fictive and the real, the metaphorical and the literal, become irrelevant. To be sure, their late twentieth-century visions of other worlds or coming worlds arrive in the wake of a long and privileged history of poetic representations of apocalypse and rebirth, but dominant aesthetic ideologies placed the latter's source in a foundation outside language itself, whether in God, nature, or the imagination. The absence of such a foundational appeal for Burroughs and Merrill means that their judgments about the meaning and prospects of contemporary Western civilization apparently find no ground on which to stand. Such judgments must rest, these writers tell us, on the productivity and inventiveness of language alone—language bereft of transcendental authority, idealizing assumptions, or reliable argumentative procedures. Burroughs and Merrill are by no means equally successful if measured by this project, but their respective failures and successes have something to teach us, I believe, about the prospects and dangers of a posttheoretical political discourse.

Writers on postmodernity have noted striking similarities between the deconstruction of metaphysics and what they perceive to be kindred strategies at work in such postwar American fiction as the novels of Thomas Pynchon, Don DeLillo, and William S. Burroughs, among others. Both the theory and the fiction of the postwar period, as Charles Russell points out, eschew the modernist dream of inventing a radical alternative to the existing social order. They also share an awareness—sometimes celebratory and sometimes critical, but rarely elegiac or nostalgic—that a writer in the late twentieth century no longer has recourse to a privileged standpoint from which to judge or transcend the existing order and its dominant cultural codes.[7] Like much postwar literary theory, political theory, and philosophy, postmodern fiction cultivates a sensibility that, though critical of the established order, has abandoned the heroic oppositional impulses of modernism that drove a Pound (or a Marx) to project countercultures of their own and to posit the subjectivity of the artist (or the theorist) as a resource adequate to the threats posed by technology, the state, and mass culture.

Postwar theory and fiction are alike in their skepticism toward modernist claims about the privileged status of the theoretical gaze or the privileged position of the writer. Yet it is also true that they often resort to critical strategies traditionally dependent on such figures in order to unmask the illusory plenitude of contemporary culture, exposing it as a locus of hidden forces and controls, whose dreary sameness of power is concealed by an apparently flexible cultural system. Burroughs's work, in particular, is explicitly dedicated to "subverting" dominant ideologies by exposing their role in strategies of control and administration in ways that align him with the unmasking strategies discussed in Chapter 2. Indeed, a reading of his work contributes to enumerating the limits of unmasking by showing how postmodern subversion, as Burroughs practices it, is itself entangled in the culture of the authorities it seeks to overturn, and in ways that seriously compromise his critical intentions. More important for our immediate purposes, however, Burroughs's subversions depend on breaking down received distinctions between fiction and nonfiction, and his work is therefore an apt point of departure for an attempt to complicate the Habermasian distinction just outlined.

For Burroughs, the world in which we live, the public world in which our ideals, motives, loves, and hates are recognized and discussed and acted out, is a world of manipulated needs that serve mainly to keep those who satisfy them in power. Though formidable, their power is far from absolute; for they too are manipulated by need, namely, their need to control and dominate. Burroughs relies on many images to communicate this vision of modern power: the master metaphor of addiction or "the algebra of need"; the character of the "vampire," who draws on the vitality of others to live, necessitating a constant search for new victims when the old have been exhausted; and the virus, whose artificial reproduction eventually consumes the host on which it feeds. The ultimate virus, the most pervasive and deeply rooted form of addiction to artificial pleasures that sap the vitality of those dependent on them, is language itself, whose ability to create fictions detached from reality opens up multifarious possibilities of control and seduction. Discourse, in the form of "word lines controlling thought feeling and apparent sensory impressions," lodges itself in the human host and reproduces its scripts, argumentative routines, and programs in ways that entangle the individual subject in a world it can neither master nor effectively negotiate.[8] As the host of a language virus, the individual body becomes a mere "flesh script" or "soft machine," a grid of received discourses obsessively realized through desires and needs.

These "word lines," devised in the "Reality Studio," constitute a "Garden of Delights" in which images of happiness, satisfaction, and the exercise of powers substitute for the real things.[9] The key to control in Burroughs's world is the ability of power to make individuals dependent on certain configurations of words, images, and pleasures to the point where they become predictable and hence manipulable automatons. Their dependence on linguistically fixed images and meanings puts individuals at the mercy of exploiters who manufacture such images to gratify their own need to manipulate and control. In such a manner, agents of domination exploit the capacity of words—as arbitrary, conventional signs that generate meaning as an effect of internal processes rather than through standing for real experiences—to depart from reality and create fictions of satisfaction and fulfillment. The rogues' gallery of Burroughsian characters— gangsters, conmen, pushers—have in common the theme of controlling others by mastering the art of producing vivid and convincing representations. They achieve this control in part by relying on the naïve, metaphysical urge to believe that when language appears most meaningful, it is because it has successfully established a referential relationship to the world. Thus there is a kind of Althusserian "teeth-gritting harmony" among the capacity of language to fabricate meaning and pleasure, the tendency for subjects to become dependent on this, and the need of some to exploit this dependence to experience the pleasure of domination.

Much of Burroughs's early work is animated by a kind of Beat metaphysics that attempts to abandon language altogether in favor of direct, intuitively legitimated communication in which distortion is impossible because representation itself has been abandoned. In this sense, Burroughs is a metaphysician, sharing with the tradition the conviction that representation is dangerous and must be scrutinized with care and, if possible, transcended. "What I look for in any relationship," Burroughs says, "is contact on the nonverbal level of intuition and feeling, that is, telepathic contact." [10] "When communication finally becomes total and conscious," he adds, "words will no longer be necessary." [11] It is easy to find in Burroughs elements of the classic Western myth, analyzed by Jacques Derrida in *Of Grammatology*, of the fall of language from direct pictorial mimesis into symbolic representation and the possibility of distortion. As Burroughs puts it in *The Job* (1970), "Universal literacy with a concomitant control of word and image is now the instrument of control. An essential feature of the Western control machine is to make language as non-pictorial as possible, to separate words as far as possible from objects or observable processes." [12]

A good deal of the desperate violence of Burroughs's early work may be attributable to this radical devaluation of language, which, if utterly stripped of its illusory claims to referentiality, would seem to be no more and no less than an arbitrary constraint (the moment of the "naked lunch," when the system appears for exactly what it is, fueled by an unstoppable urge to dominate and control) and would cease to obscure the richer world of simultaneity beneath the word lines' fictional linearity. This devaluation of language is to be achieved by randomizing the predominant "scripts" through such methods as the cut-up, "dicing texts with scizzors and reassembling the fragments arbitrarily in order to neutralize their power and more generally to liberate man from the traumas of early verbalization."[13] The cut-up, however, is only the instrument of a larger goal: disrupting the conventional narrative structures responsible for the illusions of temporality, causality, stable character or identity, with the additional help of such tactics as not attributing conversation to characters and refusing to explain transitions from one place or time to another.

From this perspective, Burroughs's eventual moves toward more conventional narration suggest a reconciliation with language.[14] Several writers have noted Burroughs's shift away from the sheer destruction of narrative form toward an attempt to narrativize the West's privileged self-understanding as one fiction among others.[15] But one should not overestimate the return to traditional narrative technique by underestimating the extent to which he relied on such techniques in the early work. Just as Burroughs does not completely embrace traditional narrative convensions even in the later work, he had not completely abandoned them in the earlier. Rather, all his work relies on an *implied* plot or plots that the reader may adumbrate and appeal to in order to explain the various levels of discourse and events one finds throughout the novels.[16]

The basic plot of the early work, or rather the figure of the basic plot, is the "Nova Conspiracy," in which alien criminals live parasitically off earthlings by addicting them to needs, above all to the need for power and meaning—language. These "Nova Criminals" are sought after by the Nova Police, who, however, cannot confront the criminals directly for fear that they would destroy the world to make their escape. Instead the police must fight them through insidious, clandestine means. The Nova Criminals rely overwhelmingly on divisive ideological manipulation through the state and industry, both of which rely on the mass media. This control is to be disrupted, as we have already discussed, by exposing the image-world of apparent freedom and happiness created by the Nova Criminals' "Reality Studio" as a nexus of control, enslavement, and dependence. Although the basic plot is never completely or coherently elaborated, Burroughs's practice as a writer thus becomes meaningful in terms of this narrative, which is developed enough for the reader to rely on it to make sense of Burroughs's work as a whole.

Burroughs's work organizes, I think, two sources of tension. On the one hand, much of the force of Burroughs's condemnations derives its power from the way in which he insists on calling individuals to account, emphasizing not general cultural tendencies but acts of brutality that stronger souls would shun. On the other hand, however, Burroughs charges Western civilization as a whole with stupidity, displaying individual inadequacies as the result of a perverse culture for which nobody is responsible—an argumentative turn that drains his initial gambit of some of its power. More seriously, Burroughs attacks those who will do anything to satisfy the needs they are addicted to; this, he suggests, is fundamentally what is responsible for the moral, social, and political chaos of modernity. At the same time, Burroughs opposes to the Reality Studio's regime of truth, meaning, and reference the slogan "Nothing is True—Everything is Permitted."[17] Again, this blunts the force of his own critique: if everything is permitted, what is really *wrong* with the algebra of need, the society of addiction?

At times, Burroughs suggests that the algebra of need is wrong because it violates or perverts individuality: "We oppose . . . the use of such knowledge [of domination through addiction and image] to control, coerce, debase, exploit or annihilate the individuality of another human creature." Yet this reason cannot satisfy Burroughs, for whom the concept of a definite, bounded, located, and embodied self is increasingly problematic. He notes his suspicion of his own "self" as a host of control and limitation: "I prefer not to use my own words, I don't like my own words because my own words are prerecorded. . . . My words are prerecorded for me as yours are prerecorded for you."[18] This recognition then renders ambiguous the notion of a struggle *against* power, inasmuch as among the things individuals must resist are their "own" desires, capacities, and goals.

As Charles Russell puts it, "Burroughs . . . suggests that to struggle against social control means to battle against one's prior identification with it—and, even more distressingly, that to actively oppose the enemy insures that one remains defined by them; for as long as one is obsessed by fighting the opposition, one is not free of it. In Burroughs' novels, the greatest danger is thus to allow oneself to become rigidly defined by something external to oneself, for then one's identity is restricted and vulnerable."[19]

Especially in his later work, however, Burroughs becomes wary even of the opposition between oneself and what is external to oneself. Burroughs often suspects that there *is* no preexisting, true self that will emerge once the "ersatz bullshit" of the Reality Studio is unmasked as such; that the problem is not one of distinguishing the external from the authentic but rather of accepting the chaos of fictions that is the self and resisting the blandishments of final or definitive self-descriptions.[20] Thus, again, the cut-up method, in which the writer's own sensibility is frustrated by the introduction of the aleatory into the process of composition. As his work developed, Burroughs supplemented such techniques, as I have said, with a return to narrative in which the world-creating character of narrative invention is foregrounded through both the use of abrupt, unexplained transitions from one plot line to another and a focus on the persona of the writer, storyteller, historian, or journalist.[21] Burroughs's strategy in this regard is based on a claim about the nature of authority and its undoing that resembles, in essential respects, de Man's in *The Resistance to Theory:* authority depends on the fiction of reference or meaning, and authority can be undone, therefore, by exploding such fictions, not by producing a new myth or reality— telling yet another story—but by making clear the fictitious character of reality as a narrative process and so making language useless for purposes of domination (pp. 10–11). But this is an uneasy solution at best, because it still relies on the tacit assumption that, once all our organized and mystified fictions have been unmasked as such, some other (and presumably better) principle or value might naturally make itself felt. To the extent that such metaphysical optimism is itself a fiction, Burroughs's subversion of conventional narrative might well fuel the drive for more authoritative—more intense, more vivid, more "real"—fictions, a dynamic whose political significance is neither good nor evil but strictly incalculable.

3

Burroughs's writing, early and late, embodies central concerns of postwar American fiction: paranoia, conspiracy, apocalypse, and an unrelieved suspicion of all public representations and discourses. Like his Beat colleagues, Burroughs has cultivated an identity of a "literary outlaw," an identity that associates authenticity with extremism, risk, adventure, and moral ambiguity.[22] For Burroughs, this identity takes two not entirely distinct forms: involvement in the drug world, where the postwar imperatives of "conformity" and "responsibility" are chemically revalued in favor of an approach to literary invention which abandons authorial intention for postintentional synchronicity, that is, the cut-up method. As he put it in a 1966 interview, The declarative sentence "is one of the great errors of Western thought, the whole either-or proposition. . . . I feel the Aristotelian construct is one of the great shackles of Western civilization. Cut-ups are a movement towards breaking this down."[23] But if the problem is Western metaphysics ("the whole either-or proposition") itself, the writer's task is immense indeed, encompassing a transfiguration of Western perceptions of agency and identity and overturning "responsible" cause-and-effect explanatory narrative through the ecstasy of the synchronous and its logic of displacement. Such a transfiguration, as we have seen, is not only a moral or individual concern but a political one. It has to do with the character of our shared world, and demands, in addition to a form of opposition or subversion, the articulation of new criteria for judging the order bequeathed to us by the "Aristotelian" civilization Burroughs rejects. The trilogy written during the 1980s—*Cities of the Red Night* (1981), *The Place of Dead Roads* (1983), and *The Western Lands* (1987)—confirms this assessment by extending Burroughs's criticism of "the whole either-or proposition" to a sweeping refiguration of the history and destiny of the West, imagined now in the persona of a writer-narrator who would escape Western civilization not by dissolving its logic but by creating for it a new account of itself.

In *Cities of the Red Night*, the narrator attempts to escape the temporalized destiny of Western history by insisting on the reality of multiple histories, stitching together eighteenth-century adventurers, twentieth-century private eyes, and warring, ultimately self-destructing city-states, existing one hundred thousand years in the past and obsessed with the technology of reincarnation. In the end, only the narrator is left, a disembodied figure of pseudoutopian hope hidden in the resources of language. In *The Place of Dead Roads*, gunslinger Kim Carsons explores the peak experiences of violence, danger, and extremism, governed by an ethical code of devotion to the preservation of individual authenticity in a world that will tolerate this value only as an essentially fugitive experience. The only decisive way out of such a world, we learn, is through cloning and mutation—the biologic transformation of the human animal into a creature capable of infinite self-transfiguration, something that may be achieved, perhaps, with the help of a deadly virus, for which the only "cure" is humanity's evolution into something nonhuman.

This pop-Nietzschean (or Darwinian) theme is carried over into the final novel in the trilogy, where it is combined with the story of the search for the ancient Egyptian "Western Lands," for immortality—for the chosen, pharaonic few. Much of *The Western Lands*, in fact, reads like a rehearsal of Nietzsche's reassessment of rank and severity in the context of a Christian, equalizing culture. For Nietzsche, the "terrible consequence" of Western culture is that "everyone believes he has a right to every problem."[24] The idea that *one* omnipotent God is interested in *every* human being leads to the idea that immortality—that is, escape from the modern Western conflation of logic and history—is an achievement that should be on everyone's agenda, with the result that the highest values (in this case, timelessness) are degraded into ritual and routine. All that immortality demands now is a simple contract, properly signed by man and appropriately countersigned by God in script legible to everyman. Nietzsche has a different idea: "I teach: that there are higher and lower men, and that a single individual can under certain circumstances justify the existence of whole millennia—that is, a full, rich, great, whole human being in relation to countless fragmentary men" (sec. 997). Such as Napoleon, for example.

Like Nietzsche, Burroughs considers that monotheism represents a hatred for distinction, contingency, and the unexpected, an attempt to trade the extraordinary for security: "The OGU is a pre-recorded universe of which He is the recorder. It's a flat, thermodynamic universe, since it has no friction by definition."[25] Although the literal political implications of these judgments are not edifying to contemplate, we may take the point of Nietzsche's and Burroughs's reassertion of rank and severity to be that the appeal of such a culture is precisely that it represents the achievement of immortality as a task demanding an immense labor for its fulfillment, a labor that cannot be derived from nor guaranteed by any deity, method, or formula for social harmony. "The road to the Western Lands is the most dangerous of all roads. . . . To know the road exists violates the human covenant" (p. 180). Seeking the Western Lands, then, is an unprecedented project each time it is undertaken and demands above all else a break with common, mainstream ideas of authority, certainty, and utility.

If the road to the Western Lands is so dangerous, why does the central figure of Burroughs's epic, the "old writer," seek it? The answer, of course (and here again we observe Burroughs silently reading Nietzsche) is that the present stage of Western civilization is intolerable because it has eliminated any reason to live; the nuclear holocaust we fear is simply the possibility of literalizing what is already the metaphorical truth that society and culture are *already dead*. "What happened here? Nothing happened. Cause of death: totally uninteresting. They could not create event. They died from the total lack of any reason to remain alive" (p. 180). Contemporary civilization copes with the pointlessness of modernity by constructing the illusory *appearance* of life in the form of a dominant "fixed image" or identity maintained by a "vampiric" civilizing process in which dominant figures utilize more "life" than they generate in order to preserve their identities against time and decay (pp. 157–58). Throughout, the main symbol of the civilization of the "fixed image" are the British, wedded to their identity and unable to change even when circumstances demand it. But they represent in extreme form what is true of contemporary life generally (pp. 160–66). Indeed, for Burroughs, the ultimate fixed image—the central trope, as it were, for the master trope—is nothing other than monotheism in its essentially Christian form: the idea that all can achieve salvation by following one simple, easily understood rule.

Escape from the certain death this civilization has in store for its adherents must take the form, then, of breaking with monotheism, and to think this break, Burroughs turns to the mythology of ancient Egypt. Rather than one center of power which articulates and enforces one easily comprehended rule, there are many vectors of power—an unknown number, in fact—and many rules, none too intelligible. One thing, however, is clear: surviving the Land of the Dead and attaining immortal life in the Western Lands depends on establishing a relationship with one's "Ka," the fifth soul in Egyptian mythology, the "double" whose fate is linked with that of the subject and who may therefore provide guidance but no guarantees. The conflict of cosmic powers with ambiguous and overlapping authority means, then, contrary to Christian monotheism, that most are doomed but that *a very few might prevail:*

> The Magical Universe, MU, is a universe of many gods, often in conflict. So the paradox of an all-powerful, all-knowing God who permits suffering, evil and death, does not arise.
>   "What happened, Osiris? We got a famine here."
>   "Well, you can't win 'em all. Hustling myself."
>   "Can't you give us immortality?"
>   "I can get you an extension, maybe. Take you as far as the Duad. You'll have to make it from there on your own. Most of them don't. Figure about one in a million. And, biologically speaking, that's very good odds." (P. 113)

"Biologically speaking"—the powers that Burroughs's escape artist must negotiate are as much physical as spiritual: the biologic and cosmologic worlds are both governed by the same nonlogic of "the Long Chance, the impossible odds":

> He is the God of the Second Chance and the Last Chance, God of single combat, of the knife fighter, the swordsman, the gunfighter, God

of the explorer, the first traveler on unknown roads, the first to use an untried craft or weapon, to take a blind step in the dark, to stand alone where no man has ever stood before . . . God of Mutation and Change, God of hope in hopeless conditions, he brings a smell of the sea, of vast open places, a smell of courage and purpose . . . a smell of silence confronting the outcome. (Pp. 114–15)[26]

By the same token, Burroughs expresses contempt for the attempt to artificially increase the odds, as Burroughs understands modernity's will to organizational efficiency through technology and rationality. Thus his assessment of Hassan i Sabbah's assassins, who, despite the fact that capture means certain death, refuse the possibility of escape: "To modern political operatives, this is romantic hogwash. You gonna throw away an agent you spent years training? Yes, because he was trained for one target, one kill. The modern operative, then, is doing something very different from the messengers of HIS [i.e., Hassan i Sabbah]. Modern agents are protecting and expanding political aggregates" (p. 192). The value Burroughs places on the absolute singularity of the event or project, and his rejection of the attempt to elude chance and contingency through causality and calculation, both echoe Nietzsche's *amor fati* as explicated by Gilles Deleuze:

The bad player counts on several throws of the dice, on a great number of throws. In this way he makes use of causality and probability to produce a combination that he sees as desirable. He posits this combination itself as an end to be obtained, hidden behind causality. . . . To abolish chance by holding it in the grip of causality and finality, to count on the repetition of throws rather than affirming chance, to anticipate a result instead of affirming necessity—these are all the operations of a bad player.[27]

As Deleuze explains, there is a "double affirmation" at work in the throw of the dice: a first, when the dice are thrown and all possible combinations are affirmed, and a second, when a particular combination results. Man, for Deleuze's Nietzsche, is a bad gambler because he plays only on the condition of having an infinite number of turns, thus guaranteeing that eventually the desired combination is achieved. Man affirms chance only in the throw, insisting on selecting again and again until the result meshes with his desires and expectations. Burroughs and Nietzsche agree that the sovereign, eternal god of monotheistic religions is the image of Man in this sense: "Heavy as the pyramids, immeasurably impacted, the One God can wait." [28]

The good player—*Übermensch*—affirms both the throw of the dice and the result, including the unexpected result that takes us beyond what we want and away from ourselves: "That the universe has no purpose, that it has no end to hope for any more than it has causes to be known—this is the certainty necessary to play well. The dicethrow fails because chance has not been affirmed enough in one throw." [29] This, according to Deleuze, is truly tragic thought: the traditional interpretation of tragedy as failure reflects only the slavish, resentful, metaphysical perspective, whereas an appreciation of "Dionysus" reveals the essential innocence of unexpected and unmastered happenings. Like Nietzsche's and Deleuze's Dionysus, Burroughs's god of chance "demands more of his followers than any other": "Do not evoke him unless you are ready to take the impossible chances, the longest odds. Chance demands total courage and dedication. He has no time for welchers and pikers and vacillators." [30]

The late twentieth century is precisely the place of the last chance—the freak success, the unlikely victory. It is a place representable in mythological or biologic terms as a population of "remains, kept operational by borrowed power overdrawn on the Energy Bank . . . physical bodies powered by bum life checks" (p. 150, ellipses his), or as an evolutionary backwater where all potentially viable mutations are immediately swallowed up by the larger, biologically inactive population. Thus Burroughs's NOs, "natural outlaws dedicated to breaking the so-called natural laws of the universe foisted upon us by physicists, chemists, mathematicians, [and] biologists" (p. 30). The aim of the NOs is to turn evolution toward the genesis of a creature capable of discarding earth and its temporal traps in favor of a disembodied life in space. "Only those who can leave behind everything they ever believed in can hope to escape," and chief among these beliefs is the idea that humanity's fate is linked to its body; instead, it will achieve immortality by abandoning the body (as a natural product of evolutionary history) and building an entirely artificial world in space, not time (p. 116). Indeed it is the natural outlaw who discovers the greatest barrier to space: "the monumental fraud of cause and effect," which he replaces by "the more pregnant concept of synchronicity," namely, the receptivity toward relations, events, ideas, and inventions beyond the order of intentions, plans, and values (p. 30). This in fact is the old writer's Ka: whatever enables him to *escape himself*; and these resources are discovered, precisely, through the act of writing, which can proceed along lines other than strict temporal succession. The Burroughsian writer, then, is *the* political thinker par excellence, the only figure possessed of the resources enabling one both to state, in general terms, the Western predicament ("the monumental fraud of cause and effect") and to articulate a generally applicable alternative ("the more pregnant concept of synchronicity").

4

To this point, I have discussed Burroughs's book as if it were narrated in a temporally orthodox manner, but it is not, and as the comments above suggest, the fact that it is not is very much to the point. Images of a degraded species, biologic mutation, escape into space, and the old writer's desperate attachment to these stories in his attempt to imagine for himself a fate different than the one prepared for him by his civilization do not compose part of a master narrative or plot but are juxtaposed against one another, as the ethic of synchronicity would demand. Consequently, the status of any given image is always in question: at one moment, biologic evolution stands as a metaphor for cultural evolution; at another, discourses of cultural evolution are offered as ways of imagining a biologic transformation. At some points, emigration into space is offered literally as a possible way out of the Land of the Dead; at others it remains a figure of speech. This ambiguity is maintained with almost perfect rigor throughout, underwriting the question pertaining to the claims that might be made for Burroughs's grand vision: Is Burroughs serious? His apparently straightforward answer—the admonition "not [to] take anything too seriously [but to] remember also that frivolity is even

more fatal" (p. 163)—cannot resolve these doubts, but it does suggest that the question is badly posed. Burroughs's speculation about
the nature of our civilization's predicament is serious *and* frivolous,
because, he seems to believe, such speculation can only be carried
out in a discourse that combines both registers. The frivolous, nonserious character of fiction, according to the traditional concept that
Habermas endorses, is not so much rejected by Burroughs as taken
up by him as a pose or device. It is a mask licensing his more radical,
outré speculations, allowing him the poetic license needed, for example, to disregard the fraud of cause and effect. But as Burroughs
repeatedly suggests, the extent to which fictions are *simply* frivolous or nonserious is difficult to decide; for from his perspective, it
is always within the terms of various fictional discourses that we attempt to make these distinctions.

Consider, for example, Burroughs's discussion of the Egyptian
animal gods. These gods, he tells us, which take the form of combinations of various animals (including humans), have a basis in fact:
"I venture to suggest that at some time and place the animal Gods
actually existed, and that their existence gave rise to belief in them.
At this point the monolithic One God concept set out to crush a biologic revolution that could have broken down the lines established
between the species, thus precipitating unimaginable chaos, horror,
joy and terror, unknown fears and ecstasies, wild vertigos of extreme
experience, immeasurable gain and loss, hideous dead ends" (p. 112).
On the one hand, Egyptian mythology provides an image of Burroughs's call to transcend the limits of time and evolve into entirely
different creatures, a fantasy he renders in other terms as the exploits of the NOs, who will rededicate our evolutionary heritage and
retool us for life in space. On the other hand, Burroughs claims in
his own voice that the gods were believed in because they were real:
the metaphor of the animal gods was based on the literal fact of an
approaching "biologic revolution." At the same time, the biologic
revolution serves as a metaphor for cultural transformation, especially for the work of the writer as Burroughs sees it: the attempt to
write "our own Western Lands," to invent a "land of dreams" that
is *not* "solid" and that does not exist in time. The insistence that immortality find a literal, solid form was "the error of the mummies.

They made spirit solid. When you do this, it ceases to be spirit. We will make ourselves less solid." This, Burroughs tells us, is what art and indeed all creative thought is directed toward (p. 165). But if Egyptian gods and biologic revolution serve at times as metaphors for literary invention (which is itself a figure for cultural transformation and renewal), writing itself is also a figure for life as preparation for the literalization of Burroughs's fantasies of our "biologic and spiritual destiny in space" (pp. 58–59).

Or consider "the Big Picture," Burroughs's central conspiracy story in the novel, the tale of Joe the Dead (a character who appeared earlier in *The Place of Dead Roads*), the NO who leads a secret group of evolutionary biologists planning to modify themselves for life in space, abandon Earth, and destroy the remaining population. On the one hand, the idea of a group of individuals who isolate themselves from the general population as a prelude to biologic revolution thematizes Burroughs's interpretation of the implications of the "punctual" theory of evolution, namely, the doctrine that evolutionary transformations occur rapidly through small groups of mutating organisms (p. 56). But on the other hand, as we have seen, the question of whether biologic revolution has a metaphorical or literal status in his work cannot be resolved, which casts similarly ambiguous light on the fiction of Joe the Dead. The "Big Picture involves escape from the planet by a chosen few. The jumping-off place is Wellington, New Zealand. After that, an extermination program will be activated. Needless to say, Big Picture is a highly sensitive project. Even to suspect the existence of Big Picture is unwholesome" (p. 51). Yet Burroughs is here suspecting the existence of Big Picture in public, violating his own advice, a gesture that is synecdochic for his conspiracy narratives and the genre as a whole: if the conspiracy really existed, the last thing one would do is publicize it.

Further on, Burroughs provides a reason for the need for conspiracy narrative as a public discourse: it is the terrain he knows best, and "when dealing with an adversary the strategy is to inveigle him or her into your territory" (p. 138). This might serve as the hermeneutic clue to Burroughs's narrative strategy in the book as a whole, which involves inveigling the reader into the terrain of synchronicity: "Imagine that you are dead and see your whole life spread out in a spatial panorama, a vast maze of rooms, streets, landscapes, not sequentially arranged but arranged in shifting associational patterns. Your attic room in St. Louis opens into a New York loft, from which you step into a Tangier street. Everyone you know is there" (p. 138). But the status of Burroughs's synchronous universe—whether writing practice, project of cultural transformation, biologic revolution, terrorist conspiracy—remains undecidable.

Or rather, *almost* undecidable. It is true that Burroughs appropriates an ideological concept of literature as fiction in order to indulge in otherwise proscribed political fantasies. At the same time, he is suggesting that fiction is a concept that actually comprehends language as such; it is a medium of mutation such that writing, as both real act and fictional play, becomes the political act par excellence. But it is also the case that he is not quite as good as his word. Through various textual stratagems, Burroughs both reintroduces sources of metaphysical comfort he officially rejects and betrays ideological commitments he cannot acknowledge.

In the first place, Burroughs's celebration of synchronicity and its abandonment of the logical certainty and rootedness afforded by the fraud of cause and effect is mitigated by his attraction to images of order, organization, and rigorous chains of command and by the dreamlike clarity such images offer. The account of the Big Picture is full of such language, the attractiveness of which is evident in Burroughs's lovingly detailed accounts of the sharp clarity of the relationship of leader to follower as the conspiracy unfolds. It is equally evident in Burroughs's description of the elaborate hierarchy of souls attempting to make their way over the road to the Western Lands: "Neph is letting his far-seer scouts get too far ahead. Some call them spirit guides or helpers. It is their function to reconnoiter an area so that one knows what to expect, and to alert headquarters with regard to dangers, conditions, enemies and allies to be contacted or avoided. They are bringing him instead general considerations on the area . . . valuable and interesting, but not precisely applicable in present time" (p. 156, ellipses his). The Leninist-style organization has a role to play, it seems, even after death, where tight precision and the reliable calibration of social relations are to be valued even more than before.

Furthermore, the tone of Burroughs's writing is often openly nostalgic, suggesting that the dream of a world beyond the Land of the Dead is fueled by a yearning for the prewar world of the nonadministered society: "The old-time bank robbers, the burglars who bought jewelry-store insurance inventories and knew exactly what they were looking for, the pickpockets trained from early childhood—they say the best ones come from Columbia—where are they now? The Murphy Men, the hype artists, the Big Store? Gone, all gone" (p. 32). This nostalgia for a world of "self-made men" who, in virtue of having rejected the standards and rewards of respectable society, enjoyed the freedom to invent and reinvent their lives as they lived them, suggests that Burroughs's dream of escape into space through accelerated evolution relies upon the equally nostalgic notion: the quintessentially American notion of freedom as the discovery of *empty space*, a place of innocence outside history where the fundamentally new and original may at last emerge. To the extent that this is the case, ideology plays a more powerful role in Burroughs's fantasies than he otherwise cares to admit.

Finally, Burroughs's attitude toward language and the practice of the writer betrays the view that literary invention is authorized by a plenitude existing outside language. I have already suggested that Burroughs often treats the practice of writing oneself out of Western civilization as a preparatory act for a genuine transfiguration of culture and society. To this extent he might be seen as maintaining, despite his sympathy for polytheism, the Christian doctrine of life on this earth as a preparation for the life to come. Burroughs, one senses, would really *like* to be out in space, mutating, and he resorts to writing as the only available supplement for this accomplishment. More fundamentally, Burroughs's antipathy to time (to the culture of the One God, the God who has all the time in the world and before whom, therefore, everything ultimately must perish through having been already anticipated) entails a disdain toward writing itself as an irreducibly temporal medium. Leaving time entails leaving the word; but Burroughs can only *articulate* the need to stop articulating. Hence the air of bad conscience about Burroughs's books: writing is still something that happens *in lieu of* action.

This problem is symbolized by Burroughs's obsessive use of ellipses, which represent not simple pauses but active attempts to stop temporalizing, ineluctably deferring speech so as to point to something beyond it—namely, the pure presence or simultaneity of space. Yet as the ellipses themselves demonstrate, the articulation of space occurs through the temporal unfolding of discourse, as evidenced also by Burroughs's retrieval of past forms (such as Egyptian gods) to think through a current crisis. This, in turn, is a difficulty that may be traced directly to Burroughs's central quarrel with Western civilization: the problem with the "Aristotelian construct," fundamentally, is its *inaccuracy*. "Reality" just *is* synchronous and unpredictable, whereas the declarative sentence moving ahead determinably through time makes it *appear* as if one event follows another in an orderly manner. Burroughs might attempt to write in ways that undermine the Aristotelian construct, but not without declaring *something*, and finally, as we have seen, not without becoming inveigled into this construct's seductive images of lucidity, order, control, and a plenitude beyond mere writing as fiction. *The Western Lands* ends when the old writer reaches "the end of words, the end of what can be done with words" (p. 258); one cannot *write* oneself out of history, after all. That Burroughs speaks of what can be *done* with words betrays a lingering instrumentalizing view of the task of the writer.

Burroughs's critique of metaphysics contains metaphysical motifs, then, and gives expression to metaphysical desires. His blurring of the distinction between serious and nonserious discourse is in tension with his resort to unmasking strategies, and it is the latter that ultimately predominate. The critique of the "either-or proposition" rests on the claim that it *conceals* a more fundamental order: the liberating truths of space and eternity as opposed to the oppressive lies of time and causality. Space, the absence of the constraints imposed by time and causality, is the realm where everything is possible and hence permitted. But Burroughs cannot think the leap from the time of language to that of space except in forms that indict themselves as temporalized narratives. He therefore resorts to nostalgia: for the truly marginalized outlaws, for premodern civilization, and even for the future. Yet the nostalgic yearning to escape time is, as Heidegger teaches, the most metaphysical desire there is. And to avoid finally coming to terms with the limits of postmodern subversion, as prac-

ticed by contemporary literary theory, Burroughs must finally resort to fantasies of enemies, monsters, and other power addicts who
serve as focuses of evil and whose ritual elimination might enable a
new becoming to take place. In this sense, Burroughs continues the
obsession with locating "responsibility for evil" which William E.
Connolly has identified as a central trope of Western moralists and
their critics; and he offers an ironic reversal of the "political demonology"—the creation of monsters who threaten our freedom—that
Michael Rogin has located at the center of American political culture.[31] In his conviction that the political is entirely absorbed by the
undoing of authority and that, once all public power has been thoroughly delegitimated, life, in its "pregnant" synchronicity, will take
care of itself, Burroughs, and the practices of postmodern subversion
he masterfully exemplifies, remain decisively *within* the tradition.

5

Only a god can save us.

—Heidegger

THIS IS NO AGE FOR EASY REVELATION.

— *The Changing Light at Sandover*

The Changing Light at Sandover is commonly described as a departure from James Merrill's previously exclusive concern with private,
subjective, or aesthetic experiences in favor of larger spiritual, metaphysical, and even political subjects. As David Lehman writes in his
introduction to a collection of essays on Merrill, "Without sacri-
ficing grace and nuance, . . . [Merrill's poetry from *Divine Come-
dies* onward] took on an unmistakably public character, a willingness to engage the world at its most problematic and least tractable.
'Can humanity save itself from destruction?' This . . . is the central question articulated by [*Sandover*]."[32] While acknowledging the
emergence of this public voice in Merrill's writing, however, most
commentators have chosen either to avoid confronting its political

content or to relegate its politics to a secondary, derivative status.[33] Helen Vendler, for example, finds in *The Book of Ephraim* (the first of the three long poems and one coda that comprise *Sandover*), and even (though to a lesser extent) in *Mirabell's Books of Number* (the second) primarily "the unpopular . . . [lessons] of middle age." She sees both poems' significance mainly in aesthetic and existential terms: a record of the changing meaning of love, companionship, and memory as one ages; of the need to totalize the fragmentary memories that crowd the mind as it contemplates death.[34] Judith Moffett, who reads *Ephraim* as the jewel in the crown of Merrill's poems of "progression through time from the passionate and transitory toward the domestic," acknowledges that the later episodes of the trilogy cannot be understood only on an exclusively personal register, but she seems at a loss in the face of the blatantly antidemocratic and illiberal implications of the poem's political vision, registering her unease and pointing out that it is shared by the poet.[35]

Given the manifest political content of the poem, such reactions are understandable, and commentators who do take Merrill's political imagination seriously are often quite harsh. David Bromwich sees the poem as a monumental projection of Merrill's "aesthetic bigotry," through whose lens human action is reduced to moves in a vast, impersonal game. Robert von Hallberg chastises him for his inability to empathize with the lower classes, arguing that Merrill's penchant for periphrasis, or "loaded silences," serves as a badge of class identity and superiority, "situat[ing] his writing in relation to patterns of usage which confirm social relations," in particular, his "skeptical view of that American idée fixe, the democratic or classless society." [36] Merrill's neoaristocratic sensibility, his "power to ignore," as Hallberg puts it, is figured in high-camp style as a cultivated distance from colloquial usage and a self-appointed right to judge, to discern, and to establish standards of taste which may be intuitively grasped by one's peers but not publicly, explicitly articulated. This tendency would seem to reach almost fanatical proportions in the cosmology of *Sandover*, in which earthly paradise is figured as a hierarchical society, underwritten by the gods themselves, made up of rare and perfected "soul densities" devoted to great accomplishments in art and culture. In such readings, either Merrill is unpolitical or his political sensibility is embarrassing.

Moreover, his revelations about reincarnation, or about severe cosmic powers dedicated to "thinning" and perfecting the human race, are domesticated as frankly metaphorical: the "fiction of reincarnation" becomes a figure for the shifting, irregular character of quotidian life; the figures of political order are the fantasies of an elitist, or marginalized, upper-class aesthete.[37] In any case, neither their political nor their theoretical meaning is to be taken seriously; that is, they are not to impede an appreciation of the aesthetic or stylistic achievements of the poem. In these interpretations, Merrill remains, even as his work takes on undeniably political themes, America's most insistently apolitical poet, dedicated, if anything, to privatizing the public rather than the reverse (fabricating an exquisitely crafted "private" self for public consumption, as in the Romantic and high-modernist traditions). The disdain for liberal democracy expressed in *Sandover* (and elsewhere) can thus be seen as inessential, an extension of an archetypal aesthetic anti-Americanism that begins as a disgust for the vulgarity of popular culture and ends in reaction against the democratic state that makes the dominance of such a culture possible.

In this view, American liberal democracy and popular culture are not so much good or bad as, ideally, irrelevant, and spiritual survival in such a society depends on acquiring the power to ignore them. In Merrill's poetry, as Charles Berger puts it, "One gets the sense . . . that America itself is peripheral. It is all too easy to forget that the events of *Mirabell* transpire during the Bicentennial summer of 1976."[38] For Berger, *Mirabell* is nonetheless aptly characterized as "conservative" in that it embodies a "conserving act of retrieval" — the retrieval and conservation, that is, of spiritual experiences that cannot be accommodated within a modern, essentially materialistic ontological framework. Such conservation, of course, must not be confused with political conservatism. Rather, Merrill's "retrieval" is best understood as a Heideggerian *violent* (*gewaltsam*) appropriation of discursive materials, a "saving" that inevitably transforms, often beyond recognition, what it preserves. It is also for this reason, perhaps, and not only because of his aesthetic mistrust of politics or American popular culture, that Merrill appears to Berger as "the least explicitly 'American' of our major contemporary poets." Indeed, the personalities with whom Merrill converses (with the help of his collaborator at the Ouija board, David Jackson), despite his (and their own) oft-expressed elitism, have no such aversions:

> WE MY BOY DRAW FROM 2
> SORTS OF READER: ONE ON HIS KNEES TO ART
> THE OTHER FACEDOWN OVER A COMIC BOOK.
> OUR STYLISH HIJINKS WONT AMUSE THE LATTER
> & THE FORMER WILL DISCOUNT OUR URGENT MATTER[39]

(Transcripts from sessions at the Ouija board appear in the poem in uppercase letters; Merrill's commentary and narration appear in lowercase.)

The search for a text drawing upon these "2 SORTS OF READER" might be thought of as the exemplary American cultural trope: as Stanley Cavell argues, what defines American culture is not a shared canon or a common code but a "lack of *assured* commonality." Given this "ability to move between high and low, caring about each also from the vantage of the other," Merrill's unwillingness to indulge in explicitly "American" poetry may only reflect a typically American lack of assurance about how to do so, a reluctance to acknowledge that any cultural emblem can embody an essence or totality of American culture.[40] It is odd that so many of Merrill's American readers have been willing to make good the spirits' prediction regarding how the poem will be received, keeping the "URGENT MATTER" at arm's length by assigning to it a primarily metaphorical or psychological status.

Merrill, of course, has often enough confirmed his distance from public life. If we look closely at those instances in which he intimates his distaste for it, however, we find that his suspicion of politics cannot be subsumed under such polar oppositions as the worldly and the poetic, the sublime and the mundane. Consider, for example, "18 West 11th Street," a gloss on a current event that Merrill, in a departure from principle, graces with an explanatory note.[41] The poem, he tell us, concerns "a house in Manhattan, our home until I was five, carelessly exploded by the 'Weathermen'—young, bomb-making activists—in 1970" (p. 253). For Merrill, the house had enjoyed iconic status, as a monument to his attempt to piece together in poetry the fragments of his "broken home"; after the assault by antiwar activists, it is irretrievably caught up in public discourses and images. The act of "saving" or "conserving," always problematic for Merrill, becomes problematic in a newly disturbing way.

The destruction of his childhood home crudely literalizes and, as it were, publicly disseminates Merrill's carefully constructed metaphor; his "broken home" is no longer his private property. An initial reading of the poem suggests a stark contrast between the intrusions of a vulgar outside world and the poet's attempt to redeem the sources of his private pain. Yet Merrill does much more than simply register this sense of violation; he suggests that the line between the public and private, as between the literal and figural, is permeable and unreliable:

> A mastermind
> Kept track above the mantel. The cold caught,
> One birthday in its shallows, racked
> The weak frame, glazed with sleet
> Overstuffed aunt and walnut uncle. Book
> You could not read. Some utterly
>
> Longed-for present meeting other eyes'
> Blue arsenal of homemade elegies,
> Duds every one. The deed
>
> Diffused. Your breakfast *Mirror* put
> Late to bed, a fever
> Flashing through the veins of linotype:
>
> NIX ON PEACE BID   PROPHET STONED
> FIVE FEARED DEAD IN BOMBED DWELLING
>   —Bulletin-pocked columns, molten font

"18 West 11th Street" turns on a series of oppositions contrasting the uncanniness of personal experience and the difficulties confronting the individual who attempts to craft a language to illuminate it, with the jagged prose in which the activists' blunderings are portrayed, "word by numbskull word," in the newspapers. It goes on to offer a series of images of shock, disruption, and dislocation at the way in which this family home, the encoding of which had become Merrill's personal project, has been thrown into another history, a greater disorder:

> The night she left ("One day you'll understand")
> You stood under the fruitless tree. The streetlight
> Cast false green fires about, a tragic
>
> Carpet of shadows of blossoms, shadows of leaves.
> . . . .
> The ruin. The young linden opposite
> Shocked leafless. Item: the March dawn.
>
> Shards of a blackened witness still in place.
> The charred ice-sculpture garden
> Beams fell upon. The cold blue searching beams.

Merrill speaks of the disorder of the attempt to restore order by extinguishing the fire: "black / Fumes massing once more . . . Sea serpent / Hoses recoil, the siren drowns in choking / Wind," the "Drunken backdrop of debris, airquake, / Flame in bloom." All this is enough to call into question the viability of Merrill's attempt of "forty-odd years" to deal with the "Original vacancy" of his broken home. But a sense of futility and anger yields to a certain kinship with the perpetrators. "Dear premises," he writes, blurring his efforts with theirs, "Vainly exploded, vainly dwelt upon." If the bomb makers were living according to an ideological fiction, punishing the world for failing to conform to their conviction of what it ought to have been, so, too, Merrill's poetic struggle, his attempt to undermine the premises that made possible his mourning for an illusory plenitude of the unbroken home, depended on the fiction of a carefully guarded private self protected from outside, especially public, influences. Merrill's ability to read the Weather Underground's appropriation of his poetic materials confirms the slipperiness of public and private meanings.

In this sense, "18 West 11th Street" is something of a preamble to

Sandover: it allegorizes the moment at which, and the way in which, the poet addresses the political public sphere, showing that even poetic mastery cannot preserve the meanings Merrill painstakingly articulates; and it suggests that both private and public are threatened by the lack of a language capable of negotiating the relationship between them, by the "Bulletin-pocked columns" and "molten font" that determine the limits of what can be publicly expressed, transmitted, and preserved. But whereas some critics could interpret "18 West 11th Street" in the conventionally metaphysical terms of a timeless human condition, a hopeless longing for the return of that which never was, the lessons learned in *Sandover*, despite their occult source, refer not to eternal truths but to the particular historical moment we face in the late twentieth century. Where earlier mediums used the Ouija board to escape their time-bound world for one of enduring (if evanescent) presence, Merrill's adventure moves in the opposite direction: enriching his cultivation of personal authenticity with a vivid historical appreciation of the distinctiveness of *our* moment, its crises and opportunities.

If Merrill's work cannot be dismissed as simply Hermetic and elitist, then, the suggestion that he dismisses the political is equally unhelpful. Instead, his work calls both popular culture generally, and the political public sphere more specifically, into question and, I suggest, subjects them to a penetrating critique that contributes to the most central political discussions of modernity. Rather than domesticating his politics by dismissing it as metaphorical, or being embarrassed by it because it questions certain premises of liberal democracy, we should place Merrill's political theory in relation to the problematic it embraces. That problematic, I suggest, is the crisis in liberal democracy owing to the latter's complicity with a nihilistic technological imperative, as diagnosed by Nietzsche, Heidegger, and Arendt. *Sandover*'s contribution to this problematic is to invent and enact terms and discursive strategies to detach strong political, moral, ethical, and aesthetic judgments from the equally nihilistic imperative of truth as correctness, representation, fidelity to a natural order, and the search for foundations generally and thus to bring to the foreground the question of the narrative *practice* of political theory from a postphilosophical perspective.[42]

6

Communication with the dead—that has to be learned.
                                                —Hannah Arendt

To put writing in the service of escape from dominant codes of temporality and causality, of natural laws now seen as the ultimate constraint on action and imagination, is a powerful theme of Cold War
American fiction, as we saw in the discussion of Burroughs. Yet no
amount of invention or reinterpretation of narrative convention can
alter the fact that writing is a temporally determined activity, and
such reinterpretation will necessarily be marked by what it intends
to erase, namely—in Burroughs's case—the temporality, the irreducible materiality, of writing itself. Burroughs's resentment against
time fuels his nostalgia for better, more interesting times; and this
nostalgia fuels his desire for a violent purge of the "Land of the
Dead," as he characterizes contemporary Western civilization. Merrill's not entirely unrelated attempt to link the act of writing to the
discovery of new images of order and new forms of judgment avoids
this danger by beginning with a commitment to no specific project
or ideology but with sheer *écriture*, defined, however, in the most
common, elementary, and material terms:

> Silence. Then a grave, deliberate
> Glissando of the cup to rainbow's end:
> ABCDEFGHIJKLMNOPQRSTUVWXYZ

DJ.   What's all this?
JM.   Looks like the alphabet.
Gabr.   THE NEW MATERIALS, YOUNG POET, FOR A NEW FAITH:
      ITS ARCHITECTURE, THE FLAT WHITE PRINTED PAGE
      TO WHICH WILL COME WISER WORSHIPPERS IN TIME[43]

(In *Sandover*, "DJ" refers to David Jackson and "JM" to James Merrill.) In this passage from the third part of *Sandover, Scripts for the
Pageant*, the Angel Gabriel, having presided over Gautama Buddha
and Jesus as they tell of the exhaustion of religion and its failure to
check the danger humankind poses not only to itself but to the entire

cosmos, suggests what the "powers" with whom JM and DJ converse have in mind as the next strategy for containing the destructive impulses that human nature seems to conduct. Gabriel is one of many personalities contacted through the Ouija board, which consists of nothing more than a smooth surface displaying the elements of writing: the letters of the alphabet, the ten numbers, and a "Yes" and "No." The board is operated by placing one's fingers on an inverted cup, whose movements are then followed and indicated letters transcribed.

This game, which Merrill and Jackson began to play during the 1950s, enacts in the most literal sense the meditation on textuality begun by Jacques Derrida in the 1960s: the return, from the realm of pure philosophical "ideas" or literary "imagination," to the materiality and productivity of writing, its motions, currents, and elements. In defining what might count as a form of writing that succeeded in remaining at a distance from (though admittedly parasitic upon) the binary oppositions of metaphysical thought (among which alphabetic writing itself, in opposition to both iconic writing and speech, is included), Derrida insists on the literally *marginal* status of such a writing. A criticism of metaphysics must take the form of a "fourth text," distinguishable from introductions, prefaces, or conclusions that serve to anticipate or recapitulate "the Book" that is never completed; it must, that is, keep to the form of marginal comments on *all* such texts.[44] Although the fourth text would not be "beyond" the other three in the sense of grounding itself in some independent source of authority or meaning, it would undermine them by, in Derrida's words, "fictionalizing" them, or more fully, it would "imprint upon" (*imprimer*) these texts "a movement of fiction." Annotating the book, then, is a way of *laying hands* on the oppositions of metaphysics, of getting one's fingers on them, just as JM and DJ finger the constituents of writing through the Ouija board and await the results of the cup's movements.

This fingering, handling, and motion is, we might say, the essence of the fictional itself, even etymologically, as the fashioning, forming, or molding of given raw materials. Merrill and Jackson fictionalize the alphabet and follow the lessons thus revealed. Gabriel indicates an essential lesson with his reference to the alphabet as the next locus of worship and devotion: Such "marginal" Derridean practices are the surest route to the essence of Being itself. The "sources" of power and value are the inventive capacities of writing divorced from any notion of an extralinguistic reference or resource—including, above all, the sovereign imagination of the poet and the sovereign reason of the scientist.

The instrument of divine revelation, the Ouija board, is democratic, even American, in the extreme; approaching the Other World requires no rigorous training beyond literacy, and little spiritual discipline: JM and DJ worry when their informants ask them to stop drinking and smoking for a time. Although the medium seems democratic, however, the order this work of fiction reveals to them is emphatically not: the Other World is unambiguously hierarchical. The immediate significance of the vision of a hierarchical order linking This World with the Other is not, however, political, but existential, as the self is revealed to be not autonomous or private, but relational. The first glimpse of this relational self takes the form of the revelation, given by Ephraim, a Greek slave of the first century C.E., that any given, current, subjective identity is but one term in a complex system of events and identities constituting the universe or Being as a whole:

> on Earth
> We're each the REPRESENTATIVE of a PATRON
> —Are there that many patrons? YES O YES
> These secular guardian angels fume and fuss
> For what must seem eternity over us.
>
> (P. 9)

Far from private egos working out the terms of their existence according to their individual inclinations, our subjectivities are established on the basis of a "POWERFUL MEMORY OR AFFINITY" with others, including the dead (p. 24). As the poem unfolds and more voices of the dead are heard, it transpires that Plato, Wallace Stevens, and Merrill, as well as Rimbaud and T. S. Eliot, for example, are linked in a powerful series of representation, lineage, and patronage. The fates of the patrons are linked to those of the representatives: the former move up the "NINE STAGES" of heaven to the extent that their representatives are able to gain a foothold on the lowest stage—a scheme that foreshadows more dramatic accounts of natural-supernatural connections later in the poem. As a patron advances, he achieves "a degree of PEACE FROM REPRESENTATION," which Merrill characterizes as "a motto for . . . Autocracy," anticipating the chilling vision of order that is to come (p. 10).

The political import of Merrill's understanding of how the self is constituted through a relational matrix of other voices, subjects, and lives, and his figuring of this as reincarnation or immortality, becomes clearer if we situate *Sandover* in terms of Hannah Arendt's discussion of how the ancient Greek distinction between immortal gods and mortal humans mirrored a distinction among human beings themselves. For the ancients, on Arendt's reading, the closest that humankind could come to immortality was by leaving a trace that would be remembered and discussed. Only the best would want or achieve this kind of immortality, the rest being content with whatever fleeting pleasures nature offers them, appearing and disappearing without a trace and without remembrance. Distinguishing between the eternal (that which persists unchanged, timeless, such as a god or a natural law that governs the universe) and the immortal (that which lives on and which therefore has a history that is to some extent open), Arendt offers the act of writing as the most accessible symbol of this desire for human immortality: the writer, by attempting to leave traces of his or her thought and self, signals a commitment to the immortal as opposed to the eternal. For Arendt, "immortality" is purchased at the price of contingency, openness, and unpredictability; for the fate of one's written traces—how they will be received, judged, interpreted, and used—is never fully under one's intentional control. Or, to put it still another way, we might say that the only immortal self is a public self necessarily exposed to the hazards and unpredictability of the public sphere—for traces can "live on" only to the extent that they are available to be appropriated. In a sense, then, the public sphere is coextensive with that of Derridean *écriture*. As Arendt puts it, "If . . . we define the political in the sense of the *polis*, its end or *raison d'etre* would be to establish and keep in existence a space where freedom as virtuosity can appear. This is the realm where freedom is a worldly reality, tangible in words that can be heard, in deeds which can be seen, and in events which can be talked about, remembered, and turned into stories. . . . Whatever occurs in this space is political by definition."[45]

As this passage suggests, Arendt insists on the theatrical or performative quality of the discursive events that take place in the public sphere, the essential noninstrumentality of political action. In order for virtuosity to appear and persist, it must become tangible and public, and all that is tangible and public remains open to the contingencies of further action, interpretation, and appropriation. For Arendt, then, the only durable identity human beings can possess is dependent on the preservation and transmission of words and deeds. The irony is that this identity, because public, is never identical with our "private" self, is not under our personal control, and cannot be reduced to an individual project, because the significance of what is said and done is determined by others as well as ourselves, and by contexts and circumstances we are wholly unable to anticipate. This necessary openness to the contingency of the public world is a constant theme of *Sandover*, which, as it were, virtually writes the political (in Arendt's sense) into the nature of things. In *Sandover* it takes the form of the insistence that the Other World is *not* one of eternal, unchanging laws guided by an accessible, intelligible, centered god but rather an *immortal* world of contrasting and conflicting forces whose history is open and the outcome of whose struggles remains always undecided. The immortality revealed in *Sandover*, then, is precisely *not* the survival after bodily death of an individuated ego but the deconstruction of the ego and its dispersal among the mix of voices, deeds, and memories from which a public self is generated.[46]

To be sure, Ephraim's earliest revelations suggest an eternal sphere reached by those patrons who achieve Stage Nine in the cosmic hierarchy, at which point their senses have returned and they no longer must watch over their earthly representatives, but his account is subsequently undermined by more authoritative voices in *Mirabell* and *Scripts*, where we learn that the hierarchy described in *Ephraim* is only a very small component of a much more complex state of affairs. Something of this complexity begins to come through in *Mirabell*, when JM and DJ are suddenly confronted with grave and urgent voices, the "dark angels" or fallen, negative powers (not human souls and hence not part of Ephraim's system of representation and patronage). From a civilization "B4 MANKIND," whose existence had been hinted at in *Ephraim* but who were not heard from there directly, they are now feverishly at work attempting to "clone" a new human nature and thereby prevent the impending collapse of civilization. This task they attempt with the help of powers and practices far beyond what the beings in Ephraim's "BUREAUCRACY OF SOULS" are aware of.

These dark angels insist that JM use his poetic skills to communicate a message of the utmost importance:

> UNHEEDFUL ONE   3 OF YOUR YEARES MORE WE WANT   WE MUST HAVE
> POEMS OF SCIENCE   THE WEORK FINISHT IS BUT A PROLOGUE
> ABSOLUTES ARE NOW NEEDED   YOU MUST MAKE GOD OF SCIENCE
> TELL OF POWER   MANS IGNORANCE FEARES THE POWER WE ARE
> THAT FEAR STOPS PARADISE

(P. 113)

The urgency conveyed by the voices is explained by the fact that humanity's problems are no longer its own; the development of modern Western civilization threatens the entire cosmos. Again, this much had already transpired in *Ephraim*:

> NO SOULS CAME FROM HIROSHIMA U KNOW
> EARTH WORE A STRANGE NEW ZONE OF ENERGY
> Caused by? SMASHED ATOMS OF THE DEAD MY DEARS

(P. 55)

Humanity's increasing command over atomic power threatens not only the planet's current inhabitants, then, but the entire cosmic order, which relies on an influx of new souls in order to fuel the mechanism of promotion through the nine stages of heaven:

> Wait—he couldn't be pretending YES
> That when the flood ebbed, or the fire burned low,
> Heaven, the world no longer at its feet,
> Itself would up and vanish? EVEN SO

(P. 56)

The gravity of this threat becomes evident when we reflect that "Heaven" has been rendered in *Sandover* not as an eternal sphere of enduring, self-identical subjects but as the continually evolving, continually reappropriated and reappropriating voices, articulations, and energies of *all* who have lived and left traces of their experiences and actions. What is threatened with destruction is not so much heaven, as conventionally understood, but the world as human action. The threat at issue here is not only that of nuclear holocaust but the whole array of processes, forms of life, and assumptions associated with modernity, including the technological drive to master nature, mass "democracy," overpopulation and the depletion of resources, and pollution. Much of the second and third parts of *Sandover* are in fact taken up with conflicting and complementary versions and elaborations of the origins and meaning of Western modernity.

The picture that emerges from *Mirabell* is one of successive attempts, by "God Biology" (who is also, we learn, "HISTORY" and perhaps the "EARTH ITSELF"), to construct a viable civilization. Mirabell himself is (among other things) the trace of one such failed attempt, in which artificially evolved, intelligent beings outgrew their masters (whom they enslaved) and created a civilization in the sky which then perished owing to its members' distraction and carelessness—and, it is hinted, their access to nuclear energy. God Biology's next attempt was humanity, which, however, was problematic owing to the very qualities—curiosity, a zeal to survive, resistance to the given world and an insistence upon reinventing it anew—that make humans fascinating. God Biology does not create humanity ex nihilo but fictionally, through the modification and perfection of elements already present. The "BASIC SOUL" fabricated in the "Research Lab" by the dark angels, and introduced into an ape child, causes the species to mutate rapidly:

A SERVICEABLE SOUL.   IT GUARDED MAN & ESTABLISHD

HIM AS A SPECIES APART   PROUD   UNABLE TO REVERT

. . . .

THEY SUBJECTED THEIR FRIGHTEND

FOREBEARS & CHANGED WITH EACH GENERATION, LEAVING BEHIND
THE SOULLESS HORDES.

(P. 236)

Originally nomadic and sparse, each individual human could be spared one high-quality soul, a gift from God Biology to ensure survival under difficult conditions. But when the human species abandoned nomadism and began to create cities, the resulting population explosion meant that there were fewer and fewer souls to go around, leading to a degradation of the species as a whole. God Biology attempted various expedients, such as religion, the state, and technology, to control, temper, or placate humanity's drive to mastery and independence. The emergence of rulers, for example, was God Biology's response to urbanization and the subsequent degradation of subjectivity:

PRIOR TO
AKHNATON HAD BEEN ONLY CHANCE   FRESHNESS & WIT   WE DEALT
IN STRONG SOUL INTENSITIES   BUT AS THESE GREW URBANIZED
& BASIC SURVIVAL INTELLIGENCE BEGAN TURNING
INTO ACQUISITIONAL CHANNELS, TOOLS INTO WEAPONS,
A NEED AROSE FOR CLONING THE RULERS. WE REINFORCED
AS WITH THUNDER & LIGHTNING THE PROCESS WHEREBY A MERE
MAN BECAME GOD   SO AROSE ASSYRIA AND EGYPT

(P. 179)

After the failure of religion and politics, humanity was given mastery over the machine to remedy the effects of overpopulation: "MAN ... GETS CLEVERER WITH HIS TOOLS, / CONTRIVING NEARLY PERFECT SUBSTITUTES FOR GOD'S NATURAL / POWERS" (p. 464). But "NEW DISCOVERIES CREATE NEW PROBLEMS" (p. 182):

THRU TYPES
LIKE DICKENS & ZOLA THE DREAD MACHINE BECAME MAN'S FRIEND.
TODAY HOWEVER, FACED WITH NUCLEAR DISASTER, HOW
IS MAN NOT TO DESPAIR? YR 6 YEARS AGO CAME
WEEPING TO US 'THEY IN ANGUISH'

(P. 183)

All these attempts—religion, the state, technology—have backfired, and the population continues to increase to the point where animal soul "densities" are currently being used for most humans:

DAILY NEED 5

MILLION SOULS (DENSITY 1:20,000) & HAVE NOT
HALF THAT NUMBER   QUALITY FAILS   EVEN WITH PLAGUE & WAR
TO DEFUSE POP EXPLO, EVEN WITH THOSE SUICIDES WE
MORE AND MORE APPLAUD (O YES THEY ARE A GREAT BOON TO US
WHEN OF RETURNING LAB SOULS WHOSE INTENSEST WORK IS DONE)
WE HAVE IN THE PAST HALF CENTURY HAD TO RESORT TO
SOULS OF DOMESTIC ANIMALS   MOST RECENTLY THE RAT.
BY 2050 THESE TOO WILL BE EXHAUSTED   & THEN?
WILDER STRAINS   MOUNTAIN CATS & FOREST MONKEYS

(Pp. 145–46)

The resulting vision, of course, is that of a strictly divided world in which most humans rise very little above an animal level, while a few are cloned with the better densities (a select group that includes the "FIVE IMMORTALS," Akhnaton, Homer, Montezuma, Nefertiti, and Plato, whose souls recycle endlessly, as well as others whose soul densities are doled out bit by bit, and still others whose souls have been perfected at Stage Nine). Those few are responsible for the "V WORK" that makes civilization possible by creating culture worth preserving. "THE MASSES WE NEED / NEVER CONSIDER"; for "THEY REMAIN IN AN ANIMAL STATE" (p. 188). The role of modern politics is brutally simple: to thin humanity's ranks through war and famine and thus prepare the way for a new order of more resilient souls:

MILK TO CREAM TO BUTTER   WE ONLY WISH TO PURIFY
CERTAIN RANCID ELEMENTS FROM THIS ELITE BUTTER WORLD.
THE HITLERS THE PERONS & FRANCOS   THE STALINS & THE
LITTLE BROTHER-LIKE AUTHORITIES ARE NEEDED   EVEN
ALAS INEVITABLE

(P. 188)

The distinction between the elite soul densities who perform "V Work" and the animal souls who merely live and die without a trace is also rendered as the distinction between cultural and biologic evolution, or between individuals concerned only with reproduction and domesticity as opposed to those whose lives center around cultural achievement. Although this seems stark (many readers of *Sandover* have been frankly offended by it), the distinction plays in Merrill's poem essentially the same role as the one Arendt assigns to her distinction between action and labor, namely, action (political action) that enables the construction of a durable (if thereby contingent) identity, and action (social action) that has no end beyond that of sheer reproduction. For Mirabell, the massed animal souls are little more evolved than our simian ancestors:

> WHEN BY CANDLELIGHT YOU MEET & TALK DO U
> EVER THINK OF THE TWO BASIC APECHILDREN WHO IN PRE
> CARNIVOROUS PRE IN FACT FIRE DAYS MET FOR ONLY
> ONE REASON WHICH THEN, SAD TO SAY, OFTEN RAN DOWN A LEG?
> (P. 241)

JM and DJ speculate that their receptivity to the voices stems from the childlessness of their homosexual marriage: "Are we more usable than Yeats or Hugo, / Doters on women, who then went ahead / To doctor everything their voices said?" (p. 154). Their imposed alienation from the sphere of domestic reproduction prevents them from convincing themselves that biologic traces will suffice, placing them squarely in the field of *action* and therefore making them fully aware of the necessity of the preservation of the public sphere: "THE CHILDLESSNESS WE SHARE . . . TURNS US / OUTWARD TO THE LESSONS & THE MYSTERIES," as it did "AKHN & NEF," who "AFTER PRODUCING 5 STILLBORN MONSTERS / . . . SAW THEIR LOVE DOOMD TO GIVE BIRTH TO IDEAS ALONE" (pp. 216, 225). Mirabell confirms this rigid distinction between the production of bodies and the work of culture:

> LOVE OF ONE MAN FOR ANOTHER OR LOVE BETWEEN WOMEN
> IS A NEW DEVELOPMENT OF THE PAST 4000 YEARS
> ENCOURAGING SUCH MIND VALUES AS PRODUCE THE BLOSSOMS
> OF POETRY & MUSIC, THOSE 2 PRINCIPAL LIGHTS OF
> GOD BIOLOGY. LESSER ARTS NEEDED NO EXEGETES:
> ARCHITECTURE SCULPTURE THE MOSAICS & PAINTINGS THAT

FLOWERD IN GREECE & PERSIA CELEBRATED THE BODY.
POETRY   MUSIC   SONG INDWELL & CELEBRATE THE MIND . . .
. . . .
NOW MIND IN ITS PURE FORM IS A NONSEXUAL PASSION
OR A UNISEXUAL ONE PRODUCING ONLY LIGHT.
FEW PAINTERS OR SCULPTORS CAN ENTER THIS LIFE OF THE MIND.
THEY (LIKE ALL SO-CALLD NORMAL LOVERS) MUST PRODUCE AT LAST
BODIES   THEY DO NOT EXIST FOR ANY OTHER PURPOSE

(P. 156)

Actions observed and discussed, then, traces left in public—and at the limit, traces invented and preserved *only* through the necessarily public, intersubjective medium of language, as opposed even to the more "material" enterprises of painting and sculpture—and not sheer reproduction, are what matter:

SO WHAT IS MOST REWARDING OF MAN'S V WORK? HIS CULTURE
& THIS? HIS ENTIRE LIFE-FABRIC WOVEN OF LANGUAGE.
. . . .
                THINK AGAIN OF THAT LEAP FROM
THE HALTING PATH TO WATER OVER FALLEN ROPY VINES
TO THE GREAT JETFLIGHTS ABOVE YR LANDSCAPED MINDS

(P. 241)

Although provocative, this elitism enables Merrill to avoid confusions that might otherwise be engendered by *Sandover*'s deep politicization of the cosmos, and again, a comparison with Arendt is illuminating. Arendt could distinguish between thinking, which is private, and writing, which is irreducibly public because it involves a commitment to leaving a trace, a distinction that authorizes a rigorous separation of the public and private spheres. Merrill's voices, however, insist that thinking is itself possible only owing to the accessibility of traces—an insight that moves him away from Arendt and toward Derrida but also threatens to collapse Merrill's kinds of judgments and distinctions into a generalized *écriture* that exceeds or escapes all such devices. What is at stake in *Sandover* is not a metaphysical distinction between thinking and writing but a practical distinction between the cultivation of identities that can be preserved, transmitted, developed, and transfigured (the realm of the immortal, or heaven) and the reproduction of fixed identities that cannot be recovered after their deaths.

7

The elitism of *Sandover*'s voices bears comparison with Nietzsche's reassertion of rank and severity in the context of a critique of democracy. Democracy, for Nietzsche, is the modern political expression of the "slave morality" diagnosed and criticized in *On the Genealogy of Morals:* an insistence on equality grounded in the idea of the essential evil and depravity of power, an evaluation that, carried to extremes, results ultimately in the disparagement of life itself in favor of an other-worldly realm of purity. Of the many consequences Nietzsche draws from this interpretation of the demand for equality, one is especially relevant for an understanding of the political theory of *Sandover:* slave morality is *nihilistic* because it affirms that which cannot be, namely, the fiction of an eternal world of timeless and enduring truths; and it engenders a subjectivity addicted to such fictions, unable to act without them. Liberal democracy, in this sense, is not the empowerment of the people but the generalization of powerlessness; or rather, democracy is the ideology that renders meaningful, and hence tolerable, a society of organized powerlessness. Those who suffer from powerlessness in this sense—that is, from the inability to posit values, an inability to fabricate narratives that would give sense, direction, and coherency to their lives—are therefore exploitable by figures who offer interpretations that render such a condition meaningful. This, according to Nietzsche, is the function of the "ascetic ideal," according to which powerlessness is a privilege: "The meaninglessness of suffering, *not* suffering itself, was the curse . . . *and the ascetic ideal offered man meaning!* . . . In it, suffering was *interpreted*, the tremendous void seemed to have been filled" (bk. 3, sec. 28). The meaning, of course, is slave morality: that the weak who suffer from powerlessness and an inability to do anything in the world, the "ordinary people," are in fact privileged because they, having avoided the corruptions of worldly power, will inherit the kingdom of heaven; their suffering in this world is expiation for earlier sins and pushes them ever closer to heaven. Platonic dialectic, Christian virtue, scientific objectivity, and democratic equality are so many versions of the ascetic idea that salvation depends on the renunciation of power. Similarly, Mirabell criticizes the public discourses of modern democracy for the way in which they institutionalize powerlessness and mediocrity by fabricating for them a seductive and satisfying meaning:

POLITICIANS HAVE LED MAN DOWN A ROAD WHERE HE BELIEVES
ALL IS FOR ALL   THIS IS THE FOOL'S PARADISE   ALL WILL BE
FOR ALL ONLY WHEN ALL IS UNDERSTOOD

(P. 247)

Democratic ideology allows humanity to imagine that its most banal pursuits somehow fulfill a grand design with profound significance: "IMAGINING ONLY THAT THE GAP MUST BE / FILLD, HE RESPONDS TO NATURE'S . . . SIGNAL: REPRODUCE!" (p. 248).

For Nietzsche, "Europe's democratic movement" yields a nihilistic culture, a pastiche of forms, masks, costumes, and identities that do not cohere into a meaningful identity or cultural project: "Modernity" . . . the abundance of disparate impressions greater than ever . . . the impressions erase each other; one instinctively resists taking in anything, taking anything deeply."[47] The clashing "impressions" that Nietzsche speaks of here derive from the immense variety of cultural systems that the nineteenth century's obsession with exotic cultures (and with Europe's exotic origins) makes available to the modern historical subject, for whom the present is therefore relative and derivative. In the face of a Christian, equalizing culture that parades "empowerment" to disguise the institutionalization of mediocrity, Nietzsche, with Merrill's informants, "teach[es] that there are higher and lower men," or, in the dark angels' words, that "ABSOLUTES ARE NOW NEEDED."[48] But such teachings must be seen in the context of Nietzsche's "perspectivism," or the view that all such judgments are embedded in particular forms of life or practices and that the Western attempt to construct a metalanguage with which to judge Being as such has disastrous consequences. The aristocratic stress on rank and distinction, accordingly, is not "truer" than Christian equality but rather, more useful in addressing certain limitations of the latter.

More fundamental is the strategy of the perspectivist as opposed to the thinker of ascetic ideals, the theorist: whereas the latter is skilled in making rapid inferences, correct deductions, and rigorous distinctions, the perspectivist is adept at coming to terms with the nuances of competing outlooks and sensibilities, at shifting from one perspective to another, and at fabricating new perspectives on the basis of the cultural materials available to the modern subject. In this way, the perspectivist combats the lure of a nihilism that would will the void to cope with modernity's chaos and confusion. Merrill's informants agree: the "EVIL" that is growing in modernity is "THE VOID   CALL IT IN MAN   A WILL TO NOTHINGNESS" (p. 120). They also affirm a perspectivist rather than a Platonic approach to the "V work" that "holds back" these negative forces. Their maxim "ALL WILL BE USED . . . NOTHING IS EVER EVER LOST" (pp. 116–17) is confirmed by the powers' and shades' tales of tempering the human drive for mastery with qualities of the plant and mineral worlds and by the revelations as a whole, which draw upon and employ all cultural sources irrespective of their origins: Near and Far Eastern mythology, aristocratic politics, Western science (and science fiction), twentieth-century aesthetics, high culture, and popular imagery. God Biology, Michael and Gabriel, and the dark angels are nothing if not pragmatic.

Modernity's will to nothingness, in Heidegger's interpretation of Nietzsche's doctrine, is the completion of metaphysics. To say, as Nietzsche does, that man would rather will the void than be void of will is to establish, in Heidegger's phrase, "the will to will"—sheer, empty instrumentality—as the final aim and meaning of Being. Far from ensuring human freedom, however, the way in which humanity achieves autonomy—constituting all that makes up its world as *means* to ends *willed* by humans—results in a world that, owing to its elimination of contingency, traps the human in a routinized and prefabricated technological identity. As Aristotle's definition of the slave as a tool suggests, the transformation of humanity into an instrument through the human attempt to achieve dominance and independence by instrumentalizing the world means the triumph of slave morality. In Nietzsche's words, modernity constitutes the individual as a "handy, multi-purpose" subject of "mechanical activity," where action has meaning "only from the point of view of the whole, for the sake of the whole."[49]

Yet "the point of view of the whole" possesses at best an ironic meaning, given that "the thousand-fold atrophy of all individuals [into mere functions]" implies that in modernity, the "what-for? and for-whom? are lacking" (sec. 69). Far from producing smooth efficiency, the transfiguration of human culture into raw information, functions, and resources generates anarchy: "The past of every form and way of life, of cultures that formerly lay right next to each other or on top of the other, now flows into us 'modern souls'; thanks to this mixture, our instincts now run back everywhere; we ourselves are a kind of chaos."[50] Merrill's informants too stress the chaotic consequences of humanity's identification of freedom and growth with independence and domination, the will to control and master nature or, as they phrase it, his "RESISTANCE" to Being and insistence upon controlling it for his own endlessly expanding needs (p. 408), "PLAY[ING] SO FREELY WITH OUR ATOMS," "CARELESSLY PLUNG[ING] INTO THE WATCHWORKS OF OUR GENETIC CELL," ending in nuclear pollution from which "NOTHING OF USE SURVIVES" (p. 455). Instead, they imagine a world where humanity negotiates with, listens to, and speaks with the forces and elements of nature. Like the Nietzsche of *Beyond Good and Evil* and *The Gay Science,* and like Heidegger after the *Kehre*, they see the growth of chaos as linked to the technological successes of the will to truth and mastery, and against chaos they prescribe not more control but a "thinning" of the will to control. The postscientific civilization that emerges is less attuned to control and autonomy and more to openness to the richness of Being:

> TIME WILL STOP
> AND LONG FRUITFUL SPACES BE GIVEN HIM TO LEARN THROUGH
>   SONG AND POETRY
> OF HIS OLD HELPLESS FEELINGS & WEARY PAST
>
> THE RESISTANCE? NONE. HE WILL, YES, SWIM & GLIDE,
> A SIMPLER, LESS WILFUL BEING. DULLER TOO?

IF SO, IS THAT SHARP EDGE NOT WELL LOST
WHICH HAS SO VARIOUSLY CUT AND COST?

(P. 512)

A less willful being, his autonomy reduced, the world in which man lives no longer appears as the exclusive product of his own sensibility; with "NO ACCIDENT," human life will be more determined and deterministic. But in return, man enjoys an expanded sense of the richness of the histories, memories, and relationships that determine him and that determine humanity's Being as Becoming. JM learns this lesson in the most direct way when he is given to understand that his own actions will generate meanings far beyond those he intends. In *Ephraim*, there are hints that the powers have taken an interest in JM and DJ for some time, and it transpires in *Mirabell* that much of what JM writes conveys meanings he cannot yet comprehend. Mirabell urges JM to see in this something to celebrate rather than deplore:

> I'd set
> My whole heart, after *Ephraim*, on returning
> To private life, to my own words. Instead,
> Here I go again, a vehicle
> In this cosmic carpool. Mirabell once said
> He taps my word banks. I'd be happier
> If *I* were tapping his. Or thought I were.
>
> YR SCRUPLES DEAR BOY ARE INCONSEQUENT
> .   .   .   .
>   THINK WHAT A MINOR
> PART THE SELF PLAYS IN A WORK OF ART
> COMPARED TO THOSE GREAT GIVENS
> .   .   .   .
> IS NOT ARCADIA TO DWELL AMONG
> GREENWOOD PERSPECTIVES OF THE MOTHER TONGUE
> ROOTSYSTEMS UNDERFOOT WHILE OVERHEAD
> THE SUN GOD SANG AND SHADES OF MEANING SPREAD

(Pp. 261–62)

In any case, as JM had already affirmed, "What to say? / Our lives led *to* this. It's the price we pay" (p. 218). Humanity persists, if at all, as other, as "the return of difference," in Gilles Deleuze's interpretation of Nietzsche's doctrine of the eternal recurrence[51]—the only possible persistence for publicly constituted, and therefore irreducibly open and appropriable, selves. In reality—that is, in public—our lives are not only what we make of them or *would* make of them; and the planning, calculating, sovereign individual of both scientific reason and liberal political theory cannot be considered as fundamental.

The reference to *The Will to Power* is appropriate because one of *Sandover*'s lessons is that the immortal world is preserved by power, not Christian (or other) morality: "Power itself," not "plain old virtue," is what matters in the "Cosmic Mind"; power, or "THE HELIUM OF PUBLICITY," "kicks upstairs those who possess it, / The good and bad alike" (p. 54). Indeed, as the revelations proceed through *Mirabell* and *Scripts*, with greater and greater "powers" speaking directly to JM and DJ, the very texture of Being is revealed as an array of impersonal (though invariably personified) forces whose coexistence must be continually re-negotiated. Michael and Gabriel, two archangels who, guided by God Biology, direct the dark angels in their transfiguration of human nature, emerge as equally necessary, interdependent forces of creation and destruction. Gabriel conducts the world-destroying forces of antimatter, "The Black beyond black . . . Eater of energies" (p. 440), which are periodically harnessed to eliminate various of God Biology's misbegotten creations, and which may yet be turned on humanity—not to eliminate the entire species, to be sure, but as part of a violent thinning process:

> They wash their hands of us?
> Of people? After going to such lengths—
> WE TOO ONCE DOTED FONDLY (EH CONFRERE?)
> ON EARLY WORKS WE RATHER SQUIRM AT NOW
> JM: We've threatened—therefore we must go—
> Earth and sea and air. JIMMY NO NO
>
> . . . .
>
>   THE KEY
> WORD IS ALPHA   Yes, yes—"Brave New World".
> MY BOY U GOT IT   WHAT OF THE OMEGAS?
> 3 BILLION OF EM UP IN SMOKE POOR BEGGARS?

(Pp. 441–42)

The "KEY WORD" in this passage refers to postscientific man who will succeed a human nature and society overly burdened with the chaotic, impulsive animal soul densities, driven by the will to reproduce and control but living without purpose, in "TIME WITHOUT GOD OR NATURE RUNNING WILD / IN THE BAD DREAMS AND BRAINCELLS OF ITS CHILD" (p. 440). Gabriel offers a Machiavellian justification for the horror and trauma that such a transfiguration may require:

> WHEN NEXT WE MEET TO STROLL THE GROUNDS OF OUR
> WORLD, TWO SCIENTISTS ADMIRING THEIR HANDIWORK,
> APPROVED BY GOD,
>   YOU AS ONE OF THIS NEW GENERATION, AN ALPHA MAN, WILL TELL
>   ME WAS I KIND OR NOT
>
> (P. 439)

Michael, in contrast, personifies creative, generative forces associated with the sun. But there are dozens of other powers, including Nature as an integrative, shaping power; Psyche; and the dark angels of the Research Lab who clone soul densities but who are also associated with the negative electrical charge of the atom, antimatter, and Chaos itself. As the stories of creation and destruction, success and failure, on the part of God Biology and his minions are elaborated, the Christian opposition between worldly power and heavenly truth is displaced by the realization that power must be met by power, force by force; but the apparent one-dimensionality of this conclusion is offset by the multiplicity, plurality, and continual development and readjustment of powers and forces. Personifications are qualified as mere metaphors: "ADAM & EVE," we are told, "ARE IMAGES / FOR DEVELOPMENTS IN THE VERY NATURE OF MATTER," and the dark angels insist that their existence is one of abstract concepts and mathematical formulas (p. 115); but these too are rendered not as disembodied ideas but as drives at work in matter itself:

> SHALL WE BEGIN OUR HISTORY   THE FALL   WE ARE KNOWN AS
> THE BAD ANGELS. . . .
> I SPEAK OF COURSE IN SYMBOLS
>
> . . . .
>
>   PUT SIMPLY THE ATOM IS L SIDED
> ITS POSITIVE SIDE GOOD   ITS NEGATIVE AH WHAT TO SAY

A DISAPPEARANCE   AN ABSOLUTE VOID   ASTRONOMERS
HAVE AT LAST SEEN OUR BENIGHTED WORK   THE BLACK HOLES
THEY GROW

(P. 119)

Merrill's account is simultaneously about the rise and fall of civili-
zations and their unpredictable destinies and about of relationships
that inhere in matter at both subatomic and cosmic levels. And at the
same time as personifications and qualities are seen as abstract forces,
raw natural elements are seen to embody specific forms of intelligence. In fact, natural elements are presented as evolving, through
the intervention of the Research Lab, in the direction of intelligence, as the souls of some of the poem's personalities, such as W. H.
Auden, are reborn as minerals or elements:

I'LL SHIFT THRU VEINS OF METAL
GETTING THE FEEL OF IT, THEN SURFACING

.   .   .   .

THEN INTO
THE WORLD   A CLIFF? A BEACH? OUR WORK BEGINS:
COVERING THE SINS OF MULTITUDE
WE MARCH WE GRAINS OF SAND! Creating famine.
Time's latest cover story tells it all—
"Nature's Revenge: The Creeping Deserts". INDEED

(P. 507)

Other souls, such as that of scientist George Cotzias, are shat-
tered and distributed among various human beings in laboratories
around the world, to frustrate or encourage scientific research. The
vision that emerges toward the climax of the poem is thus one of
a world saturated with meaning, intelligence, and significance, in
which oppositions such as self versus other, animal versus human,
or even animal versus mineral (and of course life versus death) are
displaced in favor of a world of flux, becoming, and transfiguration
that generates and finally supersedes all such distinctions. The world
given in *Sandover* is one of constantly developing, constantly conflicting forces and powers whose negotiation requires, on the part
of beings who would live in it, active and continual care, vigilance,

and concern. Merrill's vision here thus recuperates and conserves the acute sensibility toward power and its centrality in human experience that Sheldon S. Wolin finds in the ancient Near Eastern creation myths.[52] In Genesis, for example, as Wolin interprets it, the powers available to Yahweh must be ranged also against the powers of his creation, Man, who ultimately forces Yahweh to grant some scope and legitimacy to his drive for power. For Wolin, Genesis and other such myths testify to a "pagan" understanding of power that has been obscured by Christianity and by scientific civilization's devaluation of myth; modern discourses of power tend both to sanitize power and to denude it of its specificity, its open and contingent character. In Merrill, however, this sensibility is reinvented and preserved, although thematically *Sandover* represents a correction of Genesis: whereas in the latter, Man is given dominion over everything on Earth, in Merrill's vision the scope of humanity's power is to be drastically curtailed.

Merrill's discovery of immortality as the negotiation and renegotiation of an always already voiced, already textualized universe recapitulates Heidegger's insight in *Being and Time* that "fundamental ontology" is inevitably hermeneutic, and Merrill's qualification of human "resistance" (the will to domination and independence) in favor of a more nuanced openness to Being accords with Heidegger's turn away from subjectivity toward Being itself. According to Heidegger, the phenomenological return to the things themselves can only mean an understanding of Being as interpretation or textuality: "*Only as phenomenology, is ontology possible,*" Heidegger writes, adding, "The phenomenology of Dasein is a *hermeneutic* in the primordial signification of this word."[53] We may take Heidegger as meaning here that since Dasein's Being appears as a finite, "thrown" projection, the "thing" itself to be investigated is, precisely, interpretation. Because Being "as a whole" is never fully present to Dasein, but always only particular beings or entities, Being is a hermeneutic process in which Dasein projects a Whole on the basis of particular existential experiences and then interprets the meaning of particular experiences on the basis of an understanding of the meaning of Being as a whole, in a continuous, circular process.

Being, then, for Heidegger and Merrill, is not enduring presence but interpretation, an insight that *Sandover* confirms not merely as a matter of doctrine but by way of the texture of the revelation itself. The informants' accounts are not delivered dogmatically but instead take the form of seminars or investigations, with personalities of various levels of authority and experience offering a variety of facts and interpretations. Their accounts are then questioned, amplified, and reconstructed by voices of souls between lives, mentors of JM and DJ such as Auden, Cotzias, Maria Mitzotakis, and others. So seriously do these voices undermine the "authoritative" accounts of the powers that it becomes clear at one point in *Mirabell* that the powers are not telling the entire story. By the end of the middle section of *Scripts*, where JM's and DJ's mentors vainly attempt to fix clear and distinct identities on the voices the two have heard, it becomes almost impossible to credit *any* version, especially as the possibility is raised of stronger, unnamed dark forces whose presence is known but whose effects are incalculable. Such ambiguities are confirmed in the poem's coda, *The Higher Keys*, where Ephraim is revealed to be Michael, and throughout the poem, as more authoritative voices qualify earlier revelations, only to be themselves qualified as the poem goes on. Although we eventually hear the presumably authoritative voice of God Biology, it transpires that he is only one of a Pantheon, about whom we know little except that he was given Nature to shape only on the condition that he admit the presence of another force, the "Monitor." The scope of God Biology's power, then, though vast, is not absolute, and the extent of the forces of the Monitor, though known to exist, are unspecified. Contact with the Other World, far from offering metaphysical comfort, shatters the comforting modern ideologies of technology, progress, and certainty. Even toward the final revelations of *Scripts*, Nature's "LAST RESOUNDING YES / TO MAN, MAN IN HIS BLESSEDNESS," which DJ hopes to interpret as having settled the question in favor of humanity (p. 489), cannot silence Auden's doubts:

> Nature said Yes to man—the question's settled.
> SHE SAYS DEAR BOY EXACTLY WHAT SHE MEANS
> LOOK IT UP "A last resounding Yes."
> LAST? The fête was ending. JM: Or

Because man won't be hearing Yes much more?
AH SHE SETS MEANING SPINNING LIKE A COIN.

(P. 492)

In such ways, all putative foundational or master tropes are rela-
tivized, but, more profoundly, the rational pride that would reject
any claim to truth lacking in official Enlightenment credentials is
itself revealed as one more revisionist trope, useful for certain forms
of life but damaging, perhaps deadly, to others. Philip Kuberski describes this aspect of Merrill's work as follows: "Merrill's revelations . . . occur in the transpositions of keys, letters, numbers, selves,
and atoms. In this exchange of figures and myth, doubt is itself subject to doubt, skepticism to skepticism. The divisive model of reality
is replaced by a musical elaboration of relations, so that the baroque
and the artificial—the impossible—are no less real than the realistic
and low-keyed." [54] By subjecting doubt to doubt, Merrill avoids en-
trapment in what Michael Roth calls "the ironist's cage," the deaden-
ing, all-embracing skepticism that rules out strong moral or political
judgments by reducing reality to "mere" fiction. [55]

JM's and DJ's engagement with their powers and shades begins as
a mere board game—the most banal of fictions—but gradually becomes more real than "real life," taking over their imaginations to
the extent that they feel the loss of friends less because they can communicate with them through the Ouija board. When, owing to the
game becoming *too* real and JM and DJ becoming overly dependent
on it, JM asks his former psychiatrist for advice, they find that the
latter's Freudian explanation cannot compete, in imaginative power,
with Ephraim's revelations. Less important than Ephraim's status—
symptom, revelation, hallucination—is what his existence in their
lives sustains:

> The question
> Of who or what we took Ephraim to be,
> And of what truths (if any) we considered
> Him spokesman, had arisen from the start.
>
> .   .   .   .
>
> As through smoked glass, we charily observed,
> Either that his memory was spotty

(Whose wouldn't be, after two thousand years?)
Or that his lights and darks were a projection
Of what already burned, at some obscure
Level or another, in our skulls.

. . . .

Ephraim's revelations—we had them
For comfort, thrills and chills, "material."
He didn't cavil. *He* was the revelation
(Or if we had created him, then we were).
The point—one twinkling point by now of thousands—
Was never to forgo, in favor of
Plain dull proof, the marvelous nightly pudding.

(Pp. 30–31)

The point here, again, is the Nietzschean insight that an imaginative perspective generates effects of power in virtue of offering an interpretation of reality that orders, ranks, directs, and so suggests possibilities for action, so that the question is not only one of literal truth but of the generative potential of the revelation in question. "Composition," in this sense, as JM puts it, is "a cleaner use for power" (p. 81). Neither ingenuously accepting of the politicometaphysical diagnoses he encounters nor glibly contemptuous of them, Merrill, in learning to negotiate the movement of fiction he both initiates and is caught in, offers a vision of how to cope with what Nietzsche calls "this life—your eternal life."

8

The systematic ambiguity and openness of *Sandover*'s revelations applies most fundamentally to questions concerning the status of the poem as a whole: it is irreducibly a blend of fact *and* fiction, if only because the transcripts from the Ouija board originate in real experiences while the texts they generate are at the same time fictional, that is, they concern personalities and events whose existence is imaginary. Returning to Habermas's distinction, JM and DJ never fully bracket their demand that their informants demonstrate the validity of what they say; far from relaxing the demand that validity claims be redeemed, formulating the latter are among JM's and DJ's most urgent tasks. But they also heed what *Sandover*'s Auden insists on, that "FACT IS IS IS FABLE" (p. 263): proof is in some sense moot; for the personalities they encounter generate effects in their lives regardless of the partners' understanding of their validity or reality. An essential lesson of the poem is the need to create and maintain in existence this sphere that is both real and apparent, fact and fiction—the importance, as Mirabell, Michael, and Gabriel put it, of "belief" or "idea" as against "THOUGHT." Thought's demand for clear and distinct proofs, naturalistic explanations, and in general for seriousness *as opposed* to fiction risks concealing the generative capacity of the ideas that are neither serious nor nonserious but simply revealed. According to Mirabell, the "FEATHER OF PROOF" is a literalism of "CHEAP NOTORIETY," appealing only to "DULLD WIT" (p. 258), and the demand for a full and complete proof is simply the formalization of the modern's attempt, in Nietzsche's words, to "resist . . . taking anything deeply," keeping all at arm's length.

In *Scripts*, Gabriel expands on this theme by linking thought or reflection to humanity's destructive impulses:

> I PROMOTE THOUGHT, AGGRESSION,
> DREAD, AS THROUGH WOOD & COAL & OIL & ATOMS AND YES,
> LIVES
>   I GO UP IN FLAME
>
>   (P. 344)

The stress on the corrosive effect of thought on "THE NATURE OF IDEAS" suggests Nietzsche's interpretation of the Platonic dialectic and its hostility to appearance and illusion, a dialectic that ultimately ends in objective thought's self-destruction as the will to truth turns on itself and is exposed as one more illusion (p. 343). Thought, in this sense, enables humanity to dominate the world and secures its independence from it, but its discrediting of "values" threatens also, in Max Weber's terms, to disenchant the world and thus rob humanity's independence of its raison d'être. According to Max Horkheimer and Theodor W. Adorno, the drive to objectify nature and render it calculable reflects a deeper dread of nature and the need to be independent of it, a theme that, in *Dialectic of Enlightenment*, allows them to link reason with myth (pp. 3–42). Merrill's practice in *Sandover*, in contrast, seeks to temper the instrumental rationality of thought with openness to revelatory ideas, an attitude distinguished from myth *and* reason by virtue of its willingness to engage nature's otherness rather than fear or fight against it.

For Merrill, then, Being is revealed as Becoming, a world of strife and balance, negotiation and evolution. It is for this reason that the direct, "natural" language that Merrill first thought to use to tell the story of his experiences with the Ouija board would in fact have betrayed the truths yielded by that experience; for naturalistic fiction conceals the political truth of the embeddedness of immortality in publicity, contingency, and transformation:

> Admittedly I err by undertaking
> This in its present form. The baldest prose
> Reportage was called for, that would reach
> The widest public in the shortest time.
> Time, it had transpired, was of the essence.
> Time, the very attar of the Rose,
> Was running out. We, though, were ancient foes,
> I and the deadline. Also my subject matter
> Gave me pause—so intimate, so novel.
> Best after all to do it as a novel?
>
> (P. 3)

The baldest prose reportage and the kind of novel JM abandons embody the most fateful characteristic Arendt attributes to modernity, namely, the replacement of experience by fiction. Ideology and the atomization of individuals combine, as Arendt argues in *The Origins of Totalitarianism*, to form a "fictitious world," one that replaces the real world constituted in a genuine public sphere. Such a fiction departs from the world in that it presents events as inevitable, ordered, and necessary; it tells a story with a beginning, a middle, and an end implicit in the beginning; it seems to consist of particular experiences that follow from some general principles; and above all, it conceals the radical contingency of political life, in which purposes are transmuted into unanticipated projects and acts take on meanings their agents could not have intended or predicted.

In Arendt's sense of these terms—and this, paradoxically, is the chief reason why the novel, or plain reportage, was finally unsuitable to convey the poem's meaning—the world Merrill reveals is as far removed from *fiction* as can be, although Arendt's fiction is here very close to Habermasian seriousness as the concern for consistency and rationality. As a poet, that is, as a witness to and reporter of events in speech and deed, Merrill neither brackets the question of validity nor appeals to a theoretical foundation. Instead, both alternatives are eclipsed by an entirely unexpected project that emerges not because communication has respected quasi-transcendental norms or critical ideas embedded in language, but in virtue of the fortunate accidents of linguistic revelation itself: the imperative to articulate the value of, and preserve, the contingent revelations of meaning of publicly accessible utterances. In the next, concluding chapter, I explore how that understanding might modify our conception of the *practice* of political theory through a reading of Arendt's *On Revolution*.

CHAPTER FIVE

Practicing Political Theory Otherwise

1

James Merrill, like Proust, experiences the opposition of Athens and Jerusalem.[1] His encounters teach him that the question of whether to be guided by reason or revelation rests ultimately on the false presupposition that the two constitute a contrary pair. He discovers that the pursuit of the truth cannot avoid unmasterable moments of revelation which, however, far from constituting a "miraculous" exception to the lawful work of reason, are opened up by the movements of discourse itself. Over the course of the events resumed in *Sandover*, JM and DJ learn that the world of meaningful, significant relationships they inhabit cannot be fully appreciated or preserved by regarding it merely as the artifact of actions of subjects. Instead, language itself, as a medium that cuts across or through even the distinction between the living and the dead, emerges as a fundamental, yet abyssal, "ground."

As we have seen, this stress on how meaning emerges, willy-nilly, from the traces of language (or from the traces of traces)[2] in such a way as to escape determination or mastery by conscious, rational agency, connects the lessons of *Sandover* to the Arendtian concern for the autonomy of the meaningful political world in relation to "life" or instrumentalizing action. In Arendt's view, that perspective narrows the significance of things, actions, and events to the subject's purposes of preservation and enhancement.[3] In Merrill's poem, the horizon of meaning that emerges in the course of JM and DJ's investigations and experiments cannot be reduced to their own subjective projections. That does not mean, however, that meaning is to be located in a metaphysical beyond; rather, JM and DJ learn that meaning's source is as near to hand as conceivable. For it is nothing less than the unpredictable twists and turns of their own speeches and deeds, which always *turn* out to mean more and other than originally intended, expected, or received. The interactive or intersubjective character of language virtually guarantees that the meaningfulness of the world they explore escapes their conscious mastery and so constitutes it *as* a world, that is, as something more than the projection of a subject and so something that resists the subject's wishes and intentions. The novelty of *Sandover* is its articulation of the way in which the very solidity of the world requires no more ground than the exchange and circulation of linguistic signs.

The modern concept of fiction can act, has acted, as a source of *reassurance* about the boundaries between the real and the unreal, the clear and the obscure, the direct and devious. The earliest novels, literary historians tell us, were not novels at all, but literal deceptions: an invented narrative was presented as "real" through the device of its author pretending to be its editor or discoverer.[4] The concept of fiction in its modern sense, however, depends on the reader's voluntary submission to the unreal time, space, and voice constructed by the novel, the Coleridgean "willing suspension of disbelief." That phrase repays some reflection. Because disbelief is *willed* by the agency of the reader, and because disbelief is only *suspended* and not entirely abandoned, the treatment of the novel as a fiction serves to bolster the reading subject's confidence in its own cognitive powers. Modernity thus understands the novel as a "fiction" in the sense given the term by legal usage: as something "stipulated" to be the case for certain purposes but about which a definitive judgment or commitment to believe is reserved. Keeping the novel in its place by determining it as an experience about which one need not feel called upon to arrive at a definitive judgment or commitment is a strategy that rests ultimately on the epistemological subject's firm control over the real and the unreal. By means of such assumptions and devices, then, the reader, even in giving himself or herself over to the world of the novel and letting it work its effects upon him or her, is still *willing* the suspension of critical powers; the reader remains a subject of will at all times. It is this power that enables fiction to assume the status of an artifact of an experience neither true nor untrue but simply, neutrally, "unreal."

The American fictions explored in Chapter 4 upset these formal delimiters along with the epistemological subject upon which they rest and, for that reason, should perhaps be considered "postmodern." Merrill's poem, especially, withdraws any such cognitive reassurance for the very simple reason that the experience it testifies to is unavailable to the reader who insists on approaching it in the conventional "conditional mode." To reduce the matter to a formula, the work of Burroughs, and even more powerfully (as I argued) that of Merrill, is *both* true *and* untrue, or, perhaps better, in Umberto Eco's and Jean Baudrillard's terms, it is neither real nor unreal but "hyperreal." This is because their work foregrounds mechanisms that link the text of the "fiction" to the larger narratives to which it refers, upsetting the epistemological reliability necessary to the idea of the reader entering into a stable contractual relationship between reader and author in which the reader willingly suspends his or her belief in return for a vivid aesthetic experience.

According to M. M. Bakhtin, this commingling and interpenetration of fictive and nonfictive elements is virtually constitutive of the modern novel as a distinct genre. The novel is distinctive, Bakhtin argues, in that it not only transforms other literary genres (through parody, reformulation, and changes in tone and emphasis) but also maintains a constant relationship with "extraliterary genres, with the genres of everyday life and with ideological genres": "constructed in a zone of contact with the incomplete events of a particular present," the novel therefore "crosses the boundary of what we strictly call fictional literature."[5] Bakhtin himself regards the formal incompleteness of the novel—its relentless appropriation and transformation of extranovelistic and extraliterary discourse—as a symptom of its immaturity, attributing it to the fact that the novel remains but a "developing genre." But if one dispenses with this teleological perspective and ceases viewing the novel's "border violations," as Bakhtin calls them, as steps on the way to a purified and perfected genre, the phenomenon of the confusion of the fictional and the real becomes evident in its own right—and as *Sandover* indicates, there is no reason to restrict it to the novel.

The political relevance of this phenomenon is that it helps capture what has commonly been felt to be at stake politically in literary forms such as the novel: their inherent connectedness to an outside world of extraliterary discourses, making them in some sense strongly worldly in character. This is why Merrill's poem unexpectedly reveals a political engagement: it is a virtual allegory of the transformation of self-contained poetic concerns into a far broader series of discursive phenomena, and that in itself makes for political engagement despite Merrill's oft-expressed hostility to political discourse. That hostility is founded on a suspicion of intellectual systems generally, and rigid patterns of thought and evaluation in particular, which Merrill associates with both political systems and the leveling, generalizing gaze of the theorist.[6] To such an image of the intellectual, Merrill prefers an intelligence that employs beliefs and modes of thought in the pursuit not of Truth but of fulfillment. What matters in such a project is access to beliefs, which includes the ability to take up and leave off ideas pragmatically as opposed to the demands of a coherent or deductive system. The discourse of politics is antithetical to such a project primarily owing to the unsupple character of ideological contestation, and it is for this reason that poetry cannot survive its politicization: "The trouble with overtly political or social writing," as Merrill told an interviewer in 1969, "is that when the tide of feeling goes out the language begins to stink."[7]

On this view, political discourse is by its very nature inextricably linked to the grossly articulated feelings of the moment, so it cannot result in genuinely significant writing, that is, writing that creates its own context and readers. It is evident, however, that Merrill limits his rejection of political writing to that which is "overtly" political, to that which trades in received understandings and is "engaged" in especially direct or obvious ways. Merrill is not, absurdly, ruling out the possibility of politically significant poetry or literarily significant political writing (say, Yeats's "Easter 1916," or *The Declaration of Independence*, or Thoreau's *Walden*), but rather, aesthetically or literarily significant writing that depends directly on ephemeral policies, causes, or "issues" for its emotional impact. What is commonly read as Merrill's apoliticism, then, is better understood as a rejection of the stupefying ideological belief systems that crowd the postmodern public sphere—dominating for a moment, only to disappear without a trace—in favor of the invention of beliefs and perspectives worth preserving for discussion and hence open to transfiguration. To the extent that the latter is in fact what we might want to mean by "the political," Merrill's un- or antipolitical attitudes seem superficial indeed.

One might argue that this amounts to no more than that Merrill's elitism and aestheticism are not un- or antipolitical but, more narrowly, antidemocratic or elitist. Those who criticize Merrill often stress just this point, acknowledging a political turn but deploring the direction. And Merrill himself has seemed to confirm such fears, associating the cultivation of the sensibility he espouses with the lives of the few: "Some will always have a more complex emotional or intellectual life than others, which a more complex art will be called upon to nourish."[8] No matter how equitable the society, Merrill appears to be saying, the distinctions that matter for culture cannot be erased; the difference between oppressor and oppressed may be eliminable, but not that between popular and high culture, because the latter is rooted in intractable human differences, however distorted their expression in a given society. This is a genuine form of elitism, though it is not for that reason unpolitical; indeed, it thrives on and nourishes acute political judgments, as the framework that emerges in *Sandover* makes clear. Whatever the truth of that judgment, however, the significance of Merrill's work for political theory lies elsewhere—not in its appraisal of democracy but, rather, in its conception of how one transcribes or represents the emergence of the event itself, or better, how one testifies to the emergence of the contingent through practices that escape the grasp of sovereign will and the certitudes of the epistemological subject.

At issue here is the question of the particular. To draw on Adorno's reflections in *Negative Dialectics*, Merrill pursues strategies designed to show up the insufficiency of Western, theoretical, "conceptual thinking." Adorno rejects the concept because it presents the particular only as an example of the general, grasped conceptually in a manner independent of any experience of a particular; the problem is that this is prejudicial to the disclosive power of the contingent particular, which loses its specificity and peculiarity, becoming an example rather than a particular. Adorno suggests thinking through models rather than concepts, that is, unfolding the contents of particular events and problems in order to acknowledge and preserve their peculiarity rather than to fold them into a larger conceptual scheme; indeed, the point is to disrupt any such scheme.[9] The strategy (comparable in some respects to Derrida's) involves an acknowledgment of, even an affinity for, the concrete particular. But a strange conundrum haunts such writing: the excavation of the particular contingent, supposed to be so disruptive and transgressive, is placed within the service of a larger narrative lesson about the virtues of the contingent. In other words, there is a danger that the peculiarities at stake get buried under the abstract, general, conceptual "lesson" about the importance of the contingent, open-ended performativity of discursive action. The demand that the contingent be preserved, that the model not be sacrificed to the concept (even a concept of contingency), if taken seriously, places severe discursive pressures on the would-be theorist, whose very success in articulating the contingent would then seem to undermine his or her fundamental intentions.

I think that the importance of Merrill's strategy lies in his scrupulous attention to this dimension. On the one hand, he has commingled discourses such that his poem cannot be considered a purely imaginary artifact because, no matter how strange or occult, it maintains a contact with the real that can never be entirely bracketed. On the other hand, Merrill's basic commitment to a poetic discourse means that the generalizing judgments he does hazard are inevitably folded back into the particularity and uncertainty of the experiences that generate them. They remain, on Kant's terms, reflective not determinant judgments: the question mark of the poem as a whole hangs over every "final" interpretation offered, decisively undermining its finality without, however, making possible its simple dismissal.

The perspective JM and DJ ultimately adopt meshes, as we have seen, with Hannah Arendt's revision of the political as the site of an identity that lives on only in discourse, "free" not in the sense of being the vehicle of unconstrained will but in the sense of being unconstrained *by* will, undetermined by subjective manipulation and therefore open to continual revision and renewal, to the ceaseless *transformation* and *transfiguration* of identity as the price of the "immortality" that preservation through discursive remembrance offers. That conception answers to Arendt's desire to counter the nihilistic worldlessness that for her characterizes modernity by identifying a source of meaningful action that, however, does not rely on the transcendental grounds of Platonic, "other-worldly" metaphysics but instead issues from and remains within the entirely relative and variable world of discourse, act, and event. To avoid nihilism and subjectivism, the world of meaningful relationships must not be reducible to the "anthropological" projections of a willful subject; to avoid Platonism, such a world must not refer for its stability and solidity to meaning grounded in an extra-human agency.[10] For Arendt, the "political" satisfies these exacting demands because the virtually infinite variety and plurality brought to bear on events through public discussions of them ensure the continual irruption of fresh meaning even as such meaning remains self-referentially tied to the actions and speeches of individual actors themselves, because actors' public identity always fails to coincide with their own willed self-identification and therefore possesses a measure of tangibility and reality that transcends the merely psychological or private self.

Such a world of meaningful, significant relationships, actors, and events, far from constituting a solid foundation, is inherently fragile, evanescent, transitory. By its very nature, it cannot reliably be got hold of, managed, produced, or reproduced at will. The evanescent and transitory character of the meaning generated by political action in Arendt's sense has the effect, however, of transforming the enterprise or practice of political theory. If the meaningfulness of political action, and the identities formed through it, are not such that it can be produced or organized in the manner of purposive or instrumental action, then the raison d'être of political theory cannot be (as in already discussed the Platonic traditions criticized by Lyotard) to gain a clearer theoretical understanding of the truth of politics, the better to instantiate it in practice "here below." Put differently, the Platonic appropriation of the model of craftsmanship, in which the vision of the product precedes and governs the actual production of the artifact itself, becomes not only useless but positively harmful once the reality of the horizons of meaning within which action takes place is seen to depend on a *dislocation* of event and its anticipatory vision. Arendt's task would be rather to preserve, by testifying to, actual events of the emergence of political meaning. The problem, in other words, is how to *write* political theory, not in order to secure a pristine theoretical vision, to establish the unchanging truth of the political in theoretical form, but rather to register, or better to celebrate, the emergence of unexpected and unprecedented meanings through discursive action.

From Arendt's perspective, I hazard, what we might call "writing the political" involves not telling the whole truth about the nature of political action in the sense of achieving a comprehensive and exhaustive theoretical vision but something more like "remaining true" to the political in the sense of being faithful, in one's own discursive practice, to the specific texture of political action, its simultaneous openness to revision and resistance to a singular, manipulative will. Such writing is not only political theory; it possesses a quasi-political force in that it serves to illuminate, and thus preserve for appreciation, the value of events that are free precisely in so far as they are unprecedented. Far more effectively than by appealing to normative criteria, however well grounded, such writing contributes to stimulating and refining our political sensibilities by articulating the political emergence of political events themselves. The light *Sandover* can shed on our understanding of the practice of political theory, then, concerns above all else the imperative to eschew the deductive argumentative routines of "Platonic" theory in favor of forms of narrative more adequate to capturing the peculiar contingency and overdetermination of the emergence of political meaning.[11] It suggests that the thought of postmetaphysical political theory cannot be far removed from considerations of narrative practice and textual articulation, or at least that an encounter with such problems is unavoidable.

There is good reason, then, as Ronald Beiner has observed, to view the theorist as a storyteller.[12] But what, exactly, might that mean—how *does* the theorist write when the aim is not comprehensive illumination but the disclosure of a partial, contingent meaning and the celebration of contingency? For Beiner, doing theory as storytelling means "true stories that help us to see our nature more clearly, and . . . serve to disclose (or remind us of) possibilities of human life that are hidden from us by our immersion in the needs and preoccupations of the present" (p. 10). Arendt's narrative political theory, according to Beiner, articulates historical events with an eye to rescuing them from the oblivion of forgetting so as to enlarge our sense of what is possible and what is closed off, and so to enhance our reflection on who we are and what we might do. Beiner seems ultimately, however, to want to yoke this use of narrative to the practical project of making judgments about conduct; the point of enriching political theory to include narrative is that it deepens and widens the ensemble of relationships and possibilities within which we act and so, widens the field of our judgment. In Beiner's vision, then, the narrativization of theory remains instrumentally tied to the (rather traditional) project of passing judgment on political and moral phenomena. However necessary that enterprise may be, Arendt's interest in the political is at least as concerned with the identification of sources of meaning and significance in a world threatened by nihilism and ideology as with the making of ethicopolitical judgments.[13] Given the concern for retrieving sources of meaning, it makes sense to look closely at Arendt's narrative practice, one of the most remarkable exemplifications of which is her reading of the founding of the American Republic in *On Revolution*.

2

For Arendt, the fundamental affinity between political theory (as narrative) and the political itself (as the ever-changing, doxastic world of witnessed and interpreted human interaction and event) lies in the irreducibly textual, interpretative character of each. George Kateb captures this identity when he points out that "Arendt frequently distinguishes between words and deeds, or between talking and doing, as the basic modes of action. But given all that she excludes as not properly political, the distinction cannot stand. It must collapse, with the result that there is only one true mode of political action, and that is speech, in the form of talking or occasionally writing, as with the Declaration of Independence and other manifestoes or addresses to the world, writing that should be read aloud." [14] Kateb allows that deeds count as political only in so far as they are primarily communicative in character, and as the mark of the primacy of the communicativeness of a deed, he points to the quality of "luminosity[,] . . . exemplariness, [and] instantaneous intelligibility."

Kateb's stress on "instantaneous intelligibility" seems to me, however, to be at odds with Arendt's insistence on the unpredictable and initiatory character of political action, the way in which such action discloses a personality quite distinct from the actor's own subjectivity. As she puts it in her essay on Hermann Broch, "We can only agree with the Gospel phrase: 'For they know not what the do'; in this sense no acting person ever knows what he is doing; he cannot know and for the sake of man's freedom is not permitted to know." [15] Arendt does, it is true, affirm that the public identity constituted and disclosed through action, while invisible to its bearer, "appears clearly and unmistakably to others." But the clarity and distinctness of such appearances ought not to be assimilated to notions of self-evidence or an incontestable identity of meaning, if only because for Arendt that would be sufficient to identify them as *anti*political in character: for Arendt, both self-evident and rational truths are, from the point of view of political action, simply "that which we cannot change," whereas the utterly relativistic, doxastic world of political action is change itself. [16] To be sure, changeability, initiation, and beginning cannot be celebrated in every sphere of human existence; the freedom of authentic political action is both limited and transitory, but no less relevant as a source of meaning and significance for that. What must be appreciated, then, is what we might call the existential relevance of the transitory and contingent, and, as we shall see, a narrative approach to theory is essential to shaping that appreciation.

Arendt's turn to narrative reflects her appreciation of the systematic bias with which political action has traditionally been viewed in the West: she warns of "an inevitable flaw in all critical examinations of the willing faculty," namely, that "every *philosophy* of the Will is conceived and articulated not by men of action but by philosophers, . . . who in one way or another are committed to the *bios theoretikos* and therefore by nature more inclined to 'interpret the world' rather than to 'change it.'"[17] Professional thinkers, Arendt continues, "have not been 'pleased with freedom' and its ineluctable randomness; they have been unable to pay the price of contingency for the questionable gift of spontaneity, of being able to do what could also be left undone." To remedy the fact that the Western philosophical tradition has described and evaluated action from the point of view of those for whom action necessarily takes place on a lower ontological or spiritual plane, Arendt suggests turning away from thinkers to "men of action, who ought to be committed to freedom because of the very nature of their activity" (2:198).

The hope that we might discover in the "men of action" an articulation that would provide us with a different inheritance than that of the philosophers proves, however, to disappoint; and that disappointment, I argue, is central to understanding the meaning of Arendt's use of narrative. The basic perplexity involved in action that is free in the sense that it appears as an interruption in the chain of previous causes is easily stated: "An act can only be called free if it is not affected or caused by anything preceding it and yet, insofar as it immediately turns into a cause of whatever follows, it demands a justification which, if it is to be successful, will have to show the act as the continuation of a preceding series, that is, renege on the very experience of freedom and novelty" (2:210). The quality of freedom characteristic of authentic political action is, if you like, immediately obscured by the fact that its very politicalness calls forth a retrospective interpretation that presents it as justified, that is, as responsive to a pre-existing moral or political or spiritual imperative rather than an unprecedented departure in the scheme of things. The "men of action," then, unwilling or unable to face up to the "abyss of freedom," resort instead to the expedient of presenting their innovations as "re-establishments and re-constitutions, not absolute beginnings" (2:213). As a result, the "men of action" themselves, the innovators and founders, are blind to the true dimensions of their distinctiveness and originality, and their interpretations of their deeds blind others to them as well.

At the end of *The Life of the Mind*, Arendt underscores the failure of her turn to the articulations of political actors: "When we directed our attention to men of action, hoping to find in them a notion of freedom purged of the perplexities caused for men's minds . . . we hoped for more than we finally achieved. The abyss of pure sponta-neity . . . was covered up by the device . . . of understanding the *new* as an improved re-statement of the *old*" (2:216). We will not, then, discover, ready-made, an articulation of authentic political action as sheer spontaneity in the accounts of the actors themselves; there is no "other" tradition of discourse, outside philosophy and thus free from its prejudice against action "here below," with whose aid we might free ourselves of those prejudices; no other ground on which to stand but that of our own tradition of reflective thought. Yet that tradition is singularly unhelpful in thinking authentic freedom; within it, only Augustine's concept of the human as a beginner, or natality, suggests a still-to-be-developed alternative (2:216–17).

There is, however, a third alternative: the narrative reinterpreta-tion of the words and deeds of the men of action themselves, a re-interpretation so constructed as to bring to the foreground the dis-tinctiveness and originality of their actions even at the cost of doing violence to their own understanding of them. This is the strategy Arendt pursues in *On Revolution* (and elsewhere), and it is wholly consistent with her more general claim in *The Human Condition* that "action reveals itself fully only to the storyteller, that is, to the back-ward glance of the historian, who indeed always knows better what it was all about than the participants" (p. 192). That action might reveal itself "fully" means, presumably, that it reveals those qualities that mark it as originary, distinctive, and novel, that is, free in Arendt's sense. Clearly, such a revelation is available to the storyteller not be-cause the latter is in possession of more facts or regards events with greater objectivity than the participants but because of the reinter-pretation of events the storyteller is able to accomplish. Narration— by foregrounding some aspects at the expense of others, which are pushed into the background, by placing events in contexts other than those imputed by the actors themselves—can textually isolate that in the event which is indeed distinctive and originary and which thus opens up the possibility of a new beginning. For Arendt, at least in "the modern age," after the definitive destruction not of the past but of the *authority* of the past, the enterprise of political theory can never stray very far from considerations of language and interpretation: "Any period to which its own past has become as questionable as it has to us," as she writes in her essay on Walter Benjamin, "must eventually come up against the phenomenon of language, for in it the past is contained ineradicably."[18]

Arendt's narratives of political action will detach the deeds, even the spoken deeds, of the "men of action" from their own reductive understandings of them and narrate them in such a way as to bring out their truly novel and distinctive features. In this regard, her much-discussed "distinction-making" can be seen for what it is: an indispensable textual strategy with which Arendt undermines the identity, emphasized by historical actors themselves, between their political innovations and the imperatives of the past, interrupting it and so isolating its interruptive character. In this manner, Arendt's narratives become themselves of a piece with the phenomenon of freedom she seeks to articulate: just as political action, in her view, brings into being the absolutely contingent by doing what might as well have been left undone, so her texts operate by discovering unexpected meanings and innovative departures by single-mindedly refusing to read the present as a mere continuation of the past. Thus totalitarianism is not the return of tyranny but "a novel form of government," and the founding of the American Republic did not yield "Rome anew" but rather "a new Rome."[19]

Given her understanding of the open, revisionary character of free political action, it is hardly surprising that Arendt should be drawn to literature as a model for the practice of political theory; for in her view, "literature imposes no binding edicts. Its insights do not have the compelling character of the *mythos* which it serves in an intact religious view of the world. . . . Neither does art, and especially literature, possess the coercive forcefulness, the incontrovertibility, of logical statements; although it manifests itself in language, it lacks the cogency of *logos*."[20] Contained in Arendt's understanding of literature, it seems, is the intuition that narrative, literary meaning emerges in a thoroughly immanent manner and cannot be reliably determined in advance by the reader's vision of the meaning or of the structure of the text. The experience of literary meaning in Arendt's sense would then suggest the very opposite of Plato's metaphorics of craftsmanship, in which everything is guided and judged according to the stable, end-determining vision possessed by the author of the fabrication process; in literature, on the contrary, such meaning as one finds could not have been posited or even imagined in advance of the reading process, at least not determinately. Moreover, the meaning that emerges through the acts of writing and reading does not itself come to stand as a permanent or definitive delimiter of the further emergence of meaning. The antipolitical quality of "compelling necessity," then, which is "the common denominator of the mythical and logical world view," is singularly absent from storytelling, which "reveals meaning without committing the error of defining it" and so stifling further revelations (pp. 134, 105).

While literary meaning does not compel, and while, like the meaningfulness of political action itself, it is therefore evanescent and transitory (though no less real for that), it is tangible *enough* however to reveal "the meaning of what otherwise would remain an unbearable sequence of sheer happenings" (p. 104). Literature is uncompelling in the sense that it can indeed be resisted, but it is not for that reason lacking in power: the power, precisely, to illuminate, preserve, and render intelligible actors, events, and their worlds. Thus, Arendt speaks of the political not in terms of fixed human purposes, moral imperatives, or philosophically divined essential attributes but with a markedly *erotic* vocabulary: what sustains *political* freedom (as opposed to the freedom of the philosophers, freedom philosophically understood) is its sheer *attractiveness* as a way of life. Arendt celebrates the actor's "passionate openness to the world and love of it," a love of the "inexhaustible richness of human discourse," which is "infinitely more significant than any One Truth could ever be."[21] In entering the public sphere, the actor "opens up for himself a dimension of human experience that otherwise remains closed," a dimension that is compelling because of "the joy and gratification that arise out of being in company with our peers, out of acting together and appearing in public, out of inserting ourselves into the world by word and deed, thus acquiring and sustaining our personal identity and beginning something entirely new."[22] Authentic political action, one would say on the basis of the terms in which Arendt chooses to describe it, is compelling in the sense of being seductive rather than commanding, a seductiveness grounded in the attractions of what is different, plural, novel, unexpected and yet admirable and distinctive. If one would open up the world of human plurality and experience its discursive joys, one has to open oneself, as it were, becoming vulnerable to the world and allowing its discourses to traverse and affect oneself rather than attempting *only* to control or subdue. Just so the attractions of the literary, which does not "interfere with life according to a preconceived pattern" but rather allows a story to "emerge." [23]

Arendt makes a key turn in her narrative of the founding of the American Republic by introducing one of her distinctions, though in this case the distinction is indeed one held (she argues) by the actors themselves: that between power and authority. [24] The American colonists, she tells us, understood the crucial distinction between violence and power (she defines the latter, with Burke, as the ability to act in concert), but their revolution did not require but rather presupposed the establishment of power (that having been achieved over the course of 150 years of establishing and governing new communities). Thus the withdrawal of the legitimacy provided by "royal charters and the loyal attachment of the colonies to king and Parliament in England" posed a very different problem: "the establishment and foundation not of power but of authority" (p. 178). That power in Arendt's Burkean sense had long been established in America accounts, Arendt argues, for the radically different outcomes of the American and French modern revolutions; for it meant that the withdrawal of traditional, monarchical authority did not immediately pose the problem of order by shaking the entire society to its foundations:

> The rupture between king and parliament indeed threw the whole French nation into a "state of nature"; it dissolved automatically the political structure of the country as well as the bonds among its inhabitants, which had rested not on mutual promises but on the various privileges accorded to each order and estate of society. . . . The conflict of the colonies with king and Parliament in England dissolved nothing

more than the charters granted the colonists and those privileges they enjoyed by virtue of being Englishmen; it deprived the country of its governors, but not of its legislative assemblies; and the people, while renouncing their allegiance to a king, felt by no means released from their own numerous compacts, agreements, mutual promises, and "cosociations." (P. 180)

The violence of the French Revolution is to be found not only in the Terror but above all in the fact that the French understood power as a kind of natural force, "superhuman in its strength" and constituted "outside all bonds and all political organization." The salient characteristic of power so understood is that it is *mute*, manifesting itself most clearly in deeds that thrust aside institutions and conventions in order to meet the inchoate and irresistible needs of "the people." This force is not really political power so much as *strength*, the dictatorial strength that understands the birth of a polity along the lines of an almost physical, architectural shaping or fabrication process. The establishment and exercise of political power in America, in contrast, is grounded in discourse: "To [the American revolutionaries,] . . . power came into being when and where people would get together and bind themselves through promises, covenants, and mutual pledges." American power need not rely on some suprapolitical force grounded absolutely outside all institutions but is, if you like, thoroughly (and plurally) discursive in character. Thus the emergence of a distinctively American polity in the wake of the withdrawal of the traditional sanctions of British history will mean not the opening of "the political realm to this pre-political, natural force of the multitude" but, rather, the opposite, a purely discursive, deliberative political society (p. 181).

The understanding of power which spares America the inarticulate violence marking the Old World's encounter with modernity presents another problem, however, that of authority, because mutual promises and compacts, though sufficient to establish power, seem far too uncertain to provide the stability necessary for a polity that would last: "Neither compact nor promise upon which compacts rest are sufficient to assure perpetuity, that is, to bestow upon the affairs of men that measure of stability without which they would be unable to build a world for their posterity, destined and designed to outlast their own mortal lives." Arendt thus finds in the American Revolution an especially vivid instance of the basic perplexities of the authentically free, originary political action canvassed above: the peculiar way in which it both ushers in the contingently new and disruptive *and* obscures its novelty by interpreting it as responsive to a previously existing law, purpose, or imperative. This observation then provides an opportunity for a further distinction: Americans turn to law, to "the task of laying down a new law of the land, which was to incorporate for future generations the 'higher law' that bestows validity on all man-made laws," to find the authority needed for stability. This they can do because unlike the French, who ground the law in the people's power as a mute, violent force, Americans regard the law as reflective of a higher transcendental region distinct from the power constituted by discursive action: the rebirth or repetition of a great, ancient republic (p. 182). In the American Revolution, then, or more precisely in its political discourse, Arendt finds an exemplar of the way in which creative political action inevitably reneges on itself: a creative departure in the order of things, the American Revolution immediately reinterprets its practice of political power as guided by a privileged origin functioning as an authoritative, transcendental absolute, thus obscuring its originary character.

Arendt's narrative, however, leads ultimately to an *ironic* reading of the American founding in which "reflection and choice" yield not the conformity of the future course of the Republic to a pregiven rational vision but, rather, the certainty of the further generation of entirely new and unforeseen points of departure or beginnings. What the founding of the American Republic will have demonstrated is that action *creates* principles rather than derives from them (the principle at issue here being the possibility of founding a republic on nothing but deliberation and promising), and what *really* legitimates that principle, it will turn out, is not higher authority but rather the success of the republic itself—the sheer, contingent fact that over the course of its history colonial America had indeed learned to establish and maintain power discursively. At the heart of the American Revolution, then, is a virtual tautology: America's deliberative, discursive politics is legitimate because it is successful, because it does indeed "build a world," not by means of violent, dictatorial shaping but by relying on the revelatory capacities of discursive interaction (p. 166).

The Revolution, then, would merely "bring the new American experience and the new American concept of power out into the open"; and what is important here is precisely the novelty of American *experience*, the way in which the American practice of power reflects not a tradition of political thinking but the sheer force of events that dramatically distill the very essence of the political:

> It is an event rather than a theory or a tradition we are confronted with [by the early colonial compacts], an event of the greatest magnitude and the greatest import for the future, enacted on the spur of time and circumstances, and yet thought out and considered with the greatest care and circumspection. . . . No theory, theological or political or philosophical, but their own decision to leave the Old World behind and to venture forth into an enterprise entirely of their own led into a sequence of acts and occurrences in which they would have perished, had they not turned their minds to the matter long and intensely enough to discover, almost by inadvertence, the elementary grammar of political action and its more complicated syntax, whose rules determine the rise and fall of human power. (P. 173)

The grammar of political action is plural; it possesses a complex syntax because it is therefore inherently relational. Power is both plural, in that it is an attribute not of individuals but of collectives, and relational, in that it organizes individuals in terms of "joint enterprises" based on mutual accords (p. 175). Thrown back on their own resources and unsheltered by traditional European institutions, the early American colonists discovered the actual ground of purely *political* power—namely, the abyssal ground of human interaction, which is never more stable than mutual promises, agreements, and confidences can make it. This fact, however, escapes the consciousness of the "men of action" themselves and must therefore be prized loose through Arendt's narrative reinscription.

Political power itself is created by guaranteeing and extending the sphere in which individuals can conduct joint enterprises and govern their affairs in terms of mutual promises, but whence the principle of *order* according to which the liberty to create power in that sense can be absolutely guaranteed? If the constitutional order is itself the expression of power in the American (Arendtian) sense, what is to prevent it from being superseded by further political enterprise? How can, by what right does, a power defined as essentially open and revisable, that is defined in terms of interrupting the temporal chain of historical causes and introducing something new into the world, guarantee conditions "for posterity"?

The revolutionaries seek answers to these questions by turning to ancient Rome as both "model" and "precedent." That model teaches respect for "beginning," but the Founders could conceive beginning only as an occurrence in the distant past, a limitation in direct contradiction to the events of the American founding which, taking place as they did under modern conditions, could never be shrouded in the past. Thus Arendt sees in America's tendency to worship the Constitution not a secular religion but a willingness to celebrate beginning as such: the success of the revolution "was decided the very moment when the Constitution began to be 'worshipped', even though it had hardly begun to operate" (p. 197). The Founders' return to Rome is in fact a radical reinterpretation of it, one that shifts the locus of authority from the senate to the judiciary. Pointing out that the etymological root of *auctoritas* is *augere*, to augment or increase, Arendt notes that a Roman citizen cared for the city by preserving the spirit of ancestors who founded it, a care that tied the citizen to the founding through pious remembrance. In this optic, change could only mean increasing or enlarging the status quo. For the American revolutionaries, the Roman idea that foundation "automatically" develops its own stability, that authority is innovation guided by the desire to extend into the future what had been begun by others, appeared as the natural solution to the problem of "how to obtain the sanction of legitimacy for a body politic which could not claim the sanction of antiquity" (p. 202).

Thus the true authority implicit in the founding of the Republic, though anticipated, emerges or is proved only by the successes of those who come after in augmenting and improving it: "No doubt the American founders had donned the clothes of the Roman *maiores*, those ancestors who were by definition 'the greater ones,' even before they were recognized as such by the people. But the spirit in which this claim was made was not arrogance; it sprang from the simple recognition that either they were founders and, consequently, would become ancestors, or they had failed. What counted was . . . solely the act itself" (p. 203). The only authority the Founders have is the authority of founders, and that can be conferred only retrospectively. So Arendt sees that worship of the Constitution can mean not only the veneration of the written document but the celebration of "the act of constituting," which has to do with the capacity to act in concert and falls outside the scope of governmental administration as such. What is celebrated is the *act* of founding a body politic grounded in nothing but the shared, discursive performance of unprecedented political acts themselves. But that is a paradoxical authority; for unlike the Roman "return" to the ancestors and their specific deeds, American political culture involves a return to no *fixed* identity but rather to the principle of innovative, authority-creating, founding action itself. What makes American political culture distinctive is that the absolute quality of founding—the fact that political freedom is indeed abyssal and reliant only on the fragile premise of a joint enterprise—became itself a political act in virtue of having been widely witnessed and turned into discourse (p. 204). Authentic political action—action bold enough, distinctive enough, seductive enough to inspire attempts to preserve and extend it—is itself the new absolute, at once the most fragile and the most dangerous absolute imaginable.

But the Founders achieve this celebration of beginning by framing it in terms of the law. The content of authority in the American Republic is its continuous revision and reinterpretation of the Constitution: "in the American republic the function of authority is legal, and it consists in interpretation" (p. 200). That is, the American revolutionaries renege on their revolutionary acts by searching for a transmundane absolute to ground a higher, founding law, an absolute that logically would assume the shape of an "Immortal Legislator": John Adams's "great Legislator of the Universe," Jefferson's "laws of nature and nature's God" (p. 185). As Arendt puts it, "It was precisely the revolutions, their crisis and their emergency, which drove the very 'enlightened' men of the eighteenth century to plead for some religious sanction at the very moment when they

were about to emancipate the secular realm fully from the influences of the churches and to separate politics and religion once and
for all" (pp. 185–86). The need for an absolute, Arendt speculates,
was in part "an inheritance" from the time when "secular laws were
understood as the mundane expression of a divinely ordained law";
but the desire to formulate modern answers to premodern questions
is not the whole story, and in regarding the ancients as believing in a
divine origin of law, the revolutionaries simply projected their own
perplexities and concerns onto earlier periods of history (p. 189). For
the Greeks, the task of law was to establish a specially demarcated
space in which power could be practiced; for the Romans, law was
the mode whereby already constituted, mundane associations were
brought together in greater alliances or partnerships (p. 188). Such
law as practiced by the ancient Greeks and Romans needs no absolute; especially in the latter case, it is "relative by definition" and
hence characteristically political.

The insistent question of the absolute was not Greco-Roman but
rather Hebraic in origin, and Arendt detects it inscribed in the very
grammar of the law itself, as understood by the American revolutionaries. Law was a commandment limiting what can be done,
and as such—*only* as such—it required a transmundane justification:
"What mattered was that . . . the laws themselves were . . . construed
in accordance with the voice of God, who tells men: Thou shalt
not. Such commandments obviously could not be binding without a
higher, religious sanction. Only to the extent that we understand by
law a commandment to which men owe obedience regardless of their
consent and mutual agreements, does the law require a transcendent source of authority for its validity, that is, an origin which must
be beyond human power" (p. 189). Western political thought, by
Arendt's account, rereads Roman practices in terms of Hebraic imperatives, and the American revolutionaries, as the inheritors of that
tradition, thus find themselves in a paradoxical search for a source of
absolute authority to lay down *external* limits on a practice of power
for which external, unchangeable limits are, precisely, irrelevant (pp.
190–91). The most original of these replacements for the absolute of
divine guidance is Jefferson's appeal, in the Declaration of Independence, to the absolutely compelling quality of "self-evident truths,"

whose validity seems to be beyond argument, decision, or justification. Compared with the ritual invocation of heaven or hell, such an appeal possesses real force in an enlightenment culture (p. 192). Precisely because it possesses such appealing plausibility, however, the idea of a divinely inspired reason becomes the most effective move by which the originary, interruptive force of founding political action is interpretatively obscured. Consequently, self-evident truth, the enlightenment's successor concept to divine revelation, covers over the abyssal quality of freedom that the withdrawal of traditional authority had brought to the fore.

Having inherited "the traditional concept of law" as command, the Americans search for, and regrettably discover, a new absolute capable of grounding the commanding sovereignty their inheritance demands, thus obscuring the originality of their own discovery of authentic political power. In a sense, the movement from originary revelation to retrospective self-obscuration describes the substance of Arendt's narrative of the founding of the American Republic. To leave the matter at that, however, would be to obscure the most essential dimension of her narrative; for Arendt equally wishes to show that the retrospective justification that "reneges" on the creative political act cannot stand and that the insufficiencies, contradictions, and gaps that attend the justifying discourse negatively testify to the originality of the act itself. "It is true enough that the men of the American Revolution remained bound to the conceptual and intellectual framework of the European tradition," she writes, but this bondage to tradition does not determine the "destinies of the American republic to the same extent as it compelled the minds of the theorists" (p. 195). In Arendt's story, the effective if only furtively acknowledged source of authority in America is not divine sanction (if it had been, the American Revolution would have gone the way of other modern revolutions with the definitive collapse of absolutes in modernity) "but the act of foundation itself" (p. 196). What finally acquires authority or becomes authoritative in America, in Arendt's judgment, is nothing less than authentic political action itself, understood as an originary, creative, and freely evolving (though strictly limited) capacity to act, to begin and begin again.

In this wise, Arendt ultimately would have us reject (though not, of course, forget) the Roman discourse of repetition and rebuilding; and she finds the recognition of its inadequacy in the rewritings and recontextualizations of ancient ideas and slogans by the revolutionaries themselves. "When the Americans decided to vary Virgil's line from *magnus ordo saeclorum* to *novus ordo saeclorum*," she writes, "they admitted that it was no longer a matter of founding 'Rome anew' [as Milton had dreamed] but of founding a 'new Rome', that the thread of continuity which bound Occidental politics back to the foundation of the eternal city and which tied this foundation once more back to the prehistorical memories of Greece and Troy was broken and could not be renewed" (p. 212). As the tradition provides no help in "thinking" the break they enacted, the break can be read only in the displacements, faults, slips, retranslations, and distortions committed by the revolutionaries; it is, if you like, a *trauma* that emerges in retrospect and cannot be experienced immediately, that is, in the absence of mediation by subsequent interpretation and judgment. Into the gaps outlined by those textual variations, Arendt boldly inserts her own reading:

> What saves the act of beginning from its own arbitrariness is that it carries its own principle within itself, or, to be more precise, that beginning and principle, *principium* and principle, are not only related to each other, but are coeval. The absolute from which the beginning is to derive its own validity and which must save it, as it were, from its inherent arbitrariness is the principle which, together with it, makes its appearance in the world. The way the beginner starts whatever he intends to do lays down the law of action for those who have joined him in order to partake in the enterprise and to bring about its accomplishment. As such, the principle inspires the deeds that are to follow and remains apparent as long as the action lasts. (Pp. 212–13)

Thus, in Arendt's hands, the story of the American founding—her interpretation is indeed that story—constitutes a new myth superseding those of the Bible and Virgil, a myth of beginning, interruption, and rebirth. Arendt's narrative of the American founding ought, in principle, to replace that of the Founders themselves; if so, their "desperate search for an absolute," prompted by "the age-old thought-customs of Western men, according to which each completely new beginning needs an absolute from which it springs and by which it is 'explained,'" would give way to an appreciation of the "measure of complete arbitrariness" that marks "the very nature of a beginning" (p. 206). The significance that Arendt finds in the American founding, then, has nothing to do with such traditional formulations as the construction of a rational order, of a polity that will last forever because its institutions mime the immutable laws of nature, or of a constitution founded in the essence of human nature. Instead, one finds an entirely different thought of the political, one grounded in discursive interaction that reveals principles and actors that persist because they are attractive to those who participate in the way of life they open up. America's principles are not derived from reason or nature but are opened up in the space of discourse itself. So Hamilton's words, when quoted by Arendt at the close of her narrative, come, in the light of that narrative, to possess a very different meaning from that conventionally applied to them: basing a government on reflection and choice *means* opening up a political culture that celebrates founding, beginning, and the plurality implied by "the combined power of the many" rather than "the strength of one architect" (p. 214). With this reinterpretation, Arendt has opened up the possibility that political action need not renege on itself: the Revolution produced what could not have been anticipated precisely because the dimension of discursivity outweighed that of violence in the founding.

That is a possibility made apparent, however, only by Arendt's narrative reinterpretation, to whose strategies and stakes I now return. The political meaning Arendt finds in the discourse of the American founding is not what the "men of the revolution" *had in mind* when they acted: hoping to build an order for the ages by returning to an originary political principle, they invented and legitimated a new principle of ceaseless new departures, augmentations, and reinterpretations. Turning to the ancients for legitimation, cloaking their original actions in the respected garb of history, the Founders in fact liberate the splendor of political action from two millennia of "borrowed light" (p. 197). As Arendt puts it, these actors engaged in what "*turned out to be* unprecedented action" (p. 196). Unprecedented action must always *turn out* to have been unprecedented; one cannot simply will to act without precedent; the unprecedentedness of Arendt's America must therefore be ironic, or indeed allegorical, an unintended consequence of the Founders' actions and in any case not identical to their publicly imputed meanings.

In the case of both authentic political moments and the literary inscription Arendt calls storytelling, then, something unanticipated emerges (whether good or evil is another question, a question of judgment);[25] and this emergence of the unexpected is a characteristic both of the world Arendt seeks to articulate *and of her narrative practice itself*. This links Arendt's narrative approach to the articulation of political action to a narrative form that Shoshana Felman refers to as testimonial literature, the discourse of *witnessing*.[26] According to Felman, much modern literature can be read as responding to a general "crisis of witnessing." She defines such a crisis as a situation in which the event to be witnessed or described so exceeds the capacity of received discourses to grasp it that it is virtually impossible even to experience; it so must take the form of a trauma—an event whose contours become apparent only long afterward, evidenced by disruptions and distortions in narrative accounts. Such accounts demand a reading practice that is attentive to the gaps, slips, and inadequacies in narrative accounts and interprets them as reflective of a larger, traumatic event, one that is necessarily accidental, intrusive, irruptive. The paradigm for this type of reading is Freud's decoding of the hysterical symptom, but Felman finds the structure in Mallarmé, Camus, Kafka, Celine, and others as well.

Felman defines narrative straightforwardly: "That 'something happened' in itself," she writes, "is history; that 'someone is telling someone that something happened' is narrative" (p. 93).[27] Narrative, then, is closely linked to historical discourses; as Felman puts it, narrative "is defined by a claim to establish a certain history" (p. 94). She goes on to suggest, however, that the apparently natural complicity between narrative and history (narrative establishes historical events; history explains events by narrating them) has been sundered by the "cataclysm of the Second World War and the Holocaust," which resist their narrativization because to the extent that, in a profound sense, they cannot have been witnessed, they exceed anyone's capacity *to* witness them. In Arendt's terms, events so unprecedented and refractory as to frustrate the attempt to describe them in conventional discourses resist being turned into stories—or at least, the stories into which they are turned insinuate their continuity with what came before rather than their originality. Faced with such events, narration responds by twisting and turning about itself, exposing its own lacks and insufficiencies, but at the same time revealing, witnessing, or testifying *in spite of itself*. It shows above all, as Felman puts it, "that one does not have to *possess* or *own* the truth, in order effectively to *bear witness* to it; that speech as such is unwittingly testimonial; and that the speaking subject constantly bears witness to a truth that nonetheless continues to escape him, a truth that is, essentially, *not available* to its own speaker" (p. 15).[28] Narrative dislocations such as these reveal the interruption of something utterly unprecedented and accidental, which is experienced immediately as a disruption of language but which ramifies outward to emerge as a symptom of a cultural transformation of the broadest and deepest sort. Such modern writers as Mallarmé, Celan, and Camus, in Felman's reading, have in common an orientation toward responding to apparently accidental or contingent formal disruptions in literary conventions which turn out to figure larger cultural catastrophes, which themselves however are not experienced at once and as a whole but only transpire gradually, fragmentarily, as we become aware of them by experiencing their discursive consequences and effects. Such literature figures the most paradoxical witnessing imaginable, that which testifies to an event that could not have been witnessed in immediate, originary form. And that, of course, is precisely the problem that authentic political action, action that does not impose norms but creates new departures, poses for those who would articulate it.

Like Arendt, Felman relies on the metaphor of natality to capture what is involved in this process:

Psychoanalysis and literature have come both to contaminate and to enrich each other. Both, henceforth, will be considered primarily as *events of speech*, and their testimony, in both cases, will be understood as a mode of *truth's realization* beyond what is available as statement, beyond what is available, that is, as a truth transparent to itself and entirely known, given, in advance, prior to the very process of its utterance. The testimony will thereby be understood, in other words, not as a mode of *statement of*, but rather as a mode of *access to*, that truth. In literature as well as in psychoanalysis, and conceivably in history as well, the witness might be . . . the one who (in fact) witnesses, but also, the one who *begets*, the truth, through the speech process of the testimony. (P. 16)

To the extent that the truth to be narrated is that of an event — contingent, accidental, and for that reason traumatic — it will have been begotten gradually, suggested by displacements and fault lines in the grammar of its articulations and not in a full descriptive account of the event as it happened, when by definition it could not have been experienced. Just so authentic, disruptive, founding political action, by Arendt's account: its sheer novelty suppressed by the need for justifications, it will emerge only gradually, begotten by the backward glance of the storyteller or historian whose relaxed need for justification enables him or her to isolate the faults in the account to reveal the departure and novelty. If authentic political action is of the order of the natal, its emergence requires the midwife of narrative.

Felman presents psychoanalysis as a narrative, testimonial discipline of that sort:

The curious thing about this stunning theoretical event [Freud's discovery of the unconscious via the most apparently random and senseless private events] is the way in which its very generality hinges, paradoxically, on its accidental nature: on the contingency of a particular, idiosyncratic, symptomatic dream. In the symptomatic and yet theoretical illumination of this radically new kind of intelligibility, psychoanalysis can be viewed as a momentously felicitous, and a momentously creative, *testimony to an accident*. (P. 17)

By Arendt's understanding, political theory as storytelling would also constitute a "momentously creative testimony to an accident," to the creativity of the accidental, if we suppress the primary meaning of *accidental* as *mishap* and instead stress the word's secondary significance of an unexpected or unintended happening. Like Felman's modern writers, Arendt's political narrative moves forward by continually breaking through its own framework (p. 48).

For that reason, Arendt's narrative articulation of political events —as distinct from her recovery of an understanding of the character of the political—bears more than a family resemblance to her experience of thinking as such, which begins, according to Arendt's testimony, when one's self-evident truths have been shaken and one's knowledge has been rendered less than reliable. Only when one has found one's concepts *wanting* in application, or when one has exhausted one's reason and has therefore been strangely "emptied," can one *genuinely* question an object, event, or experience, that is, question it in such a manner that one's investigation yields more than an augmentation or extension or restatement of original premises:

> Thinking in the Socratic sense . . . is a maieutic function, a midwifery. That is, you bring out all your opinions, prejudices, what have you; and you know that never, in any of the [Platonic] dialogues did Socrates ever discover any child [of the mind] who was not a wind-egg. That you remain in a way empty after thinking. . . . And once you are empty, then, in a way which is difficult to say, you are prepared to judge. That is, without having any book of rules under which you can subsume a particular case, you have got to say "this is good," "this is bad," "this is right," "this is wrong," "this is beautiful," "this is ugly." And the reason why I believe so much in Kant's *Critique of Judgment* is not because I am interested in aesthetics but because I believe that the way in which we say "that is right, that is wrong" is not very different from the way in which we say "this is beautiful, this is ugly." That is, we are now prepared to meet the phenomena, so to speak, head-on, without any preconceived system."[29]

To meet phenomena head-on does not mean to see them as they really are, without any concepts at all, presuppositionless, but rather to respond to their novelty by articulating them "otherwise." To take one of Arendt's most controversial judgments, totalitarianism is not evil simply in the sense that it satisfies our preexisting concept of evil; rather, the novelty of totalitarianism, which exceeds anything anticipated, itself expands and alters our conception of evil, shows us what evil is, *if* we are able, and willing, to think it. Arendt's narrative practice of political theory is predicated on the idea that the meaning attaching to political action always only *transpires*, in the strict etymological sense of the term; that it leaks out gradually through judg-ments, interpretations, stories, reconsiderations, revisions. What Felman says about Freud's discovery—that "it takes two to wit-ness the unconscious"—is true of Arendtian political action, and for essentially the same reason: the ineluctable inaccessibility of the con-tingent, the novel, the *truly* accidental to its own subject.[30]

As a practice oriented toward negotiating that paradox, Arendt's narrative approach to political theory recommends itself not so much to contemporary attempts to rethink the political as to efforts to innovate in the practice of political theory. A reading of Arendt's narrative accomplishments not only suggests links between theory and narrative but argues in favor of discovering political theory in what are commonly marginalized as "fictional" narratives. To see Arendt as writing or recommending fiction, however, requires that we ignore the "traditional" concept of fiction or fictionalizing as the shaping of raw material into a coherent order or structure or, rather, a coherency that might be derived from a fundamental source, logic, or idea. For *that* conception of fiction, Arendt has no use; it is akin to the coercive character of logic and cousin to the absurdities of ideological thinking and organization. Arendt both condemns ideol-ogy for attempting to turn the world into a "fiction" and asserts that the only way to guarantee meaning in life is to turn one's life into a story.[31] But these statements are only apparently contradictory, be-cause storytelling and fiction are not at all the same; for where fiction totalizes and organizes, storytelling reveals the unexpected revela-tions of events, an intelligibility of an entirely other kind. Arendt's political narratives are indeed like Merrill's accounts in that both are monuments to the revelatory force of contingency and event: both serve to make us not merely tolerant of, but grateful for, that over which we have no control and could not have anticipated and which, for that reason, is uncertain; for, as both would teach us, these latter are the very conditions of worldliness itself.

By constructing a narrative that finds such revelations in the founding of the American Republic, Arendt has unearthed a politi-cal meaning almost opposite to that of an entire tradition of reflec-tion. Rather than building the city as a work of art, she discovered the peculiarly fragile but powerfully revelatory strength of ungoverned discursive interaction, a politics that does not impose identities but celebrates the birth of new ones. America's attempts to "fiction" itself by deliberating and promising can be expected to maintain the greatest distance possible from the intentions of the deliberators and promisers: the deliberative, interpretative community, for Arendt, will be at the farthest remove possible from "the state as a work of art." Precisely insofar as it foregrounds deliberation, an American politics will not have committed the "sin" of attempting to "make life poetic, live it as though it were a work of art . . . or use it for the realization of an idea."[32] Against America's own understanding of itself as the realization of timeless truths, immutable principles, or absolute ideas, Arendt's narrative reveals another America, one adrift in the unpredictable, uncontrollable perlocutionary consequences of its monumental privileging of the discursive.[33]

Notes

Introduction: Allegories of America

1. See Reiner Schürmann, *Heidegger on Being and Acting.*
2. See Slavoj Zizek, *Looking Awry*, pp. 3–6.
3. For a survey of political theoretical responses to the "end" of metaphysics, see Bernard Flynn, *Political Philosophy at the Closure of Metaphysics.*
4. On Socrates' desire to "correct existence" and the hubris it reflects, see Friedrich Nietzsche, "The Problem of Socrates," in *Twilight of the Idols*, pp. 39–44.
5. Xenophon, *Memorabilia*, 1.1.11–16.
6. Jean-François Lyotard and Jean-Loup Thébaud, *Just Gaming*, p. 21.
7. For Friedrich Nietzsche's reflections, see esp. *On the Genealogy of Morals* and the notes on "European nihilism" collected in *The Will to Power.*
8. Cf., again, Nietzsche, "Problem of Socrates," p. 42.
9. See Martin Heidegger, "The Question concerning Technology," in *The Question concerning Technology and Other Essays*, pp. 3–35, and *What Is Called Thinking*, Pt. 1; and *Nietzsche*, esp. vols. 1 and 4.
10. See Hannah Arendt, *The Human Condition*, chap. 5, and "What Is Freedom?" in *Between Past and Present*, pp. 143–71.
11. Michael Oakeshott, *On Human Conduct*, p. 26.

1. The Fiction of America

1. Arendt dismisses references in the Declaration of Independence to "nature's God" and self-evident truths as anachronistic, emphasizing in-

stead the performative "we hold" as the true locus of the appeal. For a complexification of her reading of the Constitution, see Bonnie Honig, "Declarations of Independence."

Arendt redefines the absolute to mean not a "transcendent, transmundane" source of value or being but rather the sheer fact that beginnings and departures, disconnections and originations, occur in history, a phenomenon she ultimately names "natality." What is "absolute" for the historical actor, then, is the phenomenon of natality itself, not some otherworldly realm of meaning or authority. I discuss Arendt's use of narrative to register this sense of an absolute in Chapter 5.

2. Hannah Arendt, *On Revolution*, p. 195.

3. Arendt allows that the new American understanding of political power was "in a sense prior to the colonization of the continent," but she turns to the Mayflower Compact and dismisses the importance of notions of Puritan theocracy for the development of American political discourse (see *On Revolution*, p. 172). For the argument that the reinvention of Puritan modes of public discourse has worked to shape a sense of the sacred in America's "mission," see Sacvan Bercovitch, *The American Jeremiad*. For some interesting extensions and applications of this insight to the discourse of American security, see David Campbell, *Writing Security*.

4. See John Winthrop, *Winthrop Papers*, p. 282 n. 1.

5. See Thomas Kuhn, *The Structure of Scientific Revolutions*. In his *Idea of Political Theory*, Tracy B. Strong develops a concept of "normal politics" derived from Kuhn's distinction and akin to Wittgenstein's "knowing one's way about" (pp. 7–11, 124–25).

6. In fact, however, elaborate preparations had been made in Massachusetts Bay for the arrival of the founding settlers. In no sense were the voyagers of the *Arbella* facing an entirely alien land.

7. I draw here on Perry Miller's account of the peculiarities of the history of the charter in Perry Miller and Thomas H. Johnson, *The Puritans*, pp. 7–9.

8. *Winthrop Papers*, 87.

9. Again, see Miller and Johnson, *Puritans*, pp. 10–12.

10. The claim of a federal covenant is registered toward the end of the text, where Winthrop warns that the divine punishment for a breach of the covenant will be meeted out to the "people," not individuals.

11. On the persistant Western idea that the community is founded on the imitation of an essence, see Philippe Lacoue-Labarthe, *Heidegger, Art and Politics*. For a trenchant attempt to think community otherwise, see Jean-Luc Nancy, *The Inoperative Community*.

12. "Modell of Christian Charity," *Winthrop Papers*, p. 289.

13. "John Winthrop to His Wife," *Winthrop Papers*, p. 91.

14. See Lacoue-Labarthe, *Heidegger, Art and Politics*, chap. 8.

15. Lacoue-Labarthe notes that the idea of the city as a work of art is "a deep theme which derives from Plato's politico-pedagogical writings (especially *The Republic*) and reappears in the guise of such concepts as *Gestaltung* (configuration, fashioning) or *Bildung*" (p. 66). According to the *American Heritage Dictionary*, "fiction" derives from *fingere*, "to touch, form, mold," and is related to the Indo-European *dheigh-*, "to knead clay." Cf. Jean-François Lyotard's comments on Lacoue-Labarthe's thesis in the former's *Heidegger and "the Jews"*.

16. According to Lacoue-Labarthe, this tradition "culminates in Nazism" in a complex manner (p. 82). Nazism is a response to the collapse of "the beliefs of modern humanity (Christianity)," i.e., to the collapse of any and all transcendental absolutes and to the consciousness that such absolutes are really stories or myths according to which peoples fashion themselves *as* peoples (cf. pp. 94–95). In response, nazism mobilizes "the identificatory emotions of the masses" (p. 9) and seeks to realize a community by actualizing or effectuating its legends about itself. Nazism, in other words, is "the myth of myth, or the myth of the formative power of myths" (p. 94).

17. "The constraint governing *imitatio*," as Lacoue-Labarthe writes, "demands that *imitatio* rid itself of *imitatio* itself, or that, in what it establishes (or has imposed upon it) as a model, it should address something that does not derive from *imitatio*" (p. 79).

18. The true *visible* church, that is; the invisible church—those predestined for salvation—is known only to God and will become apparent to all only at the Last Judgment.

19. "Reasons to Be Considered, and Objections with Answers," *Winthrop Papers*, pp. 141–42.

20. "Modell of Christian Charity," *Winthrop Papers*, p. 283.

21. In going on to characterize the unity of the Christian community by saying "Wee must be knitt together in this worke as one man" (p. 294), Winthrop anticipates Hobbes's characterization, twenty-one years later, of the state as "one man of immense proportions," except that the glue holding together the limbs of the Hobbesian body politic, of course, is fear rather than love. Thomas Hobbes, *Leviathan*, p. 227.

22. The Lutheran and Calvinist stress on the *word* of God represents a critique of medieval ecclesiastical institutions, whose commitment to the priest's central role in transubstantiation and confession established him as the mediator between God and the individual. By arguing that the elevation

of the priest's status had no sound basis in Scripture, Luther and Calvin could mount an attack on those institutions; at the same time, it committed them to clarifying the hermeneutic bases of their own biblical readings. The result, in any case, is to elevate the *word* to a central status—to make the Bible itself, rather than the official commentary of the Roman Catholic Church, authoritative for all—and, at the same time, to energize the act of interpretation as guided by a scrupulous attention to the script-ure itself and the authentic divine intentions underlying it.

23. Martin Luther, *Martin Luther: Selections from His Writings*, p. 19.

24. The extent to which this "return" leads to a literalistic approach to biblical exegesis depends, at least in part, on the emphasis placed on the complicity of reason in the depravity of man's nature after the fall. On this topic, see Duncan B. Forrester, "Martin Luther and John Calvin." A glance at the complex biblical hermeneutics informing Roger Williams's revision of Winthrop's theocracy, however, is sufficient to put into question this essay's dismissive claim that the Puritans were crudely literalistic readers of the Bible. See Williams's *The Bloudy Tenent of Persecution*, which reinterprets the parable of the wheat and the tares in Matthew 13:24–31 and 37–43 to the effect that state power cannot be used to punish spiritual dissent in the way imagined by Winthrop.

25. John Calvin, *Institutes of the Christian Religion*, pp. 6–7.

26. This dynamic is analyzed in different ways by Perry Miller in *Errand into the Wilderness* and Bercovitch in *American Jeremiad*, which explore how anxiety about backsliding yields a public discourse of castigation of sins and of calls to rediscover the authentic impulses of pure faith; as Bercovitch emphasizes, the stress on the purity of the *impulse* can easily have the effect of de-emphasizing the need to preserve the identity of the institutions that are the vehicles for the impulses. Preserving the identity of America, according to Bercovitch's interpretation of the jeremiad, has much more to do with maintaining a perpetual vigilance and anxiousness with regard to America's mission than with the stability of its institutions.

27. See Bercovitch, *American Jeremiad*, chap. 1. Natural, social, and political disasters were to be taken as signs of divine punishment for the community's having strayed from the terms of the covenant, but they equally reinforced the community's sense of specialness by evidencing God's special concern in singling them out for punishment.

2. America's Critique of Reason

1. See Michel Foucault, *Discipline and Punish;* pp. 170–228; and *The History of Sexuality,* vol. 1, pt. 5; and Jürgen Habermas, *The Theory of Communicative Action,* vol. 2, chap. 8.

2. See Nancy Fraser, "Rethinking the Public Sphere," and Jürgen Habermas, "Further Reflections on the Public Sphere." See also his *The Structural Transformation of the Public Sphere.*

3. See Friedrich Nietzsche, "On the Uses and Disadvantages of History for Life," pp. 61–67. *Pace* the opinions of an impressive number of Nietzsche's readers, there are good reasons to conclude that Nietzsche himself understood "life" in something like this way, at least some of the time. See, e.g., Gilles Deleuze, *Nietzsche and Philosophy,* and Eric Blondel, *Nietzsche— The Body and Culture.*

4. See Peter Sloterdijk, *Critique of Cynical Reason,* p. 222 passim. The dangers of the institutionalization of unmasking go unrecognized because, in the words of Sloterdijk's reviewer Horst Hutter, the ideals governing Western theory "do not match the cynicism of events with a realism of concepts." Horst Hutter, "Cynicism," p. 72.

5. For a discussion of the parallels between Nietzsche on morality and Arendt on politics, see Dana R. Villa, "Beyond Good and Evil," pp. 281–87. Nietzsche's (and Nietzscheans') unavoidable reliance on a grammar of reference and objectivity, even as the content of his discourse questions the possibility of such a grammar, enables Habermas (and Habermasians) to accuse him of a self-defeating "performative contradiction." For a discussion of this issue, see Martin Jay, "The Debate over Performative Contradiction." For an elaborate articulation of Nietzsche's practice of performative contradiction, see Paul de Man, *Allegories of Reading,* chaps. 4–6.

6. See Alexis de Tocqueville, *Democracy in America,* vol. 2, p. 131. It should be noted that Tocqueville is not explicitly discussing the Constitution in this context. The relevant argument in Alexander Hamilton, James Madison, and John Jay, *The Federalist,* concerns controlling the "violence of faction"; see *Federalist* Nos. 9 and 10.

7. I refer here to the specifically Habermasian concept of the public sphere, which emphasizes formal and institutional conditions for guaranteeing that political consensus is reached through rational argument alone. Seyla Benhabib, Nancy Fraser, and Dana Villa have put forward other conceptions of the public sphere that stress instead crucial noncognitive or extrarational dimensions of action in public, such as the aesthetic and

agonistic formation, display, and exchange of difference, diversity, or individuation. I turn to that issue later in the chapter.

8. The phrase "rhetoric of frankness" is borrowed from Stanley Rosen, *Hermeneutics as Politics*, p. 27. I use it here, however, in a much more literal sense than Rosen does.

9. For an account of the goals of the Federalists, see Gordon Wood, *The Creation of the American Republic*. For discussions of Publius's political theory, see Douglass Adair, *Fame and the Founding Fathers*; David Epstein, *The Political Theory of "The Federalist"*; Forrest McDonald, *Novus Ordo Seclorum*; Garry Wills, *Explaining America*; and Sheldon S. Wolin, *The Presence of the Past*. On anti-Federalist political ideas, see Herbert J. Storing, Jr., "What the Anti-Federalists Were For," in Storing, ed., *The Complete Anti-Federalist* 1:1-76; and Jackson Turner Main, *The Anti-Federalists*. As Storing (among others) points out, the term *anti-Federalist* is misleading because opponents of the proposed Constitution saw it not as a proper confederation of states (such as the Articles of Confederation had established) but rather as the blueprint for a truly national government (1-3). The phrase "national government" was used in the secret discussions of the Virginia Plan at the Constitutional Convention, but language of that kind was deleted by the Committee on Style, which prepared the final version of the document. See Main, *The Anti-Federalists*, chap. 5, and Max Farrand, *The Framing of the Constitution of the United States*, p. 91.

10. On "candor," the conception of civilized debate shared by eighteenth-century Americans, see Albert Furtwangler, *The Authority of Publius*, pp. 1-5.

11. Storing, *Complete Anti-Federalist* 4:25.

12. On the anti-Federalists' view of the Framers as "naïve," see Wilson Carey McWilliams, *The Idea of Fraternity in America*, pp. 202-3.

13. On antifederalism as the "expression of diverse local narratives" embodying the values of equality, participation, particularity, and "place," see Wolin, *Presence of the Past*, pp. 82-99.

14. On the extremely bleak, "Calvinist" views about human nature held by the Founders, and the significance of these views for the fate of the idea of civic virtue in America, see John P. Diggins, *The Lost Soul of American Politics*, esp. chaps. 2 and 3.

15. According to Morton White, Publius's rejection of apodictic certainty in politics is grounded in Hume's distinction between demonstrative and experimental reasoning: demonstrative reasoning (as in mathematics) compares ideas only, whereas experimental reasoning studies facts given in

experience; political science is experimental, hence not apodictic. But that distinction is complicated in several ways. First, political science reasons in ways that can appear demonstrative, because it attempts to discover *general* facts (maxims or laws about how people behave politically) on the basis of the *particular* facts established by the historian. Because of its commitment to generality rather than particularity, political science risks looking more "demonstrative" than it actually is. Second, Publius was inconsistent: at times, he suggests that demonstrative truths *are* possible in politics. (White attributes such lapses to political pressure, which made persuasiveness more important than consistency. For a discussion that interprets this tension, not as an inconsistency but as an expression of the contrasting *political* values Hamilton and Madison attribute to their conceptions of a "science of politics," see Wolin, *Presence of the Past*, pp. 113–19.) Finally, there is a source of ambiguity in Publius's acceptance of the Lockean idea that demonstrative truths are possible in *morals*, if not in politics. See Morton White, *Philosophy, "The Federalist," and the Constitution*, chaps. 2 and 3.

16. For an interesting discussion of the impact of the Enlightenment in general, and Newtonian mechanics in particular, on eighteenth-century American political thought, see McWilliams, *Idea of Fraternity in America*, chaps. 8 and 9. Two works that do discuss Publius's reasoning and methodology are Furtwangler, *Authority of Publius*, whose work on the rhetoric of the *Federalist* essays goes far to establish the extent to which Publius innovates in the forms of political argumentation, and M. White, *Philosophy, "The Federalist," and the Constitution*, chaps. 3 and 4. On the political meanings of the conceptions of reason and science at work in *The Federalist*, see Wolin, *Presence of the Past*, pp. 111–19.

17. Isaac Newton, *Opticks*, p. 352.

18. Woodrow Wilson, *The New Freedom*, pp. 46–48; cited in Michael Kammen, *A Machine That Would Go of Itself*, p. 19. Wilson is critical of the "mechanistic" interpretation of the Constitution and suggests that we view it as a living organism that must grow and develop. Kammen (pp. 16–20) shows that, between the late 1880s and the 1920s, a shift takes place in constitutional metaphorics: instead of being figured as a "machine that would go of itself," the Constitution is increasingly modeled on the evolution of living things. Conservatives tended to adopt mechanical metaphors and to see the Constitutional "mechanism" as an architectural splendor reflecting the genius and inspiration of its designers; Progressives preferred developmental metaphors and lamented lifeless, creaking and groaning, worn-out constitutional machinery.

19. For a discussion of the Hobbesian assumptions at work in the *Federalist* explanation of the Constitution, see Martin Diamond, "Democracy and *The Federalist.*"

20. See Furtwangler, *Authority of Publius*, pp. 1–8.

21. Cf. McWilliams, *Idea of Fraternity in America*, pp. 187–92.

22. On the "disengaged subject of reason" as an essential constituent of modern identity, see Charles Taylor, *Sources of the Self*, pp. 143–58.

23. Storing, *Complete Anti-Federalist* 5:21.

24. See also "John DeWitt," in Ralph Ketcham, *The Anti-Federalist Papers and the Constitutional Debates*, p. 194, and "Brutus," in ibid., p. 270, for other examples of the call for dispassionate examination, leisurely deliberation, and candor.

25. Storing, *Complete Anti-Federalist* 5:81.

26. Ketcham, *Anti-Federalist Papers*, pp. 200–201.

27. Storing, *Complete Anti-Federalist* 5:24.

28. See also "Cato," in Ketcham, *Anti-Federalist Papers*, pp. 318–19.

29. On Publius's thematization of the national and state governments in terms of a distinction between reason and passion, see Sheldon S. Wolin, "Postmodern Politics and the Absence of Myth."

30. See Slavoj Zizek, *Looking Awry*, pp. 157–60, explicating and applying the work of Jacques Lacan. The Law's peculiar pleasure in arresting pleasure derives from the principle that the superego "feeds" off of the forces of the id, "which it suppresses and from which it acquires its obscene, malevolent, sneering quality—as if the enjoyment of which the subject is deprived were accumulated in the very place from which the superego's prohibition is enunciated. The linguistic distinction between the subject of the statement and the subject of the enunciation finds here its perfect use: behind the statement of the moral law that imposes on us the renunciation of enjoyment, there is always hidden an obscene subject of enunciation, amassing the enjoyment it steals" (p. 159).

31. In Lacanian theory, absolute alienation from the intersubjective symbolic order culminates in psychosis, a state in which the social mask becomes "nothing but" a mask. Cf. Zizek, *Looking Awry*, p. 74.

32. Hannah Arendt, *On Revolution*, p. 104—a startling interpretation of Machiavelli.

33. On Americans' romantic rejection of artificial masks in politics, see Michael Rogin, *Fathers and Children*, p. 258. For an exploration of how the American rejection of artificiality fuels the careful construction of fictions of "authentic," "sincere," or "truthful" public personalities, see Richard Slotkin, *The Fatal Environment*.

34. Furtwangler, *Authority of Publius*, p. 86.

35. See Arendt, *On Revolution*, pp. 131, 196–97. For discussions of the importance of public acclaim or reputation for many of the Framers of the Constitution, see Adair, *Fame and the Founding Fathers*, and Garry Wills, *Cincinnatus* pp. 134–38. For a detailed discussion of the theatrical sources (in Joseph Addison's play *Cato*) of George Washington's highly self-conscious public role playing, see McDonald, *Novus Ordo Seclorum*, pp. 193–99. McDonald emphasizes the centrality, for many of the Framers, of "outward esteem" as the surest ground of political virtue in a way compatible with Arendt's interpretation in *On Revolution*, although, unlike Arendt, he sees it as a modernizing departure from classical conceptions of republican virtue.

36. Jürgen Habermas, *The Philosophical Discourse of Modernity*, p. 314.

37. See Fraser, "Rethinking the Public Sphere." Cf. Seyla Benhabib, "Models of Public Space," and Dana R. Villa, "Postmodernism and the Public Sphere."

38. See Jean-François Lyotard, and Jean-Loup Thébaud, *Just Gaming*, pp. 44–59, 93–100.

39. Michel Foucault, "Politics and Ethics: An Interview," in *The Foucault Reader*, ed. Paul Rabinow, p. 379.

40. Michel Foucault, "Polemics, Politics, and Problematizations," in *Foucault Reader*, pp. 381–82. Even in the passage cited earlier from "Politics and Ethics," Foucault goes on to say that "the farthest I would go is to say that perhaps one must not be for consensuality, but one must be against non-consensuality," thus rejecting Habermas's insistence that communicative partners *necessarily* presuppose consensus or mutual understanding.

41. On his reservations about judgment, see Michael Foucault, "The Masked Philosopher," pp. 325–26.

42. On Nietzsche's legacy for Foucault, see Michael Mahon, *Foucault's Nietzschean Genealogy*.

43. Hannah Arendt, "Truth and Politics," in Arendt, *Between Past and Future*, p. 247.

44. Hannah Arendt, "What Is Freedom?," in Arendt, *Between Past and Future*, p. 153.

45. See Arendt, "Truth and Politics," p. 239.

46. See, e.g., *Federalist* No. 9.

47. On the ritual cycles of American politics as mimetic of natural cycles, see Wolin, "Postmodern Politics."

48. Margaret C. Jacob, *The Radical Enlightenment*, p. 80. The most trenchant advocate today of "pantheism" in philosophy and politics is Gilles

Deleuze; see esp. his *Expressionism in Philosophy*, chap. 2, and Gilles Deleuze and Claire Parnet, *Dialogues*, pp. 124–47.

49. See Lyotard and Thébaud, *Just Gaming*, pp. 42–43.

50. Jeffrey K. Tulis, *The Rhetorical Presidency*, pp. 41–42.

51. Lyotard and Thébaud, *Just Gaming*, pp. 16–17.

52. Max Weber, "Science as a Vocation," pp. 148–49.

53. Ketcham, *Anti-Federalist Papers*, p. 277.

54. Lyotard and Thébaud, *Just Gaming*, p. 9.

55. Richard Rorty, "Philosophy as Science, Metaphor, Politics," pp. 18–19.

56. Arendt, of course, in *On Revolution*, offers a meditation on the American founding which stresses just that aspect. For discussion, see below, Chapter 5.

57. In "Declarations of Independence," Bonnie Honig argues that a gesture toward a metaphysically reassuring constative is unavoidably tied to the performative speech acts through which revisions and contestations are borne and that the idea of a "pure" performative is self-defeating.

58. *Federalist*, p. 9.

59. Jacob Burckhardt, *The Civilization of the Renaissance in Italy*, p. 2.

60. On Hannah Arendt's concept of ideology, see her *The Origins of Totalitarianism*, pp. 468–74; on her related ideas about the coercive character of truth, see "Truth and Politics," pp. 239, 246.

3. Cold War Metaphysics

1. See Bruce Ackerman, *We the People*, p. 3.

2. See Jean-Jacques Lecercle, *Philosophy through the Looking Glass*, pp. 86–117.

3. Deleuze uses "simulacrum" to translate the Platonic "phantasm," the false image that Plato opposes to the good copy or "icon."

4. Gilles Deleuze, *Différence et répétition*, p. 92. Since *règne* can also mean "reign," the sentence speaks not only of celebrating appearances within a restricted sphere but more forcefully of affirming their priority or dominance vis-à-vis essences.

5. Maxwell Taylor, *Responsibility and Response*, p. 6.

6. William E. Connolly, *Identity\Difference*, p. 201. It should be noted that though Connolly describes this aspect of late-modern state identity, he is far from endorsing it.

7. Martin Heidegger, "Overcoming Metaphysics," p. 94.

8. Martin Heidegger, "The Question concerning Technology," pp. 3–35 in *Question concerning Technology and Other Essays;* "The Age of the World Picture," pp. 115–54 in ibid., and "Letter on Humanism."

9. *New York Times,* December 10, 1989, A1.

10. See also Louis Uchitelle, "Americans Are Just Simulating the Good Life," *San Francisco Chronicle,* June 18, 1991, C1. Uchitelle reports that with the decline of real income since 1973, Americans "pick their purchases to simulate affluence, not to achieve it," so that "purchasing a BMW or an Armani suit might be out of reach, but not other stylish clothing or elegant food, and that is where the money is going."

11. See Jean Starobinski, *Jean-Jacques Rousseau,* p. 5; Jean-Jacques Rousseau, *A Discourse on Inequality,* pp. 118–19.

12. Jean Baudrillard, *Simulations,* p. 12.

13. See Paul de Man, *The Resistance to Theory,* p. 11.

14. See, e.g., Hannah Arendt, *The Origins of Totalitarianism.*

15. Sigmund Freud, "Introductory Lectures on Psycho-Analysis: Part III," in *The Complete Psychological Works of Sigmund Freud* 16:398.

16. In Thomas H. Etzold and John Lewis Gaddis, eds., *Containment,* p. 60.

17. John Locke, *An Essay concerning Human Understanding,* bk. 2, chap. 21, sec. 8.

18. Thomas Hobbes, *Leviathan,* chap. 6.

19. In Etzold and Gaddis, *Containment,* pp. 404, 414–15.

20. See Max Weber, *The Protestant Ethic and the Spirit of Capitalism.*

21. See Miles Orvell, *The Real Thing.*

22. Herbert Marcuse, *One-Dimensional Man,* p. 75.

23. John McCain, "The Need for Strategy in the New Postwar Era," p. 43.

24. *New York Times,* November 30, 1989, A18.

25. Friedrich Nietzsche, *Untimely Meditations,* p. 79.

26. Umberto Eco, *A Theory of Semiotics,* pp. 6–7.

27. See Friedrich Nietzsche, "On Truth and Lies in a Nonmoral Sense," sec. 1.

28. Ronald Reagan, speech of January 20, 1983, quoted in Mark Green and Gail MacColl, *Reagan's Reign of Error,* p. 41.

29. Ronald Reagan, speech of July 1983, quoted in Roy Gutman, "America's Diplomatic Charade," p. 9. For a discussion of the substance of Reagan's claims, see that essay and Noam Chomsky, "Nicaragua," p. 352.

30. Oliver L. North, *Taking the Stand,* p. 352.

31. For documentation of North's views, see the section entitled "Rea-

sons for the Deception," in *Report of the Congressional Committees Investigating the Iran-Contra Affair,* p. 150 passim.

32. This document is not paginated, so further quotations from it are not referenced.

33. North, *Taking the Stand,* p. 525.

34. David M. Ricci, *The Tragedy of Political Science,* p. 157.

35. Along with Ricci's *Tragedy of Political Science,* other valuable studies of this subject include John G. Gunnell, *Between Philosophy and Politics* and *Political Theory.* For an early, trenchant, and prescient study, see Bernard Crick, *The American Science of Politics.*

36. *Army,* December 1966; *The Pentagon Papers, Senator Gravel Edition* 2:572–73. Cited in Noam Chomsky, "The Backroom Boys," in *For Reasons of State,* pp. 98, 90.

37. Ricci, *Tragedy of Political Science,* pp. 134–36.

38. David Easton, *A Systems Analysis of Political Life,* p. 367.

39. David Easton, *The Political System,* pp. 5–6.

40. Robert A. Dahl, "The Behavioral Approach in Political Science," p. 763.

41. Easton, *Political System,* p. 45.

42. David Easton, *A Framework for Political Analysis,* pp. 23–28, 47–49.

43. Easton, *Political System,* p. 125.

44. For details of the application of cybernetics to politics, see, along with Easton, *Framework for Political Analysis,* his *Systems Analysis of Political Life* and esp. Karl W. Deutsch, *The Nerves of Government.* For the general theory, see Norbert Wiener, *Cybernetics.* James Clerk Maxwell's essay "On Governors," in which he determines the conditions of stability and instability in speed governors, is regarded as having provided the foundations of control or feedback theory; see the entry for Maxwell by C. W. F. Everitt in the *Dictionary of Scientific Biography,* ed. Charles Coulston Gillespie, vol. 19. Georges Canguilhem, in *Ideology and Rationality in the History of the Life Sciences,* tells us that "the word *cybernetics* . . . [was] first coined by Ampère in 1834 to denote the science of government" (p. 82).

45. See also Canguilhem, *Ideology and Rationality,* pp. 82–83.

46. Hannah Arendt, *The Life of the Mind* 2:97–98.

47. G. W. F. Hegel, *Phenomenology of Spirit,* p. 127.

48. In Freud, *Complete Psychological Works* 21:149–57.

49. Primary documents for the containment and rollback doctrines can be found in Etzold and Gaddis, *Containment.*

50. Easton, *Systems Analysis of Political Life,* p. 475.

51. Dean Acheson, *Present at the Creation,* p. 209 (emphasis added).

52. M. Taylor, *Responsibility and Response*, p. 6.

53. Easton, *Systems Analysis of Political Life*, p. 486.

54. Richard J. Barnet, *The Roots of War*, p. 109.

55. "Secord's Last Day: Questioners Issue Challenges and Defenses," *New York Times*, May 9, 1987.

56. "The Philippines: Another Iran?" *Newsweek*, November 4, 1985. The assessment (emphasis added) is attributed to former U.S. ambassador William Sullivan.

57. Heidegger, "Age of the World Picture," p. 153.

58. Easton, *Framework for Political Analysis*, pp. 134–35.

4. Fiction and the Dilemma of Postmodern Politics

1. For a critical exploration of Habermas's distinction between the action-coordinating and world-disclosive aspects of language which links it to two contrasting ethicopolitical attitudes, "responsibility to act" and "responsibility to otherness," see Stephen K. White, *Political Theory and Postmodernism*, pp. 23–30 passim.

2. See Jürgen Habermas, *The Philosophical Discourse of Modernity*, pp. 194–95, where he follows arguments offered by J. L. Austin and John Searle to the effect that a fictional promise, for example, is conceivable only as a nonserious instance of a real one.

3. See Jonathan Culler's discussion in his *On Deconstruction*, pp. 121–27, Habermas's discussion of Culler and Derrida in *Philosophical Discourse of Modernity*, pp. 185–210, and the debate between Jacques Derrida and John Searle in Searle, "Reiterating the Differences," and Derrida, "Limited, Inc."

4. Friedrich Nietzsche, "On Truth and Lies in a Nonmoral Sense," p. 84.

5. See also Jürgen Habermas, "Philosophy as Stand-In and Interpreter."

6. In *Philosophical Discourse of Modernity*, Habermas presents this view (that the logic of an argument is always undercut by the rhetoric of the text or discourse in which it is made) as Derrida's. That is probably an oversimplification. For discussion, see White, *Political Theory and Postmodernism*, pp. 13–17.

7. See Charles Russell, "Individual Voice in the Collective Discourse."

8. Gregory Corso and Allen Ginsberg, "Interview with William Burroughs," cited in Michael Skau, "The Central Verbal System," p. 402.

9. The idea of the "Reality Studio" is sketched in Burroughs's novels *The Soft Machine*, *The Ticket That Exploded*, and *The Nova Express*.

10. William S. Burroughs, *Junky*, p. 152.

11. William S. Burroughs, *The Ticket That Exploded*, p. 145.

12. Quoted in Eric Mottram, *William S. Burroughs: The Algebra of Need*, p. 147. That Burroughs's work can nevertheless be interpreted as an anticipation of Derridean and other "postmodern" themes is argued by Robin Lydenberg, *Word Cultures*.

13. William S. Burroughs, in Sinclaire Beiles, *Minutes to Go*, p. 44.

14. This move is evident in such works as *The Wild Boys* and *Port of Saints* and is consolidated in the trilogy of the 1980s: *Cities of the Red Night*, *The Place of Dead Roads*, and *The Western Lands*.

15. See Jennie Skerl, *William S. Burroughs*, and Lydenberg, *Word Cultures*.

16. Donald Palumbo, in "William Burroughs' Quarter of Science Fiction Novels as Dystopian Satire," notes that despite Burroughs's violations of narrative conventions, something like a plot can be reconstructed. He goes too far, however, when he says that "each volume contributes to a single plot" (p. 322). There is no "single" plot but, rather, a recourse to what, in the context of the novels, become signifiers of a master plot, for purposes of *optional* conceptual orientation. Plot, one might say, is reduced to the status of one more character or event in the text, as opposed to a logical structure that "contains" the events and characters in the novel as a whole. For this reason, I think Palumbo is wrong to compare Burroughs's work to "the spots and blobs of paint in an impressionist painting [which] form a coherent image when viewed from a sufficient distance" (pp. 322–23). The parts of a Burroughs novel do not take their shape from the whole; the point is rather that the very idea of a larger logic becomes a trope introduced at various moments to produce an effect.

Skerl's observations in her *William S. Burroughs* support this point. As she points out, Burroughs's narrative style is adapted from popular literary genres (such as science fiction and adventure), and it is the very flatness of the plots and characters that prompts the reader to see each as merely a transitory form, or momentary arrest, in a larger process of flux and transformation (see pp. 81–82). Finally, Lydenberg, in *Word Cultures*, emphasizes the changed status of conventional narrative in Burroughs with her argument that his writing explores the same strategies as Derrida's deconstruction, "tracking binary opposition to its origin in language, reversing its implied hierarchies, and finally disrupting its dual structure with an unassimilable third element" (pp. 122–23). Having revealed narrative as arbitrary by deconstructing it, Lydenberg argues, Burroughs can use it without a sense of coercion. In these ways, Burroughs preserves the advantages of conventional narrative while avoiding its ideological traps.

17. William S. Burroughs, *Nova Express*, p. 40.

18. William S. Burroughs, *APO-33 Bulletin*, pp. 16–17. Quoted in Skau, "Central Verbal System," p. 409.

19. Russell, "Individual Voice," p. 31.

20. Burroughs, *Nova Express*, p. 15.

21. Cf. Skerl, *William S. Burroughs*, pp. 91–92.

22. See Ted Morgan, *Literary Outlaw*.

23. "Interview with William S. Burroughs," in William S. Burroughs and Brion Gysin, *The Third Mind*, pp. 5–6.

24. Friedrich Nietzsche, *The Will to Power*, sec. 860.

25. William S. Burroughs, *The Western Lands*, p. 113. "OGU" is Burroughs's acronym for "One God Universe."

26. The ellipses are Burroughs's. See also p. 199.

27. Gilles Deleuze, *Nietzsche and Philosophy*, pp. 26–27.

28. Burroughs, *Western Lands*, p. 113.

29. Deleuze, *Nietzsche and Philosophy*, p. 27.

30. Burroughs, *Western Lands*, p. 114.

31. See William E. Connolly, *Identity\Difference*, and Michael Rogin, *"Ronald Reagan" the Movie, and Other Episodes in American Political Demonology*.

32. David Lehman, "Introduction," in David Lehman and Charles Berger, eds., *James Merrill*, p. 17.

33. An exception is Clara Clairborne Park, "Where 'The Waste Land' Ends," pp. 532–35.

34. Helen Vendler, *Part of Nature, Part of Us*, p. 229.

35. Judith Moffett, *James Merrill*, p. 188.

36. David Bromwich, "Answer, Heavenly Muse, Yes or No," pp. 459–60; Robert von Hallberg, "James Merrill," p. 571.

37. Vendler, *Part of Nature*, p. 214.

38. Charles Berger, *"Mirabell,"* p. 182.

39. James Merrill, *The Changing Light at Sandover*, p. 147.

40. Stanley Cavell, "The Thought of Movies," in *Themes Out of School*, p. 8, emphasis added.

41. In James Merrill, *From the First Nine*, pp. 253–57.

42. I turn to the question of textual practice in Chapter 5.

43. Merrill, *Changing Light at Sandover*, p. 446.

44. Jacques Derrida, *La dissemination*, p. 65.

45. Hannah Arendt, *Between Past and Future*, pp. 154–55.

46. In this context, Arendt's comments in her speech at the public memorial service for Karl Jaspers are striking: "What is at once the most fleeting and at the same time the greatest thing about him—the spoken

word and the gesture unique to him—those things die with him, and they put a demand on us to remember him. That remembering takes place in communication with the dead person, and from that arises talk about him, which then resounds in the world again. Communication with the dead—that has to be learned" (Hannah Arendt and Karl Jaspers, *Correspondence, 1926–1969*, p. 686).

47. Friedrich Nietzsche, *Beyond Good and Evil*, sec. 242, and *The Will to Power*, sec. 71.

48. Merrill, *Changing Light at Sandover*, p. 113.

49. Nietzsche, *Will to Power*, sec. 275.

50. Nietzsche, *Beyond Good and Evil*, sec. 224.

51. See Gilles Deleuze, *Nietzsche and Philosophy*, pp. 47–77 and *Différence et répétition*, pp. 12–20.

52. See Sheldon S. Wolin, "Postmodern Politics and the Absence of Myth," p. 218.

53. Martin Heidegger, *Being and Time*, pp. 60, 62.

54. Philip Kuberski, "The Metaphysics of Postmodern Death," p. 251.

55. See Michael Roth, "The Ironist's Cage."

5. Practicing Political Theory Otherwise

1. See Gilles Deleuze, *Proust et les signes*, p. 127.

2. See Derrida, "*Ousia* and *Gramme*."

3. Hannah Arendt, "What Is Freedom?" in *Between Past and Future*, pp. 143–71; *The Human Condition*, chap. 2; and *On Revolution*, chap. 2.

4. On the development of the modern concept of fiction, see Ian Haywood, *The Making of History;* Vivienne Mylne, *The Eighteenth-Century French Novel;* English Showalter, *The Evolution of the French Novel, 1641–1782;* and Philip Stewart, *Imitation and Illusion in the French Memoir-Novel, 1700–1750.* I am indebted to John Dolan for alerting me to these sources.

5. M. M. Bakhtin, *The Dialogic Imagination*, p. 33.

6. See Judith Moffett, *James Merrill*, pp. 5–19, 208–9; and Ross Labrie, *James Merrill*, pp. 7–9.

7. Anonymous, "Interview with James Merrill," quoted in Labrie, *James Merrill*, p. 11.

8. Ibid., pp. 11–12.

9. See Theodor W. Adorno, *Negative Dialectics*, pp. 11–12.

10. On Arendt's complex negotiation of Platonic and Nietzschean legacies, see Dana R. Villa, "Beyond Good and Evil."

11. Plato himself, of course, wrote dramatic narratives rather than deductive treatises, perhaps for the very reason that the pernicious intellectual effects of writing would at least be mitigated by a form capable of accommodating and even foregrounding intellectual aporia and inconclusiveness.

12. See Ronald Beiner, *What's the Matter with Liberalism?*, pp. 1–14. Beiner also mentions as calling for or practicing political theory as storytelling Alasdair MacIntyre, Michael Oakeshott, and Judith Shklar and offers a lucid and economical account of the entwinement in literary fiction of imagination and cognition that chimes with my reading of the implications of Merrill's poem in Chapter 4, although Beiner seems to assume that for literature to be politically and morally significant it must therefore make "normative claims," an assertion I would contest.

13. That the political is important to Arendt primarily as a source of existential meaningfulness is stressed by George Kateb in chap. 1 of his *Hannah Arendt*.

14. Kateb, *Hannah Arendt*, p. 15.

15. Hannah Arendt, *Men in Dark Times*, p. 148.

16. Arendt, *Human Condition*, p. 179, and "Truth and Politics," in *Between Past and Future*, p. 264.

17. Hannah Arendt, *The Life of the Mind*, 2:95; see also 2:3–5.

18. Hannah Arendt, "Walter Benjamin, 1892–1940," in *Men in Dark Times*, p. 204.

19. Hannah Arendt, *The Origins of Totalitarianism*, chap. 13, and *On Revolution*, p. 212.

20. Arendt, *Men in Dark Times*, p. 119.

21. Arendt, *Men in Dark Times*, p. 6, and *Between Past and Future*, p. 234.

22. Hannah Arendt, *Crises of the Republic*, p. 203, and *Between Past and Future*, p. 263. Cf. *Between Past and Future*, p. 247, where Arendt writes that we believe in equality not because it is true but because "freedom is possible only among equals, and we believe that the joys and gratifications of free company are to be preferred to the doubtful pleasures of holding dominion."

23. Arendt, *Men in Dark Times*, p. 106. The vulnerability of the political actor introduces a crucial element of risk into political action, an element absent, of course, from the literary.

24. For Arendt's discussion of the founding of the American Republic, see *On Revolution*, chap. 5.

25. See Arendt, *Life of the Mind* 2:217: "I am quite aware that the argument . . . seems to tell us no more than that we are *doomed* to be free by virtue of being born, no matter whether we like freedom or abhor its arbi-

218 Notes to Pages 194–99

trariness. . . . This impasse, if such it is, cannot be opened or solved except by an appeal to another mental faculty, no less mysterious than the faculty of beginning, the faculty of Judgment, an analysis of which at least may tell us what is involved in our pleasures and displeasures."

26. See Shoshana Felman and Dori Laub, *Testimony*.

27. Felman is paraphrasing the definition of narrative formulated by Barbara Herrnstein Smith in "Narrative Versions, Narrative Theories," in *On Narrative*, ed. W. J. T. Mitchell (Chicago: University of Chicago Press, 1981), pp. 228–41.

28. Felman was referring here to Freud's discovery of the unconscious. She also finds narrative acknowledgements of this structure of displacement in Mallarmé, Kafka, Celan, Camus, and others.

29. Arendt, transcript of remarks to the American Society for Christian Ethics, quoted in Elisabeth Young-Bruehl, *Hannah Arendt*, pp. 452–53.

30. Felman and Laub, *Testimony*, p. 15.

31. See Arendt, *Origins of Totalitarianism*, chap. 13, and "Isak Dinesen, 1885–1963," in *Men in Dark Times*.

32. Arendt, *Men in Dark Times*, p. 109.

33. Of course that is not Arendt's only or last word on America, as her misgivings about representative government indicate.

Bibliography

Acheson, Dean. *Present at the Creation: My Years at the State Department.* New York: New American Library, 1970.

Ackerman, Bruce. *We the People: Foundations.* Cambridge: Harvard University Press, 1991.

Adair, Douglass. *Fame and the Founding Fathers: Essays by Douglass Adair.* Ed. Trevor Colbourn. New York: Norton, 1974.

Adorno, Theodor W. *Negative Dialectics.* Trans. A. B. Ashton. New York: Seabury, 1973.

Ampère, André-Marie. *Essai sur la philosophie des sciences. ou, Exposition analytique d'une classification naturelle de toutes les connaissances humaines.* 2 vols. 1834–1843. Paris: Mallet-Bachelier, 1856.

Arendt, Hannah. *Between Past and Future: Eight Exercises in Political Thought.* Enlarged ed. 1968. New York: Viking Penguin, 1987.

——. *Crises of the Republic.* New York: Harcourt Brace Jovanovich, 1969.

——. *The Human Condition.* Chicago: University of Chicago Press, 1958.

——. *The Life of the Mind. Vol. 1, Thinking. Vol. 2, Willing.* New York: Harcourt Brace Jovanovich, 1977.

——. *Men in Dark Times.* New York: Harcourt Brace Jovanovich, 1968.

——. *On Revolution.* New York: Viking, 1963.

——. *The Origins of Totalitarianism.* 1951; rev. ed. 1958. New York: Harcourt Brace Jovanovich, 1979.

Arendt, Hannah, and Karl Jaspers. *Correspondence, 1926–1969.* Ed. Lotte Kohler and Hans Saner. Trans. Robert Kimber and Rita Kimber. San Diego: Harcourt Brace Jovanovich, 1992.

Bailyn, Bernard. *The Ideological Origins of the American Revolution.* Cambridge: Harvard University Press, 1967.

——. *The Origins of American Politics.* New York: Random House, Vintage, 1967.

Bakhtin, M. M. *The Dialogic Imagination*. Ed. Michael Holquist. Trans. Caryl Emerson and Michael Holquist. Austin: University of Texas Press, 1981.

Barnet, Richard J. *The Roots of War: The Men and Institutions behind U.S. Foreign Policy*. Baltimore: Penguin Books, 1972.

Baudrillard, Jean. *Fatal Strategies*. Ed. Jim Fleming. Trans. Philip Beitchman and W. G. J. Niesluchowski. New York: Semiotext(e) and Pluto, 1990.

———. *Simulacres et simulation*. Paris: Galilée, 1981. *Simulations*. Partial trans. Paul Foss, Paul Patton, and Philip Beitchman. New York: Semiotext(e), 1983.

Beiles, Sinclaire, et al. *Minutes to Go*. Paris: Two Cities Editions, 1960.

Beiner, Ronald. *What's the Matter with Liberalism?* Berkeley and Los Angeles: University of California Press, 1992.

Benhabib, Seyla. "Models of Public Space: Hannah Arendt, the Liberal Tradition, and Jürgen Habermas." In Calhoun, pp. 73–98.

Bercovitch, Sacvan. *The American Jeremiad*. Madison: University of Wisconsin Press, 1978.

Berger, Charles. "*Mirabell:* Conservative Epic." In *James Merrill*, ed. Harold Bloom, pp. 181–88. New York: Chelsea House, 1985.

Bliss, Michael. "The Orchestration of Chaos: Verbal Technique in William Burroughs' *Naked Lunch*." *Enclitic* 1 (1977): 59–69.

Blondel, Eric. *Nietzsche—The Body and Culture: Philosophy as a Philological Genealogy*. Trans. Seán Hand. Stanford: Stanford University Press, 1991.

Bromwich, David. "Answer, Heavenly Muse, Yes or No." *Hudson Review* 39 (1979): 455–60.

Burckhardt, Jacob. *The Civilization of the Renaissance in Italy*. Trans. S. G. C. Middlemore. Oxford: Phaidon, 1945.

Burroughs, William S. *APO-33 Bulletin: A Metabolic Regulator*. San Francisco: Beach Books, 1966.

———. *Cities of the Red Night*. New York: Holt, Rinehart and Winston, 1981.

———. *The Job: Interviews with William S. Burroughs*. Rev. and enl. ed. New York: Grove, 1974.

———. *Junky*. 1953. New York: Penguin, 1977.

———. *The Nova Express*. New York: Grove, 1964.

———. *The Place of Dead Roads*. New York: Holt, Rinehart and Winston, 1983.

———. *Port of Saints*. Berkeley: Blue Wind, 1980.

———. *The Soft Machine*. 1961. New York: Grove, 1966.

———. *The Ticket That Exploded*. 1962. New York: Grove, 1968.

———. *The Western Lands*. New York: Viking Penguin, 1987.

———. *The Wild Boys*. New York: Grove, 1971.

Burroughs, William S., and Brion Gysin. *The Third Mind*. New York: Viking, 1978.

Calhoun, Craig, ed. *Habermas and the Public Sphere*. Cambridge: MIT Press, 1992.

Calvin, John. *Institutes of the Christian Religion*. 1556–1559. Trans. Henry Beveridge. London: Clarke, 1949.

Campbell, David. *Writing Security: United States Foreign Policy and the Politics of Identity*. Minneapolis: University of Minnesota Press, 1992.

Canguilhem, Georges. *Ideology and Rationality in the History of the Life Sciences*. Trans. Arthur Goldhammer. Cambridge: MIT Press, 1988.

——. *The Normal and the Pathological*. Trans. Carolyn R. Fawcett with Robert S. Cohen. New York: Zone Books, 1989.

Cannon, Walter B. *The Wisdom of the Body*. 1932; rev. and enlarged ed., 1939. New York: Norton, 1963.

Cavell, Stanley. *Themes Out of School*. Berkeley: North Point, 1989.

Chomsky, Noam. *For Reasons of State*. New York: Random House, Vintage, 1973.

——. "Nicaragua." In *The Chomsky Reader*, ed. James Peck, pp. 351–61. New York: Pantheon, 1987.

Connolly, William E. *Identity\Difference: Democratic Negotiations of Political Paradox*. Ithaca: Cornell University Press, 1991.

Crick, Bernard. *The American Science of Politics: Its Origins and Conditions*. Berkeley and Los Angeles: University of California Press, 1967.

Culler, Jonathan. *On Deconstruction: Theory and Criticism after Structuralism*. Ithaca, N.Y.: Cornell University Press, 1982.

Dahl, Robert A. "The Behavioral Approach in Political Science: Epitaph for a Monument to a Successful Protest." *American Political Science Review* 55:763–72.

Deleuze, Gilles. *Différence et répétition*. Paris: Presses Universitaires de France, 1968.

——. *Expressionism in Philosophy: Spinoza*. Trans. Martin Joughin. New York: Zone Books, 1990.

——. *Nietzsche and Philosophy*. Trans. Hugh Tomlinson. New York: Columbia University Press, 1983.

——. *Proust et les signes*. Paris: Presses Universitaires de France, 1964.

Deleuze, Gilles, and Claire Parnet. *Dialogues*. Trans. Hugh Tomlinson and Barbara Habberjam. New York: Columbia University Press, 1987.

De Man, Paul. *Allegories of Reading: Figural Language in Rousseau, Nietzsche, Rilke, and Proust*. New Haven: Yale University Press, 1979.

——. *The Resistance to Theory*. Minneapolis: University of Minnesota Press, 1986.

Derrida, Jacques. "Differance." In Jacques Derrida, *Speech and Phenomena. And Other Essays on Husserl's Theory of Signs*, trans. David B. Allison, pp. 129–60. Evanston, Ill.: Northwestern University Press, 1973.

——. *La dissemination*. Paris: Seuil, 1972.

——. "Limited Inc abc." *Glyph* 2 (1977): 162–254.

——. *Of Grammatology*. Trans. Gayatri Chakravorty Spivak. Baltimore: Johns Hopkins University Press, 1976.

——. "*Ousia* and *Gramme:* Note on a Note from *Being and Time*." In Jacques Derrida, *Margins of Philosophy*, trans. Alan Bass, pp. 29–67. Chicago: University of Chicago Press, 1982.

Deutsch, Karl W. *The Nerves of Government: Models of Political Communication and Control*. New York: Free Press, 1963.

Diamond, Martin. "Democracy and *The Federalist:* A Reconsideration of the Framer's Intent." *American Political Science Review* 53 (1959): 52–68.

Diggins, John P. *The Lost Soul of American Politics: Virtue, Self-Interest, and the Foundations of Liberalism*. 1984. Chicago: University of Chicago Press, 1986.

Easton, David. *A Framework for Political Analysis*. Englewood Cliffs, N.J.: Prentice-Hall, 1965.

——. *The Political System: An Inquiry into the State of Political Science*. New York: Knopf, 1953.

——. *A Systems Analysis of Political Life*. New York: Wiley, 1965.

Eco, Umberto. *A Theory of Semiotics*. Bloomington: Indiana University Press, 1976.

Epstein, David E. *The Political Theory of "The Federalist."* Chicago: University of Chicago Press, 1984.

Etzold, Thomas H., and John Lewis Gaddis. *Containment: Documents on American Policy and Strategy, 1945–1950*. New York: Columbia University Press, 1978.

Farrand, Max. *The Framing of the Constitution of the United States*. 1913. New Haven: Yale University Press, 1936.

Felman, Shoshana, and Dori Laub. *Testimony: Crises of Witnessing in Literature, Psychoanalysis, and History*. New York: Routledge, 1992.

Feynman, Richard P. *QED: The Strange Theory of Light and Matter*. Princeton: Princeton University Press, 1985.

Flynn, Bernard. *Political Philosophy at the Closure of Metaphysics*. Atlantic Highlands, N.J.: Humanities Press International, 1992.

Forrester, Duncan B. "Martin Luther and John Calvin." In *History of Political Philosophy*, ed. Leo Strauss and Joseph Cropsey, pp. 318–55. Chicago: University of Chicago Press, 1987.

Foucault, Michel. *Discipline and Punish: The Birth of the Prison* 1977. Trans. Alan Sheridan. New York: Random House, Vintage, 1979.

——. *The Foucault Reader*. Paul Rabinow. New York: Pantheon, 1984.

——. *The History of Sexuality*. Volume 1: *An Introduction*. Trans. Robert Hurley. New York: Pantheon, 1978.

———. "The Masked Philosopher." In *Michel Foucault: Politics, Philosophy, Culture: Interviews and Other Writings, 1977–1984,* ed. Lawrence D. Kritzman, trans. Alan Sheridan and et al., pp. 323–30. New York: Routledge, Chapman and Hall 1988.

———. "Nietzsche, Genealogy, History." In *Language, Counter-Memory, Practice: Selected Essays and Interviews by Michel Foucault,* ed. Donald F. Bouchard, trans. Donald F. Bouchard and Sherry Simon, pp. 139–64. Ithaca: Cornell University Press, 1977.

Fraser, Nancy. "Rethinking the Public Sphere: A Contribution to the Critique of Actually Existing Democracy." In Calhoun, pp. 109–42.

Freud, Sigmund. *The Complete Psychological Works of Sigmund Freud.* Ed. and trans. James Strachey. London: Hogarth, 1974.

Furtwangler, Albert. *The Authority of Publius: A Reading of the Federalist Papers.* Ithaca: Cornell University Press, 1984.

Green, Mark, and Gail MacColl. *Reagan's Reign of Error.* New York: Pantheon, 1987.

Gunnell, John G. *Between Philosophy and Politics: The Alienation of Political Theory.* Amherst: University of Massachusetts Press, 1986.

———. *Political Theory: Tradition and Interpretation.* Cambridge: Little, Brown, 1979.

Gutman, Roy. "America's Diplomatic Charade." *Foreign Policy* (Fall 1984).

Habermas, Jürgen. "Further Reflections on the Public Sphere." In Calhoun, pp. 421–61.

———. *The Philosophical Discourse of Modernity. Twelve Lectures.* Trans. Frederick Lawrence. Cambridge: MIT Press, 1987.

———. "Philosophy as Stand-In and Interpreter." In Jürgen Habermas, *Moral Consciousness and Communicative Action,* trans. Christian Lenhardt and Shierry Weber Nicholsen, pp. 1–20. Cambridge: MIT Press, 1990.

———. *The Structural Transformation of the Public Sphere: An Inquiry into a Category of Bourgeois Society.* Trans. Thomas Burger with Frederick Lawrence. Cambridge: MIT Press, 1989.

———. *The Theory of Communicative Action.* Vol. 2, *Lifeworld and System: A Critique of Functionalist Reason.* Trans. Thomas McCarthy. Boston: Beacon, 1987.

Hallberg, Robert von. "James Merrill: 'Revealing by Obscuring.' " *Contemporary Literature* 21(4) (1980): 549–17.

Hamilton, Alexander, James Madison, and John Jay. *The Federalist.* Ed. Jacob E. Cooke. Middletown, Conn.: Wesleyan University Press, 1961.

Haywood, Ian. *The Making of History.* Rutherford, N.J.: Fairleigh Dickinson University Press, 1986.

Hegel, G. W. F. *Phenomenology of Spirit.* Trans. A. V. Miller. Oxford: Oxford University Press, 1977.

Heidegger, Martin. *Being and Time.* Trans. John Macquarrie and Edward Robinson. New York: Harper and Row, 1962.

——. "Letter on Humanism." In Martin Heidegger, *Basic Writings*, rev. and expanded ed., ed. David Ferrell Krell, pp. 213–65. New York: Harper and Row, Harper-Collins, 1993.

——. *Nietzsche.* Trans. David Farrell Krell. San Francisco: HarperCollins, 1991.

——. "Overcoming Metaphysics." In Martin Heidegger, *The End of Philosophy*, trans. Joan Stambaugh, pp. 84–110. New York: Harper and Row, 1973.

——. *The Question concerning Technology and Other Essays.* Trans. William Lovitt. New York: Harper and Row, 1977.

——. *What Is Called Thinking?* Trans. J. Glenn Gray. New York: Harper and Row, 1968.

Heims, Steve J. *John von Neumann and Norbert Wiener: From Mathematics to the Technologies of Life and Death.* 1980. Cambridge: MIT Press, 1987.

Hobbes, Thomas. *Leviathan: or, The Matter, Forme, and Power of a Commonwealth Ecclesiasticall and Civil.* 1651. Ed. C. B. Macpherson. Harmondsworth: Penguin, 1968.

Hoffmann, E. T. A. "The Sandman." In *Tales of E.T.A. Hoffmann.* Ed. Leonard J. Kent and Elizabeth C. Knight. Chicago: University of Chicago Press, 1972.

Honig, Bonnie. "Declarations of Independence: Arendt and Derrida on Founding a Republic." In *Rhetorical Republic: Governing Representations of American Politics*, ed. Frederick M. Dolan and Thomas L. Dumm, pp. 201–25. Amherst: University of Massachusetts Press, 1993.

Horkheimer, Max, and Theodor W. Adorno. *Dialectic of Enlightenment.* 1972. Trans. John Cumming. New York: Continuum, 1991.

Hutter, Horst. "Cynicism." *Canadian Journal of Political and Social Theory* 8 (Spring 1984): 207–19.

Jacob, Margaret C. *The Radical Enlightenment: Pantheists, Freemasons, and Republicans.* London: Allen and Unwin, 1981.

Jay, Martin. "The Debate over Performative Contradiction: Habermas versus the Poststructuralists." In *Philosophical Interventions in the Unfinished Project of Enlightenment*, ed. Axel Honneth, Thomas McCarthy, Claus Offe, and Albrecht Wellmar, pp. 261–79. Cambridge: MIT Press, 1992.

Jensen, Merrill. *The Making of the American Constitution.* Princeton: Van Nostrand, 1964.

Kammen, Michael. *A Machine That Would Go of Itself: The Constitution in American Culture.* 1986. New York: Random House, Vintage, 1987.

Kant, Immanuel. *Critique of Judgment.* Trans. James Creed Meredith. Oxford: Oxford University Press, Clarendon, 1989.

Kateb, George. *Hannah Arendt: Politics, Conscience, Evil.* Totowa, N.J.: Rowman and Allanheld, 1984.

Ketcham, Ralph, ed. *The Anti-Federalist Papers and the Constitutional Debates.* New York: New American Library, Mentor, 1986.

Kuberski, Philip. "The Metaphysics of Postmodern Death." *English Literary History* 56(1) (Spring 1989): 229–54.

Kuhn, Thomas S. *The Structure of Scientific Revolutions.* 2d ed., enl. Chicago: University of Chicago Press, 1970.

Labrie, Ross. *James Merrill.* Boston: Twayne, 1982.

Lacoue-Labarthe, Philippe. *Heidegger, Art, and Politics.* Trans. Chris Turner. Oxford: Blackwell, 1990.

Le Carré, John. *The Looking Glass War.* 1965. New York: Ballantine, 1992.

Lecercle, Jean-Jacques. *Philosophy through the Looking Glass: Language, Nonsense, Desire.* La Salle, Ill.: Open Court, 1985.

Lee, A. Robert. "William Burroughs and the Sexuality of Power." *Twentieth Century Studies* 2 (1969): 74–88.

Lehman, David, and Charles Berger, eds. *James Merrill: Essays in Criticism.* Ithaca: Cornell University Press, 1983.

Lemaire, Gérard-Georges, and Brion Gysin. "23 Stitches Taken by Gérard-Georges Lamaire and 2 Points of Order by Brion Gysin." In Burroughs and Gysin, *Third Mind*, pp. 9–24.

Locke, John. 1689. *An Essay concerning Human Understanding.* London: Dent, 1961.

Lodge, David. *The Novelist at the Crossroads and Other Essays on Fiction and Criticism.* London: Routledge and Kegan Paul, 1971.

Luther, Martin. *Martin Luther: Selections from His Writings.* Ed. John Dillenberger. Garden City, N.Y.: Doubleday, 1961.

Lydenberg, Robin. *Word Cultures: Radical Theory and Practice in William S. Burroughs' Fiction.* Champaign: University of Illinois Press, 1987.

Lyotard, Jean-François. *Heidegger and "the Jews."* Trans. Andreas Michel and Mark S. Roberts. Minneapolis: University of Minnesota Press, 1990.

Lyotard, Jean-François, and Jean-Loup Thébaud. *Just Gaming.* Trans. Wlad Godzich. Minneapolis: University of Minnesota Press, 1985.

McCain, John. "The Need for Strategy in the New Postwar Era." *Armed Forces Journal International*, January 1990, pp. 43–47.

McDonald, Forrest. *Novus Ordo Seclorum: The Intellectual Origins of the American Constitution.* Lawrence: University Press of Kansas, 1985.

McHale, Brian. *Postmodernist Fiction.* New York: Methuen, 1987.

McWilliams, Wilson Carey. *The Idea of Fraternity in America.* Berkeley and Los Angeles: University of California Press, 1973.

Mahon, Michael. *Foucault's Nietzschean Genealogy: Truth, Power, and the Subject.* Albany: State University of New York Press, 1992.

Mailer, Norman. *Harlot's Ghost.* New York: Random House, 1991.

Main, Jackson Turner. *The Anti-Federalists: Critics of the Constitution, 1781–1788.* Chapel Hill: University of North Carolina Press, 1980.

Malmgren, Darryl Carl. *Fictional Space in the Modernist and Postmodernist Novel.* London: Associated University Presses, 1985.

Marcuse, Herbert. *One-Dimensional Man: Studies in the Ideology of Advanced Industrial Societies.* Boston: Beacon, 1964.

Merrill, James. *The Changing Light at Sandover.* New York: Atheneum, 1984.

——. *From the First Nine: Poems, 1946–1976.* New York: Atheneum, 1982.

Miller, Perry. *Errand into the Wilderness.* Cambridge: Harvard University Press, 1956.

Miller, Perry, and Thomas H. Johnson. *The Puritans.* Rev. ed. New York: Harper and Row, 1963.

Moffett, Judith. *James Merrill: An Introduction to the Poetry.* New York: Columbia University Press, 1984.

Morgan, Edmund S. "Government by Fiction: The Idea of Representation." *Yale Review* 72 (1983): 321–39.

Morgan, Ted. *Literary Outlaw: The Life and Times of William S. Burroughs.* New York: Henry Holt, 1988.

Mottram, Eric. *William S. Burroughs: The Algebra of Need.* London: Boyars, 1977.

Mylne, Vivienne. *The Eighteenth-Century French Novel.* Cambridge: Cambridge University Press, 1981.

Nancy, Jean-Luc. *The Inoperative Community.* Trans. Peter Connor et al. Minneapolis: University of Minnesota Press, 1991.

Nelson, Carry. *The Incarnate Word: Literature as Verbal Space.* Urbana: University of Illinois Press, 1973.

Newton, Isaac. *Opticks; or, a treatise of the reflections, refractions, inflections, and colours of light.* 1718. New York: Dover, 1952.

Nietzsche, Friedrich. *Beyond Good and Evil.* Trans. Walter Kaufmann. New York: Random House, Vintage, 1989.

——. *The Gay Science.* Trans. Walter Kaufmann. New York: Random House, Vintage, 1974.

——. *On the Genealogy of Morals.* Trans. Walter Kaufmann and R. J. Hollingdale. New York: Random House Vintage, 1969.

——. "On Truth and Lies in a Nonmoral Sense." In *Philosophy and Truth: Selections from Nietzsche's Notebooks of the Early 1870s,* ed. and trans. Daniel Breazeale, pp. 79–91. Atlantic Highlands, N.J.: Humanities Press, 1979.

——. *Twilight of the Idols.* Trans. R. J. Hollingdale. New York: Penguin, 1990.

——. *Untimely Meditations.* Trans. R. J. Hollingdale. Cambridge: Cambridge University Press, 1983.

——. *The Will to Power.* Trans. Walter Kaufmann and R. J. Hollingdale. New York: Vintage, 1967.

North, Oliver L. *Taking the Stand: The Testimony of Lt. Col. Oliver L. North.* New York: Pocket Books, 1987.

Oakeshott, Michael. *On Human Conduct.* Oxford: Oxford University Press, Clarendon, 1991.

Orvell, Miles. *The Real Thing: Imitation and Authenticity in American Culture, 1880–1940.* Chapel Hill: University of North Carolina Press, 1989.

Palumbo, Donald. "William Burroughs' Quartet of Science Fiction Novels as Dystopian Social Satire." *Extrapolation* 20 (1979): 321–29.

Park, Clara Clairborne. "Where 'The Waste Land' Ends." *Nation*, May 3, 1980, 532–35.

The Pentagon Papers: The Defense Department History of United States Decision-making on Vietnam. The Senator Gravel ed. 5 vols. Boston: Beacon Press, 1971–72.

Prospects for Containment of Nicaragua's Communist Government. Washington, D.C.: U.S. Department of Defense, c. 1984.

Quinn, Arthur. *The Confidence of the British Philosophers: An Essay in Historical Narrative.* Leiden: Brill, 1977.

——. "On Reading Newton Apocalyptically." Los Angeles: University of California, Clark Library, 1989.

Report of the Congressional Committees Investigating the Iran-Contra Affair. Washington, D.C.: U.S. Government Printing Office, 1987.

Ricci, David M. *The Tragedy of Political Science: Politics, Scholarship, and Democracy.* New Haven: Yale University Press, 1984.

Rogin, Michael. *Fathers and Children: Andrew Jackson and the Subjugation of the American Indian.* New York: Random House, Knopf, 1975.

——. *"Ronald Reagan" the Movie, and Other Episodes in American Political Demonology.* Berkeley and Los Angeles: University of California Press, 1987.

Rorty, Richard. "Philosophy as Science, Metaphor, Politics." In *Essays on Heidegger and Others*, pp. 9–26. Cambridge: Cambridge University Press, 1991.

Rosen, Stanley. *Hermeneutics as Politics.* New York: Oxford University Press, 1987.

Roth, Michaels. "The Ironist's Cage: Kojève, Foucault, Derrida." *Political Theory* 19:3 (1991): 419–32.

Rousseau, Jean-Jacques. *A Discourse on Inequality.* Trans. Maurice Cranston. New York: Penguin, 1984.

Russell, Charles. "Individual Voice in the Collective Discourse: Literary Innovation in Postmodern American Fiction." *Sub-Stance* 27 (1980): 29–39.

Schürmann, Reiner. *Heidegger on Being and Acting: From Principles to Anarchy.* Trans. Christine-Marie Gros. Bloomington: Indiana University Press, 1987.

Searle, John. "Reiterating the Differences: A Reply to Derrida." *Glyph* 1 (1977): 198–208.

Seltzer, Alvin J. *Chaos in the Novel/The Novel in Chaos.* New York: Schocken, 1974.

Showalter, English. *The Evolution of the French Novel, 1641–1782.* Princeton: Princeton University Press, 1982.

Skau, Michael. "The Central Verbal System: The Prose of William Burroughs." *Style* 15 (1981): 401–14.

Skerl, Jennie. *William S. Burroughs.* Boston: G. K. Hall, Twayne, 1985.

Sloterdijk, Peter. *Critique of Cynical Reason.* Trans. Michael Eldred. Minneapolis: University of Minnesota Press, 1987.

Slotkin, Richard. *The Fatal Environment: The Myth of the Frontier in the Age of Industrialization.* New York: Atherton, 1985.

Starobinski, Jean. *Jean-Jacques Rousseau: Transparency and Obstruction.* Trans. Arthur Goldhammer. Chicago: University of Chicago Press, 1988.

Stewart, Philip. *Imitation and Illusion in the French Memoir-Novel, 1700–1750.* New Haven: Yale University Press, 1969.

Storing, Herbert J., ed. *The Complete Anti-Federalist,* 7 vols. Chicago: University of Chicago Press, 1981.

Strauss, Leo, and Joseph Cropsey, eds. *History of Political Philosophy.* Chicago: University of Chicago Press, 1987.

Strong, Tracy B. *The Idea of Political Theory: Reflections on the Self in Political Time and Space.* Notre Dame: University of Notre Dame Press, 1990.

Taylor, Charles. *Sources of the Self: The Making of the Modern Identity.* Cambridge: Harvard University Press, 1989.

Taylor, Maxwell. *Responsibility and Response.* Baltimore: Penguin, 1971.

Thiher, Allen. *Words in Reflection: Modern Language Theory and Postmodern Fiction.* Chicago: University of Chicago Press, 1984.

Tocqueville, Alexis de. *Democracy in America.* 2 vols. Trans. Phillips Bradley. New York: Vintage, 1945.

Tulis, Jeffrey K. *The Rhetorical Presidency.* Princeton: Princeton University Press, 1987.

Vendler, Helen. *Part of Nature, Part of Us.* Cambridge: Harvard University Press, 1980.

Villa, Dana R. "Beyond Good and Evil: Arendt, Nietzsche, and the Aestheticization of Action." *Political Theory* 20(2) (1992): 274–308.

——. "Postmodernism and the Public Sphere." In *Rhetorical Republic: Governing Representations in American Politics,* ed. Frederick M. Dolan and Thomas L. Dumm, pp. 227–48. Amherst: University of Massachusetts Press, 1993.

Virilio, Paul. *Speed and Politics.* Trans. Mark Polizzotti. New York: Semiotext(e), 1986.

Virilio, Paul, and Silvere Lotringer. *Pure War.* New York: Semiotext(e), 1983.

Weber, Max. *The Protestant Ethic and the Spirit of Capitalism.* Trans. Talcott Parsons. New York: Scribner's, 1958.

——. "Science as a Vocation." In *From Max Weber: Essays in Sociology*, ed. H. H. Girth and C. Wright Mills, pp. 129–56. New York: Oxford University Press, 1977.

Wiener, Norbert. *Cybernetics: Or Control and Communication in the Animal and Machine.* 1948. Cambridge: MIT Press, 1961.

——. *The Human Use of Human Beings: Cybernetics and Society.* 1950. New York: Avon, 1954.

White, Morton. *Philosophy, "The Federalist," and the Constitution.* New York: Oxford University Press, 1987.

White, Stephen K. *Political Theory and Postmodernism.* Cambridge: Cambridge University Press, 1991.

Wilde, Alan. *Horizons of Assent: Modernism, Postmodernism, and the Ironic Imagination.* Baltimore: Johns Hopkins University Press, 1981.

Williams, Roger. *The Bloudy Tenent of Persecution for Cause of Conscience Discussed; and Cotton's Letter Examined and Answered.* 1644. London: J. Haddon, 1848.

Wills, Garry. *Explaining America: The Federalist.* New York: Doubleday, 1981.

——. *Cincinnatus: George Washington and the Enlightenment.* Garden City, N.Y.: Doubleday, 1984.

Wilson, Woodrow. *The New Freedom.* 1913. Garden City, N.Y.: Doubleday, 1921.

Winthrop, John. *The Winthrop Papers.* Boston: Massachusetts Historical Society, 1929–.

Wolin, Sheldon S. "Postmodern Politics and the Absence of Myth." *Social Research* 52 (Summer 1985): 217–39.

——. *The Presence of the Past: Essays on the State and the Constitution.* Baltimore: Johns Hopkins University Press, 1989.

Wood, Gordon. *The Creation of the American Republic.* Chapel Hill: University of North Carolina Press, 1969.

——. "Interests and Disinterestedness in the Making of the Constitution." In *Beyond Confederation: Origins of the Constitution and American National Identity*, ed. Richard Beeman et al., pp. 69–109. Chapel Hill: University of North Carolina Press, 1987.

Young-Bruehl, Elisabeth. *Hannah Arendt: For Love of the World.* New Haven: Yale University Press, 1982.

Zizek, Slavoj. *For They Know Not What They Do.* London: Verso, 1991.

——. *Looking Awry: An Introduction to Jacques Lacan through Popular Culture.* Cambridge: MIT Press, 1991.

Index

CONTESTATIONS

Cornell Studies in Political Theory
A series edited by
WILLIAM E. CONNOLLY

The Other Heidegger
by Fred Dallmayr

Allegories of America: Narratives, Metaphysics, Politics
by Frederick M. Dolan

united states
by Thomas L. Dumm

Intimacy and Spectacle: Liberal Theory as Political Education
by Stephen L. Esquith

Political Theory and the Displacement of Politics
by Bonnie Honig

The Inner Ocean: Individualism and Democratic Culture
by George Kateb

*The Anxiety of Freedom: Imagination and Individuality in
Locke's Political Thought*
by Uday Singh Mehta

Signifying Woman: Culture and Chaos in Rousseau, Burke, and Mill
by Linda M. G. Zerilli